THE DIRECT CINEMA OF DAVID AND ALBERT MAYSLES

JONATHAN B. VOGELS

The Direct Cinema of David and Albert Maysles

SOUTHERN ILLINOIS UNIVERSITY PRESS
CARBONDALE AND EDWARDSVILLE

The Library of Congress has cataloged the hardcover
edition as follows:
Vogels, Jonathan B., 1965–
    The direct cinema of David and Albert Maysles /
Jonathan B. Vogels.
        p. cm.
    Includes bibliographical references and index.
    I. Maysles, David—Criticism and interpretation.
    II. Maysles, Albert—Criticism and interpretation.
    III. Title.
    PN1998.3.M3975V64 2005
    791.4302'33'092273—dc22
    ISBN 0-8093-2643-4 (cloth : alk. paper)   2004029614

    ISBN 978-0-8093-2643-3 (cloth : alk. paper)
    ISBN 978-0-8093-3009-6 (paperback)
    ISBN 0-8093-3009-1 (paperback)
    ISBN 978-0-8093-8601-7 (ebook)
    ISBN 0-8093-8601-1 (ebook)

To my wife, Heidi Chesley

Contents

Illustrations

Preface: Fate, Faith, and Reality

Albert and David Maysles are two of the most important nonfiction film-makers this country has produced. Born in Brookline, Massachusetts, in 1926 and 1932, respectively, the Maysles brothers and their older sister grew up in the ethnically diverse Dorchester area of Boston. Their parents, both first-generation Russian-Jewish immigrants, instilled in their children a respect and curiosity for people of all backgrounds and in all walks of life. In their early adulthood, both brothers initially transferred that curiosity to the study of psychology; they majored in the subject at Syracuse University, and Albert taught psychology at Boston University in the mid-1950s. But their interest in the social sciences soon yielded to a stronger passion for filmmaking, which for them proved to be a more stimulating and humanistic means of encountering the world. In 1955, Al traveled to the Soviet Union to make a film about the psychiatric field there, and in 1957, David relocated to Hollywood where he served as an assistant producer of such films as *Bus Stop*, starring Marilyn Monroe. By the early 1960s, they reunited in New York City in order to make documentary films exclusively, joining forces first with the budding production company Drew Associates, then venturing out on their own.

Their collaboration from 1962 until David's death in 1987 at age 55 consisted of thirteen major works as well as numerous promotional and industrial films. Despite their joint contributions to nonfiction film, however, no full-length treatment of the Maysles brothers' career has yet appeared. They are mentioned in every historical survey of nonfiction film and prominently in those that focus on direct cinema, but they have not received the same extensive notice that some of their contemporaries have. (The prolific Frederick Wiseman, for instance, has been the subject of extensive study, including two books and numerous articles.) Although their dual careers spanned twenty-four years, the Maysles brothers' films have generally been treated monolithically, and film historians have failed to consider the subtle shifts in the brothers' approach over time. *Salesman* (1968) and *Gimme Shelter* (1970), probably the best-known of their films, have received individual attention and deservedly so, but both would benefit from being considered as two parts of a lengthy career.

This study remedies that oversight by investigating the films from an interdisciplinary perspective and by advancing three interconnected arguments. First, the brothers' innovative contributions to direct cinema, one of the late-twentieth century's major film styles, helped usher in a new era of nonfiction films and left a legacy for filmmakers of all genres. Direct cinema's ambiguous nature played a principal role in the hotly contested debate over authenticity in film. The Maysles brothers' films offer crucial case studies for testing the merits and shortcomings of direct cinema's claims to the authentic. Second, their films remain significant cultural artifacts that speak to the larger cultural issues of the 1960s and 1970s. This study examines the films as both shapers and reflections of the culture from which they emerged, arguing that these works offer insights into a wide range of contemporary topics, including materialism, celebrity, modern art, and the American family. Third, careful, scene-by-scene analyses allow for a consideration of the Maysles brothers' films *as films*, a tactic not frequently employed in nonfiction film studies. The Maysles brothers' artistic achievements resulted from an unusual combination of direct cinema methods, a modernist/humanist aesthetic, and a collaborative working process that often involved one or two other editors and/or directors. Albert and David Maysles remained essentially true to the precepts of direct cinema but also departed from them as required by the overarching goals of their specific film projects. The admittedly uncontrollable nature of the Maysles brothers' filmmaking process necessitated a certain amount of truth-shaping and imposed subjectivity, especially in the editing phase. Ambiguity and inconsistency are inherent aspects of life; the brothers achieved success through the effective inclusion and management of these factors. In doing so, they created a unique aesthetic that has distinct connections to other modernist art forms.

Nonfiction films like those of the Maysles brothers deserve more attention, not only because they often have important things to say about their subject matter but because the way they are or were made speaks to where, as a culture, we are or how we were when a given film was made. How do we wish to represent ourselves? How do we seek to document truth? And how do we use film as a vehicle for truth-gathering? An investigation of the complete Maysles catalog therefore sheds light on the issues of direct cinema as a whole, highlights the technical and aesthetic achievements of specific works, and delineates two artists' quest for an authentic means of creative expression.

Acknowledgments

Many thanks to Bruce Schulman, whose insightful feedback on the first few versions of the manuscript served the final text extremely well; what he saw (or in many cases didn't see) in the manuscript always led to considerable improvement and a much sharper critical edge. In general, he helped train me (and many others) to understand and internalize the parameters of being an American studies scholar, which, in turn, informed this work significantly.

James Palmer introduced me to the wonders of film studies—and it was in his Film and the American Dream class at the University of Colorado that I first saw a Maysles film (*Christo's Valley Curtain*). Jeremy Murray-Brown inspired me to think of documentary films in new ways and provided the excuse for me to begin my serious research into the Maysles brothers. His ongoing support of my projects is most appreciated. Thanks also to those who have given me their comments on all or some portion of the manuscript: James Lane, Marilyn Halter, Lori Kenschaft, and Chris Walsh. My thanks to Albert Maysles and Xan Parker at Maysles Films and especially to Susan Froemke for permission to use material from my interview with her.

Thanks to the patience and perseverance of those at Southern Illinois University Press. The editors with whom I have worked—John Stetter, Jennifer Williams, and Kristine Priddy—have been helpful and politely nudging when I needed them to be. Completing this book at the same time that I have encountered several major life changes has not been an easy task, but the people at the press have believed in and been supportive of the final product all along.

Finally, my biggest thanks go to my wife, Heidi Chesley. She's read through the many and various drafts of this manuscript, making it better with each review, has listened to me drone on about documentary films, has watched more of them than I can count, and has even saved me from various computer malfunctions and printer problems. Her loving support and constant encouragement still mean more to me than anything I can imagine.

THE DIRECT CINEMA OF DAVID AND ALBERT MAYSLES

1
Direct Cinema and the Maysles Brothers

During the late 1950s, an energetic group of young filmmakers led by Robert L. Drew and Richard Leacock championed a new approach to nonfiction film. Eschewing the authoritative voice-over narrator, didactic scripts, and traditional problem-and-solution format used by the majority of their predecessors, these filmmakers instead tried to capture life as it happened. They regarded authentic drama to be superior to the manufactured story lines of earlier documentaries. They chose topics of general interest, but their films lacked any preconceived plots; nothing in the films was rehearsed. Because they found direct manipulation of the audience an anathema, they avoided telling an audience how it ought to feel about what it was watching or what ought to be done to remedy a social ill.

New technology, including lighter, hand-held cameras and more sophisticated sound-recording equipment, made possible this new style of filmmaking. With more portable equipment, camera operators no longer had to rely on wide shots, nor did directors have to revert to stock footage. In his memoir, Leacock describes the freedom: "The important thing was that we were experimenting. All the rules were new. We were, in fact, developing a new grammar which was entirely different from that of silent filmmaking and of fiction film-making."[1] As part of the new grammar, the camera operators and directors preferred the close-up, scanning the faces of their subjects, frequently holding the shots for long takes, in order to capture their emotions and reactions. State-of-the-art sound-recording technology meant that the subjects could be filmed speaking as they would in real life, oftentimes off the cuff; audiences could hear these people's

1

voices and decide for themselves about the subjects' credibility and integrity. As a result, the style was particularly well-suited to telling the stories of individuals (often famous) by employing a kind of day-in-the-life approach. Interesting, spontaneous moments emerged, but the process did require patience and diligence, as photographers had to shoot many hours of film before a theme or story emerged. In order to "eschew all intervention," filmmaker/historian James Blue explained at the time, these American filmmakers had to "cultivate an alert passivity. They seek self-effacement. They want the subject to forget they are there."[2]

This new approach still demanded some kind of organizing principle. One common way of shaping the material was through a crisis structure, in which the subject or subjects of the film would face a particularly challenging moment in life or where a filmed situation would come to a dramatic climax. Drew even titled one of his early efforts *Crisis: Behind a Presidential Commitment* (1963); his film team observed the Robert Kennedy–George Wallace showdown over the integration of the University of Alabama. Stephen Mamber, one of this cinema's earliest and most articulate defenders, itemized three distinct advantages to this crisis structure:

- Because he or she is so engrossed in the crisis at hand, the subject is less aware of the camera.
- The drama inherent in a crisis provides excitement in what are typically more slow-moving, less-structured films.
- A subject reveals his or her "true" identity or "character" when put to the test of a crisis.

For such a structure to pay dividends, the filmmaker must choose a subject whose life might provide conflict-oriented episodes, or the filmmaker must seek out situations in which a crisis is imminent, where a winner-or-loser outcome is inevitable. This structure also relies on a subject whose actions under pressure are visually interesting; the ideal crisis hero is what Mamber refers to as a "man of action." (The problems and limitations of the crisis structure are numerous, as Mamber also readily admitted. These limitations will be discussed in greater depth in the chapter on the Christo films, which have crisis structures but which also question the value of relying on crisis structures.)[3] For Drew, the crisis structure provided the best opportunity for the audience to see something interesting and revelatory about the subject or subjects of the film.[4]

The growing popularity and increased presence of television played a significant role in the ascendancy of this new style of documentary observation. Drew, for example, saw himself as a journalist, one who would use the new broadcast technology to disclose information more objectively, allowing his viewers to decide for themselves how they should feel or what if anything they should do about the issue presented. Drew was interested in allowing television journalism to do "something absolutely unique" by providing the "experience of what it is like to be somewhere else, seeing for yourself into dramatic developments in the lives of people caught up in stories of importance."[5] The immediacy and intimacy of the style worked well on television, and for the first few years of the movement, networks enthusiastically aired these new kinds of documentary programs. Three Drew-Leacock collaborations aired on the *Omnibus* series; others appeared on programs with diverse offerings, such as the *Ed Sullivan Show* and the *Tonight* show. Drew and Leacock also produced four hour-long documentaries for ABC's *Close-Up* program in 1960–1961.

Drew's early films for television established parameters for a distinctly American cinéma vérité. *Primary* (1960), a look at the John F. Kennedy–Hubert H. Humphrey race for the Democratic nomination in 1960, *Yanki No!* (1960) about Fidel Castro's rise to power in Cuba, and *The Chair* (1963), exploring a capital punishment case, survive as three prominent examples, all making effective use of on-the-scene portable cameras and synchronized sound to elicit a spontaneity not found in earlier documentaries. Camera shots were sometimes unsteady or grainy, and the soundtrack was occasionally inaudible, but such features gave the audience a novel sense of being on the scene, amidst unfolding events. It should be noted that these American films differed from the other cinéma vérité appearing simultaneously in France and Canada. In those countries, the films of Jean Rouch and Chris Marker, for example, employed a much more assertive and self-reflexive approach. Documentary historian Erik Barnouw has described the differences:

> The direct cinema documentarist took his camera to a situation of tension and waited hopefully for a crisis; the Rouch version of cinéma vérité tried to precipitate one. The direct cinema artist aspired to invisibility; the Rouch cinéma vérité artist was often an avowed participant. . . . Direct cinema found its truth in events available to the camera. Cinéma vérité was committed to a paradox: that artificial circumstances could bring hidden truth to the surface.[6]

Apart from the aesthetic and technical developments, Drew and his associates became featured players in a broad-based American cultural sea change. During the 1960s, cultural truths of all kinds were questioned, even discredited. Those who were dismayed by the stultifying conformity of Cold War America sought a higher form of authenticity, the "really real," as some called it. A diverse array of social critics, such as Susan Sontag, Norman Mailer, and Paul Goodman, frustrated by the perception that large, faceless bureaucracies and a greedy technological elite had lulled Americans into a materialistic stupor, called for people to "experience more immediately" their lives. A new wave of social scientists and cultural historians, armed with new theoretical approaches, gathered and presented information about the world and its people in what they believed was a less biased way, with fewer of their own cultural assumptions. College students, civil rights supporters, feminists, and idealistic politicians worked to make the American democratic process accessible to a greater number of people.[7]

Inspired by existential philosophy and frequently infused with a contemporary Christianity, many of those who looked for authenticity joined forces in the New Left. Turning away from feelings of anxiety, alienation, and political apathy, these liberal authenticity seekers believed inner wholeness could only be achieved through a more direct involvement with themselves and with their communities. In developing what has been called "America's last great experiment in democratic idealism," the New Left of the early 1960s wanted to "emerge from apathy" and make a "participatory democracy" more vibrant.[8] The *Port Huron Statement*, the political and philosophical manifesto of the New Left's Students for a Democratic Society (SDS), attacked the values of the previous generation and called for people to pursue "personally authentic" lives.

Artists in all media pursued similar goals during the late 1950s and early 1960s. Rejecting the constraints of the prevailing Cold War culture, these artists endeavored to represent the world more "authentically," whether treating different kinds of subject matter (the stories of minority groups and the underclass, for instance, were ripe for film and fiction) or featuring more controversial and more graphic modes of representation (including greater experimentation and/or products with graphic violence, explicit language, or strong sexual content). Like modernist artists of the 1920s and 1930s or the beats and the abstract expressionists of the early 1950s, artists of this period zealously counteracted an "age of anxiety" with a free flow of expression unencumbered by the cultural barriers of previous generations. Historian Daniel Joseph Singal has identified some of the key features of these artists' output: the "celebration of the animal component of human nature, the quest for spontaneity and authenticity, the desire to raze all dualisms and distinctions, . . . the quest for 'wholeness,' and the effort to expand consciousness and discover new modes of experience."[9]

Direct cinema filmmakers also equated pure creation with manipulation, the antithesis of the authentic. They, too, sought the really real. Yet, their quest for authenticity led them along a slightly different path than some of the other seekers of the era. Instead of advocating for specific social change, the direct cinema filmmakers opted to remain observers, to show rather than to preach. Their films were never polemic in nature, never jeremiads. Even when a social issue was presented, as in Drew's *The Children Were Watching* (1960) about school desegregation, there was no overt call to arms, no clear answers given as to what ought to be done to "solve" the problem. Drew had said that "the right kind of documentary programming will raise more interest than it can satisfy, more questions than it can answer."[10] In this way, direct cinema's confrontations were more detached and suggestive, reminiscent of certain modernist expressions of the 1920s and 1930s like Ernest Hemingway's *The Sun Also Rises* or the American landscapes of Charles Burchfield. Film theorist Paul Arthur has further argued that these filmmakers followed the lead of socially active documentary filmmakers of the 1930s: They conveyed "an abiding mistrust of top-down solutions" and looked beyond the traditional formulae for social change.[11] Theirs was a radical form of cinema, even more so because of the films' desire to show rather than to tell, to raise awareness rather than to prescribe remedies.

Albert Maysles's quest for an authentic means of filming people in real-life situations took him in a similar direction. With his camera, Maysles believed he could be what he called a "truthful witness" to the world around him.[12] As one of the photographers for Drew Associates, his technical style and ability to capture revelatory moments had rapidly earned him notice and respect in the early 1960s. He worked with Drew on *Eddie* (1960) and *Yanki No!*, and he was famous among his contemporaries for what is likely the most written about moment in direct cinema history: a four-minute, nearly continuous tracking shot of John Kennedy making his way through a crowd of supporters in *Primary*. By the time he formed his own film group with his younger brother David (who had worked in Hollywood as an assistant producer), Albert's reputation was secure. In 1964, French director Jean-Luc Godard called him the "greatest cameraman in America."[13] One of the leading spokesmen for an emergent American cinéma vérité, Albert coined the term *direct cinema* as a better indicator of the immediacy of his films.[14] Although he had never been formally trained in cinematography, he worked fervently on the technological aspects of film, eventually developing an even lighter (thirty-pound) camera and repositioning the viewfinder on the camera so that he had more flexibility to see what he was filming. These were advances that revolutionized the way nonfiction films were made.[15]

The Maysles brothers have been revolutionary in other ways as well. Sophisticated technology notwithstanding, a strong philosophical and artistic underpinning, constituting a distinct Maysles film aesthetic, has ensured that the films remain more than mere technical exercises. Part of this aesthetic stemmed from the brothers' search for a more authentic means of expressing themselves and of interacting with the world around them. When, for instance, Albert traveled to the Soviet Union to investigate state-run mental hospitals, he did not, as many social scientists would have done, write a report of his findings. Rather, Albert thought that making a movie [of the situation] "would be the most authentic way" of presenting what he had seen. Similarly, David, who recorded sound and oversaw the editing of the brothers' films, often spoke of putting the films together "with a minimum of structuring of the events by the film maker" and of being "truthful to what went on before our eyes."[16]

Their initial desires to create more "truthful" (that is, more authentic) films took on a nearly spiritual component as they celebrated and explored the humanity of their subjects. The brothers have both described their films as "acts of faith" and have frequently spoken of relying on faith in themselves or in their process.[17] Contemporaries have said of Albert that he was "in things cinematic . . . a religious zealot"; "both a powerful teacher and a missionary"; a man who could "mak[e] a religion or a virtue of merely looking."[18] Film critic Louis Marcorelles, after hearing the brothers discuss their film *Showman* in front of a Paris audience, reported how "encouraging" it was "to hear such a candid profession of faith in the cinema."[19] To this day, Albert Maysles uses such terminology when discussing his work: "We live in an era where fake has taken over. It's time we turn it around and live in an era of authenticity and facing the facts. That's where our humanity lies. The documentary should be where you learn what it is to be human."[20]

In making their films, the brothers strove for an unmediated presentation of people, stripped bare of pretense, their essential humanity revealed. The Maysles brothers noted that "more than ever, viewers could feel what it was like to be in the shoes of the subjects."[21] Such connectedness gives the films an egalitarian tone, with audience, subject, and filmmaker on equal ground and of equal importance. As a result, many of the usual expectations of people's behavior are reversed. Their films illustrate, for instance, that performance is a complex matter in a world increasingly steeped in performance. The celebrities in many of their films are exposed at times when they are less conscious of performing and are behaving more like "regular people." At times—as when Christo dejectedly accepts the defeat of his initial plan in California (in *Running Fence*) or when in *Gimme Shelter* members of the Rolling Stones watch footage of the Altamont murder with grim faces—the artists/celebrities even appear vulnerable, quite the opposite of their usual polished presentations of self and art. Conversely, the Maysles brothers' two major films without celebrities— *Grey Gardens* and *Salesman*—include people acting for the camera.

Furthermore, many of their films champion society's underdogs, those people struggling against societal norms, which, in the specific film's view, are reductive rather than enlightened (Paul Brennan in *Salesman*, Christo, the Beales in *Grey Gardens*). The Maysles brothers in particular used direct cinema to reassert the sanctity of the individual in a world increasingly prone to identify people as parts of large, often opposing groups (American, communist, hippie, hawk, dove). Direct cinema for them was not only about experiencing events as they happened but also reexperiencing *people* as they happened. They thereby hoped to reveal what is inherently human in all people; like other authenticity seekers, the brothers recognized that embedded within the story of one specific person's life is the narrative of all people. Albert put it more straightforwardly: "What we do is really a glorification of the human spirit."[22]

Their background in psychology underscored their interest in human behavior, yet both were unabashedly optimistic that their films were better, more *direct* explorations of what it means to be human than anything emerging from the social sciences, including psychology. There is an anti-academic strain to much of Albert's public discourse on his life's work: "When people ask me about my psychology background I have to say I don't think it has anything to do with our films. I think, in fact, that reasoning, intellectuality, is probably more than anything the enemy of art, and it would be the enemy of our way of making movies."[23] He instead has argued that the "human content" of their films is "so strong and so totally convincing, because my concentration is on what I feel I have to get of the person, rather than some artistic thing I'm trying to prove."[24] David maintained that "this kind of filmmaking can be the most emotionally involving."[25]

Still, the Maysles brothers' quest for authenticity proved to be a complex matter. Unlike others in their cohort, they publicly acknowledged that "there is no such thing as being strictly objective in anything that is at all artistic. The objectivity is just a personal integrity: being *essentially true* to the subject and capturing it essentially."[26] They believed that a truly authentic film therefore creates "some kind of relationship between truth, beauty, and art."[27] Recognizing both the inherent limits and stylistic advantages of their direct cinema, they imbued their films with what Blue identified as a "subjective-objectivity" wherein "ethics and aesthetics are interdependent, where beauty starts with honesty."[28] They admired writers like Hemingway, Mailer, Thomas Wolfe, Eugene O'Neill, Truman Capote, and photographer Bruce Davidson, all of whom engaged reality directly while still producing works of artistic merit. The key for them was trust— in themselves as sensitive filmmakers, in their subjects as real people with something interesting and human to reveal, and in their audience as discerning and intelligent viewers. The Maysles brothers hoped they could then put trust into action by using "our skills to create an intimacy between the subjects filmed and the audience."[29]

Toward that end, the brothers were not as fanatical as some nonfiction filmmakers were in avoiding conventions of traditional documentary. Like most direct cinema (and more broadly, cinéma vérité) directors, they and their coeditors shunned, whenever possible, the use of conventions such as narration, voice-over, crosscutting, music, "artistic" photography, nonsynchronized sound, and interviews. They instead preferred what Albert called the "spontaneous juxtapositions" in life itself. However, they also understood that sometimes these conventions must be used, whether for heightened effect, to emphasize the major ideas of the film, or to bolster the minimal dramatic structure of the film. They believed that used sparingly and without pretension (that is, without drawing excessive attention to themselves), these conventions, employed in what is best described as an ad hoc manner, would allow the end product to "achieve greater truthfulness."

In short, Albert and David Maysles wished to be as removed and objective as possible while filming, allowing the subjects to be themselves without manipulation or guidance from them. Still, the brothers were not hesitant to shape (or to allow their coeditors to shape) the film—through dramatic structure, a sprinkling of documentary convention, their own on-camera appearances, even a discernible point of view. "Anything that works!" Albert once replied, only half-joking, when asked what techniques he liked to apply in his films.[30] Through an ad hoc approach the brothers achieved what Richard M. Barsam has identified as a "highly structured *model* of reality" wherein the filmmakers create order out of chaos by editing.[31] The Maysles brothers thereby inscribed what might be called a planned spontaneity into their films.

THE MAYSLES BROTHERS AND MODERNISM

The Maysles brothers' highly flexible approach to filmmaking helped engender a singular kind of film aesthetic that includes many of the attributes of the modernist artist. The specific Maysles modernism that they fostered, replete with the kind of authenticity to which they aspired, was an artistry shaped and structured through film editing and augmented by a collaborative working process that often involved one or two other directors. Their particular kind of modernist aesthetic is more evident in their later work, but the philosophical seeds of it are manifest in every film. Just as their films varied in the degree to which they adhered to direct cinema convention, so, too, did they also engage modernism along a continuum. Over the course of their careers, their particular modernist aesthetic developed and sometimes shifted from one mode to another, and this book will trace the progression.

Of course, identifying any artist as modernist invites trouble. Modernism has been and remains one of the most elusive and difficult to define cultural and artistic movements in history, precisely because it covers a huge expanse of time (there is general agreement about its starting point around 1910 but its ending point, if indeed it has ended, has been widely debated). Modernism is also elusive because it encompasses a wide range of material, styles, subject matter, and art forms. In fact, modernism is in danger of becoming so inclusive that it may cease to be a meaningful designation. Nevertheless, I will venture to provide a working definition of modernism, as I believe the Maysles brothers' work can be better understood in relation to these general points.[32]

In the early twentieth century, when modernism first fully emerged, it directly challenged several assumptions of the Victorian era, including a "belief in a predictable universe"; the notion that "humankind was capable of arriving at a unified and fixed set of truths about all aspects of life"; and the idea that there were "absolute standards based on a radical dichotomy between that which was deemed 'human' and that regarded as 'animal.'"[33] Influenced by the scientific theories of Charles Darwin, Sigmund Freud, and, later, Albert Einstein, modernists were concerned with seeing and understanding a differently ordered world. In art, modernism entailed above all a loosening of the constraints of classical modes of representation. No longer satisfied with superficially realistic depictions, modernist art reflected a world that seemed increasingly splintered and fractured, especially in light of the devastation of the First World War. Latter-day modernist Michelangelo Antonioni, the Italian filmmaker, has stated, "Nothing appears as it should in a world where nothing is certain. The only certain thing is the existence of a secret violence that makes everything uncertain."[34] Even the past-present-future became fragmented: In many modernist works, there is a kind of seamless moving back and forth in time, perhaps most famously in William Faulkner's *The Sound and the Fury*.

For some modernists, a text should be autonomous; that is, it should stand alone, ostensibly ahistoric, detached from and oblivious to the more mundane concerns of the moment. Often adopting an art-for-art's-sake mentality, these modernist artists consistently described their works as unique and fleeting expressions. (Here I distinguish between modernism in general and the avant-garde, which was a politicized outgrowth of the modernist impulse.) Many modernists therefore sought to make the viewer or reader or listener acutely aware of viewing or reading or listening. They simultaneously inscribed both the reality behind what they were depicting and the artifice with which they were depicting it. In other words, much of modernist art simultaneously acknowledges both the real and the fake. Ideally, this creates an unsettled feeling in the audience, what Bertolt Brecht called the "alienation effect": the "pull and push" between involvement and estrangement has been one of the key features of modernism.[35]

Modernism in American film appeared first in the 1920s when the surrealist and avant-garde works of Man Ray, Marcel Duchamp, Charles Sheeler, and Luis Buñuel played to limited but devoted audiences, primarily in Paris, Berlin, and New York City. These films utilized nonconventional narrative techniques and were more often impressionistic than even remotely realistic. Nonfiction only in the broadest sense of the word, these films were hardly documentary; they were, like a James Joyce novel or a cubist painting, experimental, autonomous, and self-referential. Modernist filmmakers generally disregarded the commercial viability of their work, even though (in some cases, because) narrative film had become a potentially lucrative endeavor. They sought to topple the conventional boundaries of narrative structures; they shunned linear plots and traditional narratives in the name of experimentation, exploring the various ways film might be employed to create a new kind of visual aesthetic. Many of them even took a militant approach to the arts, advocating as members of the avant-garde that political systems must be challenged or overthrown and that artists should lead the way.[36]

Those seeking authenticity in the 1960s shared an affinity with the modernist filmmakers of the 1920s and 1930s. Like their predecessors, the 1960s documentarists recognized that truth is a highly complex, highly relative concept. But they, too, believed their films could get at the truth more effectively and authentically than other media could. Nonfiction directors of this period generally carried these ideas in one of two directions. Highly experimental directors like Stan Brakhage and Jonas Mekas manipulated the medium in order to create a heightened reality. Brakhage superimposed images, distorted light, or scratched directly onto film negatives, underscoring the fact that reality as he created it for his films was a highly subjective and malleable matter. A highly personal matter, too: Brakhage reveals himself making love to his bride on his wedding night in *Wedlock House: An Intercourse* and shows the birth of their daughter in *Window Water Baby Moving* (both 1960). Other directors sought authenticity via a camera-as-observer philosophy. Taken to the extreme, this philosophy led to the hyperrealistic works of Andy Warhol; in *Sleep* (1963) and *Empire* (1964), a camera was simply positioned and left to record for hours, with no editor intervening in the final product. Direct cinema took a slightly less pure, more practical approach than Warhol, opting instead to edit footage toward a more engaging storyline.

For their part, the Maysles brothers located a middle ground between pure experiment and pure observation in their films. Whereas many modernists in various disciplines have worked to make manifest their own processes and to reveal the illusion of an alternate reality, the Maysles brothers have not generally worked in this vein. Indeed, their early films strive to eliminate the revelation of the process; as much as possible, the filmmakers remain hidden. Only gradually, as their careers progressed and as they took greater artistic risks that departed even more broadly from the original intentions of direct cinema did the brothers break that barrier. In those early works, up to and including *Salesman*, they steered a slightly different modernist course, one that scholars David Hollinger and Ray Carney have connected to pragmatists like John Dewey and even William James. According to Hollinger, "What makes this particular modernism is its faith in science, its sense that what our civilization requires in order to be rescued from itself is more likely to come from communities of knowers than from a succession of artist-heroes." Hollinger thereby distinguishes these "knowers" from the "artificers" usually associated with modernism and argues that they "aspir[ed] to organize culture around the cognitive capacities of human beings."[37] While the Maysles brothers maintained suspicions about social science, they did indicate in their early films that knowledge—especially of the materialistic nature of American society—could lead to a less manipulated society, one that relied on its cognitive capacities rather than the "wisdom" imparted by authority figures or celebrities.

Carney, especially in his support of the independent filmmaker John Cassavetes, has also looked to John Dewey. Both Dewey and Cassavetes, according to Carney, "de-idealize art [and] . . . the work, its characters, and their expressions of themselves represent acts of engagement with the world. Art is not somewhere else; it is in life, and absolutely continuous with it." For Carney, Cassavetes's "pragmatic form of American modernism" aligned the filmmaker with Whitman's poetry, which similarly "celebrates the gusto of the senses; it loves the world of men and events; it relishes the social and emotional involvements of mothers, fathers, and children." Still modernist in his presentation of a chaotic world and in his assumption that art can and should comment on and reflect such a world, a pragmatic modernist also sees life as "essentially and unavoidably relational." Whereas many modernists intellectualize art to the extent that they take it out of the realm of human experience, a pragmatic modernist finds meaning only when art and experience interact.[38]

The Maysles brothers typically followed in the same direction, charting an artistic course that was decidedly pragmatic. Even when they moved toward greater self-reflexivity and openness about their own process (culminating in *Grey Gardens*, which is their most obviously and traditionally modernist film), they always saw art and experience as deeply and inextricably intertwined. In this way, their strongly held humanist ideals merged with their modernist artistic ambitions, thereby allowing them to carve out their own niche in filmmaking. Again, their films fell within a continuum of modernism, sometimes more pragmatic, sometimes more widely experimental.

Like most modernists, the brothers themselves frequently maintained that complete understanding of any situation is elusive and beyond the control of the artist and the audience with whom the artist communicates. Nevertheless, an authentic film can liberate the viewer, who, with the filmmaker, can make a few hesitant steps toward the truth, knowing full well that certainty is impossible. Resolution is not the ultimate goal; it is all about the striving. The Maysles brothers understood that their process involved a kind of journey and pursued relentlessly an ideal of presenting that journey within their films. They consistently disavowed that their work represented some universal truth, only the truth as they saw and filmed it. Sometimes that unfiltered truth made audiences feel uncomfortable—as truths that challenge often do—but the Maysles brothers were adamant that they knew no other way of making films.

Albert and David Maysles typically had to defend their films against confused audiences, reproachful film critics, disdainful film theorists, and even other filmmakers who did not appreciate or understand the brothers' aesthetic. Critics often assailed their attempts at balancing subjectivity and objectivity as ambiguous, which, of course, the attempts intentionally were. Frequently, the brothers were derided as two among a group of direct cinema idealists whose claims to pure filmmaking were misguided and naive. They were even accused of manipulating audiences and then hiding behind their allegedly authentic process. In response, their own defenses and explanations were too often inarticulate or misdirected, and they never clearly or consistently presented themselves as modernists, or anything else other than dedicated filmmakers. Not surprisingly, then, by the early 1970s, the Maysles brothers were swept up in an anti–direct cinema backlash that made few distinctions between or among individual films or filmmakers. (Subsequent chapters trace that criticism as it was directed at individual films, especially *Grey Gardens*, which brought a crescendo of backlash criticism. This movie is extensively discussed in chapter 6.)

A certain degree of naivete and blind optimism did accompany all direct cinema filmmakers' enthusiasm in the early years. They and the other practitioners of direct cinema may have hoped to capture life as it happens, but life rarely just happened in any normal way in front of their cameras. No matter how unobtrusive the sound and camera operators, no matter how advanced their technology, the mere act of filming others altered reality and replaced it with a different kind of reality, a filmed reality. Aiming a camera at someone cannot be an objective act. David Maysles once proclaimed, "We don't impose anything on the people we film. We are the servants of our subjects rather than the other way around,"[39] but these ideas do not hold up. Life is always transformed into performance for those whose lives are being recorded. This kind of cinema may have been direct, but it was also, despite its best intentions, directed.

Try though they might to suppress it or to avoid discussing it, direct cinema filmmakers maintained an authority over their work. The camera operator chose on what or on whom to focus, and the camera itself is always an authority figure that cannot be overthrown. Concealing that authoritative relationship in a film leaves a filmmaker open to being labeled disingenuous, hypocritical, and even dishonest—all words that have been used to describe the Maysles brothers and their approach to filmmaking. Moreover, the role of the editor—a role as essential to these films as those of the cinematographer and the sound recorder—further called into question direct cinema's claims of objectivity. In the brothers' films, Albert did almost all of the camera work, and the principal job of editing was always left to one or more others, generally with David supervising and contributing to the process. Albert purposely took himself out of the editing phase of the filmmaking, both because he found it exceedingly dull and because he felt it would potentially hinder his ability as a cameraman. "If I were very structured in my photography then the film would be a disaster," he argued; he therefore accepted that the editors would later impose whatever structure was necessary, trusting that they would "preserve a kind of spontaneous quality" in the film.[40] Ellen Hovde, who worked on *Salesman*, *Gimme Shelter*, *Christo's Valley Curtain*, and *Grey Gardens* (and is listed as codirector on the latter two), described the editing process as "shaping, forming, and structuring the material" and creating a "dramatically told story" from as many as hundreds of hours of film footage.[41] Albert may have affirmed that "this kind of filming is truthful . . . it's impossible for the cameraman who is shooting that fast to connive, to contrive," as he did in a 1964 interview, but he could afford to speak as the "purest of the pure" (film theorist Brian Winston's dismissive phrase) because he took no part in the editing process where "truth-shaping" would have occurred.[42]

While direct cinema did allow viewers to draw their own conclusions about what was unfolding on the screen, it was never a manipulation-free style of filmmaking. At its best, direct cinema illuminated hypocrisy, revealed personality strengths and character blemishes, or uncovered submerged truths. At its worst, it played gotcha with a camera, waiting for the moments when people let their guards down. Because direct cinema operated under the guise of authenticity, audiences may have been duped into believing they were seeing "the real" without taking into account myriad mitigating circumstances. In this sense, direct cinema may have been, ironically enough, more manipulative than the consciously and overtly subjective documentaries of the past. Even the filmed subjects who appear to be (or over time appear to become) comfortable in front of the camera may find themselves tricked into complicity with the patient filmmaker/observer. The Maysles brothers' films abound with moments in which the person in the film discloses something important about himself or herself in a way so personal, so revelatory that it makes an audience feel self-conscious, even a little guilty, about watching. Is this voyeuristic quality—the camera as a peephole—a violation of the subject's privacy, as some detractors have asserted?

The brothers usually surmounted this potential problem, however, thanks primarily to their abiding faith in three interconnected components of their direct cinema. First, the Maysles brothers were sensitive toward and respected their subjects. A greater degree of sensitivity meant that the brothers avoided condescending to or making fun of the people in their films, despite what some critics have charged (especially regarding *Salesman* and *Grey Gardens*). As a result, their films ennoble rather than degrade their subjects. Even the subjects' moments of weakness tend to enhance rather than undermine the sympathies of viewers. Where audiences could feel pity or contempt, a Maysles film encourages them to feel empathy instead.

Second, the Maysles brothers put faith in an atypical collaborative process when making their films. Unlike most nonfiction directors, whether working in cinéma vérité or not, Albert and David did not solely handle the editing or even the direction of their films. From *Salesman* on, all of their films were jointly made with the essential help of at least one other director. Like many of those seeking authenticity in the 1960s, the Maysles brothers believed collaboration was not only a desirable way of connecting with other people but also a means of producing a more truthful product. They therefore entrusted the final product to a series of skilled editors who worked with David to shape the raw material. Albert has explained the level of trust: "In [our] case it's almost the same relation as with the subjects. I trust them and they have a great deal of independence. The final product really depends on all of us."[43]

A third factor involved the brothers' faith in their viewing audience. They assumed that their audience brought a certain degree of sophistication to the theater and did not need every detail spelled out or every idea in the film elucidated explicitly. Their films reflected the complexity of life and, they believed, would not frustrate or frighten off their audience. Sometimes, as Albert argued, "An artist seeks to take the longest journey"; he and David believed the audience would willingly come along: "We can get in film something no scriptwriter can invent. Things as they come in real life are much more exciting than anything that you could invent or stage. . . . The excitement comes from seeing something revealed before our own eyes. We try to transfer that excitement to the audience."[44] It was a practical matter as well; audiences for nonfiction films were scarce already, and the Maysles brothers had to be wary of producing work so different, so loosely structured (or not structured at all) that they would alienate or confuse the majority of viewers, the brothers' trust of viewer sophistication notwithstanding. They never desired to imitate Brakhage or Warhol. They assumed they were at the forefront of a new and exciting kind of cinema that would attract a significant and devoted audience. Their assumptions were not completely borne out; only *Salesman* and *Gimme Shelter* received widespread distribution, and those films were at best moderate successes. The others completed very limited runs or faced legal obstacles that blocked their availability to a wide audience. Still, as they balanced the sometimes conflicting desire to capture spontaneous moments and to tell a compelling, emotional story, the Maysles brothers achieved critical support and established a loyal and enthusiastic following.

In assessing the artistic success or failure of the Maysles brothers' lofty ambitions, a case-by-case analysis proves most useful. Their anything-that-works approach, modernist aesthetic, and collaborative editing process combine to make a widely divergent body of work that cannot be treated monolithically. This book, therefore, considers each film in turn, noting the technological advances, significance within the direct cinema catalog, and the way each film moves forward the Maysles brothers' modernist concerns.

Their first film, *Showman* (1962), follows Hollywood film producer Joseph E. Levine as he maneuvers his way through the entertainment industry. It is a man-of-action film, with Levine bustling about, playing the role of the aggressive businessman/shark, seemingly unaware of the camera's presence. While response was mixed, with some observers rejecting the formlessness of the film and others applauding the way "we see, and interpret in our terms, the real man as he lives his life,"[45] most agreed that this film took a vastly different approach than had films of earlier eras. This film established that the Maysles brothers' films would allow a story to unfold without relying on a traditional plot or even a crisis structure. This is the subject of chapter 2.

Three short films followed over the next four years, each documenting artists or celebrities in action: *What's Happening! The Beatles in the U.S.A.* (1964), *Meet Marlon Brando* (1965), and *With Love from Truman: A Visit with Truman Capote* (1966). Without narration or an obvious structure, these films offer no overt indication as to what the viewer *should* conclude about the subjects, presenting these artists backstage, offstage, and in their homes. The films' subjects are the starting points, but the end result is far from predetermined or predictable. Direct cinema Maysles-style ushered in a new way to profile celebrities, demystifying and deglamorizing them in a way rarely done before. Indeed, part of the agenda of many of the direct cinema celebrity-based films was an implicit criticism of the concept of celebrity and of the role other forms of media play in promoting that concept. The Maysles brothers continued to develop an aesthetic in these films, but, given the nature of these commissioned assignments, it remained somewhat muted (and is further discussed in chapter 2).

Two years later, the aesthetic began to flourish with the release of *Salesman*, a film for which the brothers had complete creative control. Often cited as the quintessential example of direct cinema, the film tracks the business exploits of five door-to-door Bible salesmen. The ninety-minute film (codirected and chiefly edited by Charlotte Zwerin) presents a highly complex picture of salesmen who are sleazy, bigoted, tricky but also funny and sympathetic. Several scenes of sales meetings in which the men are cajoled into increasing their output underscore the pressures they face and illuminate why they resort to sales pitches that are a mixture of religious guilt-mongering and clever misdirection. Under Albert Maysles's watchful camera, these men slowly reveal who they are (professionally), what their job entails, and what impact it has on them in other aspects of their lives. Through an exploration of the way the language of buying and selling hinders human communication and understanding, the Maysles brothers' film questions the viability of this way of life without demonizing those engaged in it. Their modernist concern with the limits of language emerges as the central issue of the film. Chapter 3 expounds on this aspect.

The brothers' next major project, *Gimme Shelter* (1970), explores the Rolling Stones's 1969 concert tour. In addition to the expected backstage and off-stage footage of the Stones, the film also includes a murder: from a distance, the camera records a Hell's Angels bodyguard killing an audience member who attempts to rush the stage at Altamont Speedway in California. (Many critics and historians then and now have suggested this event was the "death knell" of the counterculture.) Often dark and brooding, the film continually refers to the infamous murder. Even the concert footage does not have the celebratory feel of earlier counterculture-focused films, such as D. A. Pennebaker's *Dont Look Back* (1966) and *Monterey Pop* (1968). Because of the Rolling Stones's seemingly timeless popularity, it was and remains the best-known Maysles film. The film takes the Maysles brothers' modernist aesthetic to another level, questioning whether in a world replete with images both real and constructed, it is possible to see anything clearly. Chapter 4 delves into this film.

The Maysles brothers then completed what would be the first of three films about the environmental artists Christo and Jeanne-Claude and their ambitious outdoor projects. In *Christo's Valley Curtain* (1974), a twenty-eight-minute film, Christo is shown creating and supervising a project in which he extended an immense orange drapery between two craggy bluffs in Rifle, Colorado. Christo battles community skepticism, high winds, technical complications, and even his own impatience but ultimately his project emerges from its gigantic plastic cocoon at the film's end. In Christo, the brothers found a kindred spirit, a man whose projects were like direct cinema projects on a grand scale: great leaps into the unknown. Christo approved of the honest (and ultimately supportive) treatment he and his projects received and brought the brothers back to film the making of *Running Fence* (1978) and *Islands* (1986). Still, these films were not artistic challenges for the brothers, and the results, while engaging and full of memorable "spontaneous eruptions," do not move forward their modernist concerns. The Christo films are the subject of chapter 5.

In 1976 came *Grey Gardens*, an intensely personal look at two reclusive women, Edie Beale and Edith Bouvier Beale, the cousin and aunt, respectively, of Jacqueline Bouvier Kennedy Onassis. Originally hired by Onassis's sister, Lee Radziwill, to create a documentary biography of *her* life, the Maysles brothers became fascinated by the mother and daughter who lived in virtual isolation in a ramshackle mansion on Long Island, New York. Radziwill lost interest in her film; Albert and David kept working on their own. The result is a profound, sometimes unnerving, controversial film about isolation and eccentricity. *Grey Gardens* is the Maysles film in which their modernist aesthetic reaches full flower. Complex, searching, provocative, the film also employs numerous direct cinema violations, especially the on-screen appearances of the brothers themselves. The dynamic of the mother-daughter relationship in the film recalls Tennessee Williams's plays, but the circular plot, time imagery, and repetitive language are vintage Faulkner. The Maysles brothers, with the help of masterful editing from Ellen Hovde and Muffie Meyer, created a nonfiction modernist classic, the likes of which they never again achieved. This film is covered in chapter 6.

Before David's sudden death in 1987, the brothers completed several more films: *The Burks of Georgia* (1978), a film for PBS that was part of the "Six American Families" series and that shows the struggles of an impoverished Southern clan; *Muhammad and Larry* (1980) about boxers

Muhammad Ali and Larry Holmes in preparation for a title fight; *Ozawa* (1985), a profile of the Boston Symphony Orchestra conductor Seiji Ozawa; and, again for PBS, the Emmy Award–winning *Vladimir Horowitz: The Last Romantic* (1985). In the last three, the Maysles brothers returned to the already established artist-profile film that they had mastered, relying particularly on extensive close-ups of hands as each man boxes, conducts, or performs, respectively. Having reached artistic heights but limited financial reward with *Grey Gardens*, the brothers secured more commissioned subjects and also successfully ventured into industrial and promotional films. Other projects, including a biographical portrait of the men's mother (tentatively titled *Blue Yonder*) and an exploration of train travel (*Fellow Passengers*), remain partially recorded, still awaiting completion to this day.

During their joint career, the Maysles brothers engaged some of the most controversial and complex issues facing the United States in the late twentieth century: the role and nature of art (*With Love from Truman*, the Christo films, *Ozawa*); the American fascination with celebrity (*Meet Marlon Brando*, *What's Happening!*, *Gimme Shelter*); the counterculture (*Gimme Shelter*); and the competitive, often heartless nature of business (*Salesman*, *Showman*). *Grey Gardens* has important things to say about loneliness and family dynamics, especially among the wealthy elite. That these two women are aunt and cousin to one of the cultural icons of the late twentieth century adds to the film's import. Despite that direct cinema's camera-as-observer style allegedly precluded the brothers from taking an overt stance on social issues, their pragmatic modernism freed them from the initial strictures of Drew Associates and allowed a definitive Maysles point of view to emerge in all their films. They challenged the absurdities of celebrity worship and the forms of media that foster it (*Meet Marlon Brando*, *Gimme Shelter*, *What's Happening!*), questioned the dehumanizing and money-for-money's-sake undercurrent of capitalism (*Showman*, *Salesman*), and celebrated the cause of art and process over philistinism and an unconsidered rejection of the other (Christo films). They remained true to the spirit of authenticity that infused their films with a particularly effective, frequently moving aesthetic quality. Although they did not amass as extensive a body of work as some of their contemporaries, the Maysles brothers stretched the boundaries of nonfiction film, especially in *Salesman*, *Gimme Shelter* and *Grey Gardens*.

2
Celebrity and Authenticity: The Films of 1962–1966

I want to carry movie making to the point where any story-teller can tell his story directly on film with the same personal impact as a Hemingway working with words or an Edward Hopper working with oil paint.—Albert Maysles, "Letter to the Editor of *Film Comment*," 1964

From 1962 to 1966, the Maysles brothers produced four short films, all of which focused on aspects of entertainment or culture. These initial efforts, *Showman* (1962), *What's Happening! The Beatles in the U.S.A.* (1964), *Meet Marlon Brando* (1965), and *With Love from Truman: A Visit with Truman Capote* (1966), established a distinct Maysles style and advanced direct cinema's claims to the authentic. Their modernistic aesthetic is only sporadically evident in these films because of the limitations of the subject matter and the nature of the commissions and more directly because the brothers were still experimenting with form and equipment. Like other direct cinema practitioners, most of whom had been part of Drew Associates, Albert and David Maysles were working out their own strategies and objectives for making films.

As a result, the early Maysles brothers' films may be considered exercises in a nascent direct cinema in which the brothers tested their techniques. In *Showman* and briefly in *Meet Marlon Brando*, for instance, the brothers rely on voice-over narration, an element they avoided in every other film they made. *What's Happening!* contains lengthy on-the-scene tracking shots, established in Robert Drew's *Primary* as a hallmark of direct cinema. (Soon, having been overused, this convention became cliché. Albert all but abandoned the tracking shot in later work.) *With Love from Truman* utilizes crosscutting, an editing strategy not regularly used by other direct cinema filmmakers who advocated a pure chronological approach. All of these early films lack an obvious structure, as the brothers and their coeditors were determining whether a nontraditional means of constructing a film could still lead to an interesting and artistic product. The Maysles brothers were trying to take direct cinema in new directions; at times, in these early films at least, the destination is not entirely clear.

During this period, Albert was also continually tinkering with the technical aspects of moviemaking in order to enhance his ability to observe unobtrusively. "I am interested in using the motion picture camera as a personal device," he wrote to the editor of *Film Comment* in 1964. "The closer I can bring a camera to functioning as an actual human eye, the closer I come to my goal."[1] He and David understood that their equipment needed to be built especially for them, to suit their specific needs. Albert worked at making his camera lighter and easier to shoulder. Developing a special means of balancing the camera and of positioning the viewing tube, he freed up his hands and eliminated equipment obstacles in front of his eyes.[2] The brothers also introduced a camera that could hold more film and that made less noise, leading to fewer distractions for their subjects. David's new, sophisticated sound equipment could be kept in synch with the filming, and he could, simply by watching the movement of the camera, direct his microphone accordingly. Their efforts ultimately came to fruition in 1966 when they began filming the footage for *Salesman*. Before that, the innovations brought them closer to a more effective capturing of spontaneous moments in their early films, even though the technical quality was, on occasion, still uneven and the techniques too varied.[3]

Taken as a group, these films share common thematic ground. Each deals with some aspect of entertainment or the arts, and they all make understated yet articulate points about celebrity in America. They provide visual documentation of and insight into the entertainment world of the early 1960s. In addition, they connect to some of the contemporaneous academic criticism of popular culture and celebrity worship. In 1961, at around the same time that the Maysles brothers began work on *Showman*, American historian Daniel J. Boorstin authored *The Image: A Guide to Pseudo-Events in America*, lamenting the way American society had become fascinated, even obsessed with celebrity. Relying on the emptiness of "pseudo-events" such as press conferences and news releases, the average American, according to Boorstin, "lives in a world where fantasy is more real than reality, where the image has more dignity than its original." As a result, "we become confused about what is spontaneous, about what is really going on out there." Boorstin was not alone in his concerns. Sociologist David Riesman advised an "uncommitted generation" to avoid worshiping the "images we have created" and become more involved in politics and more invested in their own lives. Students for a Democratic Society leader Tom Hayden worried that "an apathetic citizenry" was being "spoon-fed information by a monolithic media." Critical theorists, especially those whose ideas were influenced by Karl Marx, were also reading mass culture's celebrity fixation as an indisputable sign of the corrupting influences of capitalist values.[4]

Like Boorstin, many of the 1960s critics of celebrity centered on questions of authenticity. Boorstin worried that "the authentic news record of what 'happens' or is said comes increasingly to seem to be what is given out in advance," and then "the story prepared 'for future release' acquires an authenticity that competes with that of the actual occurrences on the scheduled date."[5] Would American society's boundless interest in celebrities and their performances both in their respective media and in their real lives lead a nation's people, as Boorstin believed, to think simply that "fame—well-knownness—is ... a hallmark of greatness"?[6] Would people succumb to the spoon-fed superficialities promulgated by the entertainment industry? The threat seemed real.

Direct cinema's filmmakers shared the suspicion of the public's diminishing ability to discern between an authentic and a manufactured personality. The numerous celebrity profile films of this era may be seen as efforts to retrieve the star from the mystique surrounding his or her public persona and reveal the true person within. In making *Jane* (Drew Associates, 1962), for example, the filmmakers hoped to overcome Jane Fonda's closely guarded veneer and provide the viewer with a better understanding of the "authentic" person.[7] Moreover, direct cinema filmmakers strove to bring spontaneity back into the situations their films captured. Press conferences, one of Boorstin's pseudo-events, could be made meaningful again when direct cinema revealed the machinations behind such events—and when well-known people like John F. Kennedy, Bob Dylan, Marlon Brando, and the Beatles were shown working against the superficiality of the experience.

Albert and David Maysles tackled the issue directly in their celebrity-related films. The first step involved taking an audience behind the scenes of the industry. *Showman* unflinchingly reveals the business side of show business: When Joseph E. Levine pitches movies, he is like any salesman peddling his wares—except in this case his product is viewed by millions around the world. (And part of his product is human; Sophia Loren, the star of the Levine production *Two Women*, emerges as the most compelling object for Levine to sell in this film.) *What's Happening!* takes up the issue from there, providing a vivid account of how celebrity worship and mass marketing work in tandem. Only the Beatles' awareness of and humor about their exploitation as stars saves them from completely falling victim to crass commercialism and rampant advertising. Similarly, Marlon Brando's ability to disarm his interviewers and to reassert his own identity prevents him from succumbing entirely to the trap of celebrity. In *Meet Marlon Brando*, the Hollywood actor who has never welcomed stardom stands off against interviewers who want him to play a role he finds distasteful: that of a celebrity promoting his latest vehicle. Ultimately, however, neither the Beatles nor Brando attempt to subvert the system totally; they may question or mock it, but they do not shun it. Their ironic detachment only takes them so far. Truman Capote, on the other hand, offers an alternative in the nonfiction prose of his book *In Cold Blood* (and in the Maysles brothers' film about him): an artistic expression based in reality that attempts to present its story authentically. Not surprisingly, the Maysles brothers saw Capote as a fellow traveler, as they, too, advocated an art form that would not cater, as do most of Levine's and Brando's films or the Beatles' songs, to a popular audience without challenging their sensibilities. An authentic text presents the world and its people honestly, asking difficult questions without providing easy answers. How the Maysles brothers might themselves accomplish this was still under exploration.

Showman introduces a problem (excessive selling and celebrity worship in the world of the arts and entertainment), the Beatles and Brando films show self-aware artists attempting to negotiate the problem, and the Truman Capote film offers an alternative. The problem did not prompt a solution necessarily but rather an artistic means of expression that potentially steered away from the issue of celebrity excess and commercialism. Neither Capote nor the Maysles brothers were naive enough to believe their work could ever replace the popular forms of art and entertainment that were promulgated by Levine and advanced, albeit somewhat reluctantly, by the Beatles and Brando. But the brothers held great hope that they could offer something more substantial, more "really real" than most of what was currently in movie theaters and books. David asserted in 1964, "Our purpose is to have an emotional involvement from the audience—an interest, an excitement. We want them to feel that it's worthwhile what they are seeing, that they perhaps will learn something or get some insight."[8]

Of course, the goal of seeing celebrities more authentically and of stripping away their carefully wrought pretenses and looking under the surface was more formidable than the Maysles brothers or other direct cinema practitioners realized at the time. The films that sought to unmask celebrity ironically depended on the very construct of celebrity; that is, the appeal and draw of the films were the celebrities themselves. After all, why would an audience care about meeting Marlon Brando or Jane Fonda or the Beatles if not for the fact that they were famous? Given the relative shapelessness of most direct cinema, what besides the celebrity's name value provides any kind of ballast for the films?

Such an assessment of direct cinema's celebrity-based films reveals a contradiction that shadowed much of the Maysles brothers' career. Of their thirteen major works, nine are profiles of either a popular-culture celebrity or a well-known artist. Although the brothers found ways to criticize celebrity worship in their early films and in their later films praised artists like Christo and Vladimir Horowitz for transcending the financial and personal temptations of popular culture, they nevertheless made films and profited (albeit modestly) from the fame of these particular individuals. Adopting celebrity as the subject of their films, they acceded to the process in a significant way. They were simultaneously a part of and a remedy for the problem they presented. For the Maysles brothers, it would remain an unresolved tension in much of their work.

SHOWMAN

Even before establishing Maysles Films in 1962, the brothers had been looking for a subject that would lend itself well to their preferred kind of filmmaking. With Drew Associates, they had gained valuable experience, but they were hoping to branch out, to do something more expansive artistically with the new techniques that they had helped to develop. They worried little about distribution or commissions at this point; they intended to finance the project entirely themselves and maintain total artistic control. They knew that the day-in-the-life format suited direct cinema well, but they wanted to steer away from filming an already well-known personality.

What the brothers knew about movie producer Levine intrigued them. Like the Maysles brothers, he had grown up in Boston. He had earned a reputation in Hollywood (where David had worked for four years) as a shrewd businessman and seemed like the kind of man whose life could be effectively captured in the realistic style of direct cinema. In interviews at the time, Albert and David admitted they were operating on sheer instinct; they "had a hunch" about Levine. "We wanted to find out if this hunch was correct, and we wanted to find out something about his schedule. We showed him some of the films we had made, we talked to him, we found out about his schedule, it interested us, and we told him what we were going to do." Levine was surprised but undaunted that someone would want to film his day-to-day activities and agreed to the project. Two weeks later, the brothers began filming him in action.[9] David recalled, "We didn't have any letter from any kind of a network or place that he would respect. We were just two guys. We had this camera on our shoulder and a recorder. I guess he couldn't believe that we were really making a film."[10] As a result, within the film, Levine appears to forget that the camera is watching him. Like many of the subjects of the early direct cinema films, Levine is thoroughly engrossed in his own activities (one might say engrossed in himself), so that he only rarely acknowledges the camera's presence and even then only momentarily. Indeed, one of the great advantages of the direct cinema films of the early 1960s was the relative innocence of all those being filmed. Because television was a new medium and because direct cinema films had not received wide distribution, subjects' overt performing for the camera did not yet pose a significant problem.

With *Showman*, the brothers adopted the realistic style of filmmaking that had characterized the Drew Associates films. In the opening sequence, for example, a swarm of paparazzi surrounds actress Sophia Loren. The photographers and reporters frantically call out to her and snap her picture. Albert's camera is located amidst the crowd, and, not surprisingly, the filmed images are unsteady and blurry at times. The film then cuts to Levine seated at a round table, making a deal with other producers. In both short segments, the tilted camera angles and imperfect sound recording indicate that the scenes presented are not manufactured or staged; they are actual unrehearsed moments captured on film. *Showman* immediately assures its audience that it will be witness to behind-the-scenes negotiations as well as the celebrity-centered events those deals engender. Moreover, the initial juxtaposition of scenes links the star and her producer: The film implies that the frenzy of Loren's appearance has been made possible by what has transpired around the producers' meeting table.

In the next few moments of the film, a voice-over narrator describes the scene at the table: "Showmen, promoters, gamblers, their aim is to get you to the box office." This first voice-over establishes that this film will explore the entertainment world from a businessman's perspective: Levine "builds up a title or a star; either way he gets a piece of your dollar. . . . The stakes are high, the market is the world." In between the narration, the slick and portly Levine sells. His voice has a heavily accented, nasal quality, and he punctuates his phrases with a salesman's hyperbole; when he speaks, everything is "big," and the pace is quick. His intensity as a movie producer verifies that he will indeed be an ideal subject of study. His apparent disregard for the camera aids the authenticity of the scene. In his world, it seems, the deal supersedes any self-consciousness he might feel.

The crisp writing and spare description aside, however, the decision to use voice-over narration in *Showman* compromises the authenticity. Although the copy is concise and factual, and the narrator, Norman Rosten, never dominates the film, the device does steer the audience's reactions to what is shown. The narration also proves unnecessary, as the information conveyed is provided visually or through the conversations of the filmed subjects. *Showman*'s voice-over marks a rare moment when the Maysles brothers erred on the side of greater clarity, which to the brothers generally meant overguiding the audience. In this early direct cinema effort, when some of their parameters were still being established, even Albert and David, who have trusted their audiences as much as any other team working in nonfiction film, felt they needed to provide some background information to the viewer. Had they made the same film even five years later, they would certainly have eschewed the narration. (Indeed, one of Al's six commandments, developed later in a mission statement, is to avoid narration.)[11]

Although the overall structure of the film is quite loose, one particular storyline does thread its way through the picture. We learn that Loren has won an Academy Award for her performance in Levine's *Two Women*; she could not, however, attend the ceremony to accept the award. Levine accepts for her and then delivers the Oscar personally to her in Rome. Still, to describe this film as being about Loren's Oscar win would be a gross misrepresentation. *Showman* observes Levine's life over a two-week period. The fact that the Academy Award component occurs is one of the happy coincidences the Maysles brothers hoped to find when they took on the project. Even in their earliest films, they maintained that because reality was complex, spontaneously unfolding, and frequently ambiguous, their films ought to reflect that same reality. Consequently, they never intentionally built a crisis format or any other structure into this or their later films (the Christo films provide a partial exception); rather, they believed that whatever structure could be formulated would have to come more or less fortuitously. They were adamant about not "interfer[ing] with the subject; we tried to just film it, to select scenes that were interesting to us, and we thought would make for continuity, for story."[12] Whatever structure happens occurs only after editing helps shape it, but there is no preconceived notion as to how it ought to go. In this and every subsequent Maysles brothers' film, that tension between spontaneity and edited continuity makes the finished products different from virtually any other nonfiction films—and from the 1960s to the present day also makes their films easy to misunderstand or misinterpret.

Showman, then, does what every Maysles film attempts to do: It presents a complicated world and depicts the people within it as doing their best to make their way through. Its primary subject, Levine, is neither a villain nor a saint. In the many scenes in which he is a salesman, he usually comes across as unctuous or arrogant. He wants to turn Loren's Oscar win into a major overseas distribution deal for the film and especially when on the telephone, pitches hard. "All I have to do is continue to bring you Oscars, and you'll be a smart man," he tells one distributor. But just as often, Levine is portrayed as a vulnerable man, one whose insecurities motivate him as much as his quest for profit does. Alone at breakfast following the Academy Awards, Levine solicits congratulations and opinions from the woman serving him. She appeases him but also shrewdly points out that the Oscar honor benefits Loren *and* Levine. Soon after, Levine admits he is exhausted; the tireless seller appears lonely and weak in this segment.

One pivotal sequence in *Showman* further illustrates Levine's vulnerability. He returns to his Boston West End neighborhood as the guest of honor at a special dinner. Having been introduced as a sincere and admirable man of the people, one who never forgets that for West Enders, "a smile and a handshake are genuine," Levine takes the podium and reflects about his own "difficult days in difficult times." In the portion of the speech revealed in the film, Levine does not placate the smiling crowd with humorous anecdotes and platitudes. Rather, he asserts that he "had not one day of happiness there" and that he did everything in his power to "escape" the mean streets of Boston. Without pretension, Levine surprises the assembled crowd with his candor and presents himself as an American success story, a man who through sheer determination escaped poverty and achieved wealth and notoriety. This segment, placed in the center of the film, following more than thirty minutes of Levine's negotiations and impersonal business dealings, shifts the tone of the film abruptly.

The scene that follows does even more to establish Levine as a sympathetic figure. Recounting his banquet speech the next day, Levine reveals that he was genuinely moved by the experience, not because he was honored by the old neighborhood's tribute but because he had been forced to come to terms with the demons of his past. He tells two unidentified men that he is disappointed at the way so many of his former neighbors claim to be his friends now that he is famous, when they had acted much differently forty years before. His voice nearly cracks, and his speech becomes animated as he explains at length how much he despised the difficult childhood he endured. Avoiding a manipulative technique, Albert instead keeps his camera in a medium-range close-up (a head-and-shoulders shot of a seated Levine) and allows the moment to speak for itself. In these two sequences, Levine is humanized and made likable for the first time. These scenes propose that underneath the man's all-business exterior, there is simply a man who, like most human beings, longs for meaningful communication and human connection. Despite his aggressive manner in a business setting, he is as susceptible to emotional anguish as anyone when reliving difficult childhood episodes. One critic noticed that in these reminiscence scenes, Levine "the ruthless film mogul is reduced to human proportions."[13] A better way to phrase it, in light of the Maysles brothers' aims, may be that this is one scene in which Levine is *elevated* to human proportions, in which his human side at last becomes clear.

But *Showman* never allows the audience to become too comfortable with this gentler Levine. The childhood poverty revelations are followed by a segment in which Levine makes a guest appearance on radio station WMCA, the "voice of New York." Levine squares off against cultural critic David Susskind, who dismisses most of Levine's films, especially the enormously popular *Hercules*, as trivial and insulting to an audience's intelligence. Levine brusquely defends his productions, finally boasting that he has been able to "use the same methods to sell *Two Women* that I used to sell *Hercules*." Even after the station cuts to a commercial, Levine continues to argue his point. For Levine, a film is a film, a product is a product; he makes clear he has no time or interest for a critic's distinctions between low art (i.e., mass culture) and high art.

Then, Levine is back to business in several scenes, all of which demonstrate that his business dealings never let up and that he is a master of promotion and celebrity management. First, he tries to impress rising star Kim Novak, whom Levine praises as a "nice girl" whom he wants for his next picture. He stages a grand reception and sets up a cocktail party in

New York City on her behalf, inviting many photographers to capture the events. Next, he fires one of his associates. Although the actual dismissal occurs off-camera, the audience learns from the fired man that he and Levine have "parted ways," precipitated in large part by this man's lack of production (according to Levine). Next, the producer jets to Rome, Oscar in hand, to meet with Loren. The numerous staged photographic events along the way emphasize Levine's desire to turn the award into increased box office domestically and abroad. Although Levine and Loren admit to feeling awkward and uncomfortable as they hug and pose for the camera, they endure the ordeal for the sake of publicity. They drink flat champagne and toast her victory as the paparazzi record every gesture.

Yet, suddenly, just when Levine has reestablished himself as an unfeeling, crass negotiator, his softer side reappears. Having returned to Boston for some "campaigning," as he calls it, Levine discusses his busy worldwide travel schedule with two friends. One of the friends reacts with awe and envy: "That's really great, Joe. That's something." Rather than continue to impress, however, Levine reverses: "It's *not* good. It became tiresome years ago. . . . It's not terrific. [He leans back in his chair.] It's tiresome." The film then cuts to a long shot of Levine walking away, his back to the camera, across a runway towards an airplane. Another trip, another sale, this image suggests; tiresome or not, Levine has helped create a world that now moves according to its own momentum. Even a showman may not be in total control, but the show must go on. This last image holds until the credits begin.

Not surprisingly, the complexity of the portrait produced an array of responses. Reports at the time indicated that some audience members believed the film was a "whitewash" of Levine and the Hollywood film industry, while others saw it as too harsh.[14] Some others discounted the film for its formlessness.[15] But the lack of a traditional structure supports one of the film's primary points: that Levine, like any person, is a complex and multifaceted character. Louis Marcorelles, a French film critic and one of the Maysles brothers' early admirers, appreciated the inherent contradictions: Levine "is the sore in the living flesh of the American society, the symbol of a social mechanism which has become delirious, but each second on the screen he remains a man, our brother, with all his dimensions. . . ."[16] As a result, as Charles Reynolds has correctly pointed out, "we see, and interpret in our own terms, the real man as he lives his life."[17] Albert and David were themselves pleased with the end result. They appreciated the way they had created a form that was "more organic, multi-sided and complex—many different feelings, moods, situations are reflected, the character of the man is presented in a more complex manner."[18] The brothers trusted their audience to draw meaning from the film and to learn something about the man therein. "We have faith that by filming a thing as it happens and without imposing our judgment, even if we film something that obviously shows the person to be 'bad,' then because we are letting it happen out of itself, everything from which to judge will be right there on the screen."[19] Allowing the audience to come to its own conclusions was thereby established as a key component of a Maysles Films production.

Despite the open-ended nature of both the structure and message, the film does reveal that the entertainment industry relies on the same strategies as other businesses looking to peddle a product. Levine might as well be selling soap or breakfast cereal; his methods, we can assume, would be much the same. That the product is sometimes a human one—Loren and Novak in the scenes in the film—makes little difference. Levine refuses to distinguish between or among the various films he has produced, even though *Hercules*, a frothy epic with elaborately staged battle scenes, and *Two Women*, a dark contemplation of life in post-war Italy, are markedly different. Levine's moments of vulnerability notwithstanding, the film memorably illuminates his adamant regard for profit before artistic merit. Even Loren's Academy Award win, the laurel of a dramatic performance well done, is turned into a marketing and promotion scheme. The object itself becomes tangible evidence of Levine's success.

Not every moment of *Showman* is effective at conveying that point, nor does the complete fifty-three-minute biographical portrait hold together as coherently as it might. Still experimenting with form and content, the Maysles brothers produced a film that is uneven and more ambiguous than it might have been. Given their own concerns, they could have made their critique of celebrity-oriented culture much sharper, inasmuch as Levine, not a celebrity himself, has a less ambivalent interaction with the phenomenon than the subjects of the brothers' three subsequent films. Nevertheless, *Showman* stands as an important step in early direct cinema. Without relying on a crisis or any other obvious structure, the brothers redefined the way a direct cinema film could be made. While focusing their attention on an individual man's situation, they offered universal insights into the human condition—an achievement that was central to their larger designs for filmmaking. Operating without commercial or artistic constraints, they achieved their goal of producing a different kind of documentary. The creative freedom they enjoyed on this project would not be duplicated until work on *Salesman* began four years later.

WHAT'S HAPPENING! THE BEATLES IN THE U.S.A.

Maysles Films' second major project came about unexpectedly. On 7 February 1964, the brothers received a call from Granada, a British television production company that wanted them to make a documentary of the Beatles' first visit to the United States. Although the call came only two hours before the group was due to arrive in New York City, Albert and David accepted the assignment. They met the Beatles at the airport and spent the next five days filming them as they traveled from New York to Washington, D.C., to Miami, a trip that included the group's famous appearances on the *Ed Sullivan Show*.[20] Because *What's Happening!* documents a specific moment in time—the Beatles' American invasion, 7–11 February 1964—the excitement is built into the subject matter; there is no need to create dramatic impact through structure or crisis.

As befits the subject matter, *What's Happening!* moves with great energy and fervor. Albert, still experimenting with his equipment and style of filming, tried a variety of camera angles and techniques that captured and complemented the excitement of the Beatles' first visit to America. The film features tracking shots, hand-held camera work amidst dancing crowds or screaming fans, and panning shots in which he focuses on people and scenes in the background. Albert and his camera are curious, energetic, experimental, and spontaneous in the film. The film style emphasizes the of-the-moment nature of the Beatles' stardom, and Albert's alert filming of spontaneous moments underscores the idea that the Beatles are a phenomenon, the latest craze and hottest popular commodity. The way the film was shot and edited reflected David's goal of "trying to show how they typify a great part of American youth. I feel there is a sort of restlessness."[21] The Beatles are, as New York disc jockey Murray the K repeats in the film, "what's happening."

They are also, the film illustrates, a likable group of young men. From their first on-camera appearance at a press conference to their final waves goodbye as they board an airplane to London, the "Fab Four" are charming throughout. At the press conference, they field questions with confidence and an amusing flippancy. Asked (as they constantly were) about their hair, Paul McCartney retorts, "I'm actually bald," and Ringo Starr jokes that he just had a haircut. When someone requests a song, they respond in unison, "No!" They are wise enough to know when to perform and when simply to promote their image as lovable Liverpudlians. Despite their media-savvy responses, however, their overall attitude reflects a certain innocence that was pervasive both within the group and culturally in early 1964. At this point, rock and roll was not perceived as a threat to the status quo as it would be later in the decade; the music was still a curiosity, and its musical acts were harmless novelties.[22] The Beatles themselves had just started to break through to an American audience. Although many hits would follow, only "She Loves You" and "I Want to Hold Your Hand" had charted in the United States when the Beatles first arrived.

Thus, in the film, the Beatles appear both fascinated and amused by the stir they are beginning to create in the United States. The press conference scene is followed by a shot of McCartney in a car, listening to a broadcast of the press conference. Holding a small transistor radio to his ear, he smiles at their earlier quips and responds, "Oh really?" when it is reported what the group will be doing the next day. The device of listening to or watching a recorded media appearance would become a common one in direct cinema and would be used again extensively in the Maysles-Zwerin film *Gimme Shelter*. The amused reactions of the celebrity to his or her performance allowed the filmmaker to reveal the truth behind the contrivance of the mainstream media's interview of that celebrity. The celebrity in turn becomes a surrogate for the filmmakers' criticism of popular media, and with a sort of knowing wink, filmmaker and subject reveal that they are in agreement on this issue. To some degree, McCartney and the others can control what they say and how they behave at such a pseudo-event; they can even have a good laugh about it after the fact.

For the most part, as the film takes pains to show, these four young men were enjoying their sudden and unparalleled stardom in 1964—and they were not taking it terribly seriously. In the film, we see that they are keenly aware that they are regarded as commodities but at this point in their careers seem willing to go along for the ride. They laugh and cavort with an innocent ease whenever they interact with the public, including their late-night adventures at the Peppermint Twist dance club. Starr is especially animated and friendly, and Albert's man-on-the-spot camera work in the dance scene captures the drummer's youthful vitality.

Two of the film's most effective scenes occur aboard trains carrying the group to their next gig. In the first of these, the Beatles ride from New York City to Washington, D.C., signing autographs and smiling for photographs along the way. Paul muses, "It's like running for president" as he makes his way down the train's aisle. (John Lennon, of course, would raise the stakes later when he compared the Beatles' popularity to that of Jesus.) In a meaningful role reversal, Starr absconds with as many cameras as he can manage to strap around his neck and lumbers his way down the aisle. In this brief turnabout, Ringo highlights the absurdity of the paparazzi's relentless pursuit of the band. Meanwhile, the group persistently pokes fun at the ubiquitous presence of advertising in the United States. During the train ride (and on several other occasions throughout the film), group mem--bers perform mock advertisements, including one for Marlboro cigarettes and another for Coca-Cola. In the second train scene (from D.C. to Miami), a more serious and philosophical McCartney says, "Everyone's so used to it [advertising] that it doesn't look funny anymore in America." He then relates how the evening news moves seamlessly from a tragic real event to a plug for yet-another product.

Aware of the numbing effects of advertising and celebrity, the individual Beatles also struggle to maintain some sort of unique identity apart from their collective one. On several occasions in the film, one member of the group is asked, "Which one are you?" as if it were impossible for the public to distinguish one from another. The confusion may be attributed to more than their similar hairstyles; because they are consistently mass marketed as a collective body, they are a group first and individuals only incidentally. The Beatles as a commodity were crucial in launching rock and roll into a whole new, extremely profitable orbit, and there are constant reminders in the film that the popular success of the group is a product-based cultural phenomenon.[23] The film shows bobbing-head Beatles dolls as well as posters, album covers, and the images from numerous photo shoots. Wherever the Beatles go, the screaming fans demand these by-products as well as the ultimate product: the Beatles themselves. Even when identified as individuals, they were generally only given first names (as on *The Ed Sullivan Show*) or referred to generically as the "drummer" (Ringo Starr) or "the married one" (John Lennon). In one scene in the film, the Beatles themselves call out, "Which one are you?" from their Miami hotel room to a small crowd on the beach below. This role reversal, reminiscent of Starr's acquisition of the cameras and foreshadowing Brando's deflections of his interviewers' questions, suggests the band members felt more than amusement about their lack of individuality. In this film, they consistently laugh it off, but over the years, it would take its toll on all four.[24]

Less accomplished than the more complete *Showman*, the Beatles film has certain fundamental flaws. Both train episodes are, for the most part, spontaneous and amusing, but very little is revealed about the Beatles, other than they know how to attract and entertain a crowd and that they think American advertising is a lark. The limited preparation, along with the relatively short period of time for the filming itself, conspired to create a depth problem. The viewer never learns, for instance, that George

Harrison was so ill with the flu that he almost did not perform on the first Sullivan program; or that John Lennon's first wife, Cynthia, came along with the band on this tour; or even that the group was pelted with jelly beans (in an apparent sign of affection) during their concert hall performances.[25] All of these points, in hindsight, are relevant details of a significant episode in American cultural history. Although the brothers cannot be faulted for failing to predict the enormity of the Beatles' success, the lack of probing in the film nevertheless underscores one of the potential pratfalls of direct cinema, a process that at times has difficulty getting under the surface of things.

Another weakness of *What's Happening!* is that the Beatles remain guarded and self-conscious throughout. Whenever the camera appears, they are "on"; only rarely, as when McCartney tries to sleep on the second train ride or in the aforementioned car scene do the band members let their guards down. The Maysles brothers would face a similar problem with the well-polished Rolling Stones in *Gimme Shelter*. Only the Altamont murder provided a means to break through their collective persona. As a result, much of the footage has a sameness to it, and a portion of that falls flat. During the early years of direct cinema, many of the celebrity-based films suffered the same fate; without a preconceived conceit to push the stars to open themselves to the camera, many of the celebrities simply chose not to or presented only a small portion of themselves as is the case in the Beatles film.

There is a deeper story line only tangentially covered in *What's Happening!* The Beatles themselves did not entirely avoid the trappings of celebrity. In the film, despite their bemused stance, their mocking tributes to advertising, and even their more deep-seated concerns, the Beatles never mount much opposition or try to subvert their commercial success. They dutifully appear on Ed Sullivan's show three times, politely address fans and media, and earn the praise and admiration of even people as unhip as Sullivan and the composer Richard Rodgers. Their passive acceptance of their celebrity would change in subsequent years (John Lennon's reticence in this film suggests he was already uncomfortable with it), but in 1964, they were "what's happening" and willing to be so.

The Maysles brothers, too, manifested a problematic relationship with celebrity. While they supported the Beatles' moments of resistance, they also contributed to the celebrity machine. *What's Happening!* became part of a publicity juggernaut that turned the Beatles into one of the most successful musical commodities of the twentieth century. The purpose of the commissioned film was to document and celebrate the Beatles' tour of the United States; the film was shown in Great Britain (and later on American television) and advanced further the Beatles' success. Agreeing to the commission, the Maysles brothers willingly relinquished a great deal of control. Certainly, they made the film in the way they wanted to and shaped and edited it according to their own interests and style, but they had virtually no control over what happened to the film after it was made. As a result, their film had the unintended result of becoming part of the very inauthentic system they had criticized. Thus did their critique of the entertainment business become compromised.[26]

MEET MARLON BRANDO

The making of *Meet Marlon Brando* paralleled the necessarily hurried effort in making the Beatles film. A New York producer contacted the Maysles brothers and inquired whether they would film Marlon Brando while he was being interviewed at the Hampshire House in New York City. Promoting his most recent film, *Code Name: Morituri*, Brando was going to be interviewed by a series of print and broadcast journalists, as arranged by the film's distributor, Twentieth Century Fox. The assignment seemed straightforward enough. Once on the scene, however, the brothers realized they "had something that could be a film though it was not anticipated by them or their employers. They shot more than they planned and more than they were being paid to shoot. When they put all the footage together, what had been bits and pieces of a television campaign turned out to be a film about Brando starring himself."[27] This pattern of discovering a film subject where none had been perceived would repeat itself and lead to the films *Gimme Shelter* and *Grey Gardens*. In this case, it was Brando who helped the project rise above the pedestrian nature of the assignment; the Maysles brothers, perceiving what they believed to be a self-aware artist, showed Brando in a way most viewers had not seen before.

Brando, like Levine, reveals his complexity in this twenty-eight-minute film. He is charming, forthright, passionate about Native Americans and race relations, articulate about the media; he is also sexist, hypocritical, sarcastic, and uncooperative. Although David and Albert respected Brando's ability to deflate the contrived situation, they do not present a whitewash of the man. He is revealed to be a complicated person who happens also to be a movie star. The film shows him trying to come to terms with what is for him a disturbing notion: that he, like the Beatles or Loren in *Showman*, is a mere object, a commodity in the motion picture industry. The film is remarkably simple; the vast majority of filmed footage consists of two-shots, with Brando shoulder to shoulder with his interviewer. Occasionally, Albert provides a close-up in order to capture Brando's expressions or those of his questioners. The limitations of the filmed scenes are due in large measure to the nature of the assignment, but the result gives the film an appropriately cloistered feel; Brando acts as if the interview process is trapping him, and Albert's fixed camera position supports that notion.

Brando's first audible remarks are quips, setting a tone for a good portion of his dialogue in the filmed interviews. Asked what occupation he might have taken if he had not become an actor, he muses that he might have been a masseur or a forest ranger. Disarming his interviewers in this manner is a favorite strategy of Brando's, and he deploys it frequently and effectively in the film. The strategy also marks him as being self-aware and in control of the process, qualities the brothers admired. In this same segment, the camera is positioned further back than it will be for the bulk of the film; the more removed position allows Albert to reveal the numerous paparazzi surrounding Brando—similar to the scene of Loren and the photographers in *Showman*. A brief voice-over narration follows, the conclusion of which highlights the brothers' sympathetic treatment of the subject: "The reporters asked many predictable questions. Mr. Brando gives few predictable answers. Marlon Brando has always reserved the right to think for himself, to answer for himself, and, if necessary, to go against the grain." An independent mind and a shrewd awareness of his own celebrity status allow Brando to transcend the moment, the film suggests. His self-awareness amounts to self-preservation amidst the mad rush to meet him. We understand that the interviewers have little concern with meeting Brando the man; they have come to speak with Brando the movie star who, according to the rules of the engagement, should dutifully promote his latest endeavor. Instead, Brando resists this particular role, opting instead to go against the grain.

Another of Brando's self-preserving tactics involves turning a question back at the interviewer. Those who cannot or will not play along are quickly taken to task. After the voice-over introduction, the first interviewer, a woman who describes Brando as "one of the most exciting and talented men in America today," provokes a sardonic retort: "When was the last time you saw me nude?" Brando then grumbles about his weight (which at the time was not nearly the concern it would later become for him). When another woman mentions that he has a charming personality, he challenges, "How do you know what my personality is?" Her confident but feeble reply that he "radiates his personality" prompts Brando's disappointed "Really?" Another man's question "How do you keep from getting scarred?" elicits the very same question in the other direction. This particular interviewer handles the deflection skillfully, but Brando maintains the upper hand.

Brando's most frequent disarming tactic is to elevate the mundane conversation above what he calls the huckstering of his film. Ignoring a blithe statement from one interviewer, he warns against the power of media propaganda; he similarly advises another, "I don't think that we should believe what we hear." He steers a Philadelphia reporter into a discussion of the city's brotherly love, which in turn leads to his thoughts on race relations and Dr. Louis Leakey's latest anthropological findings. Brando and an iron-jawed interviewer converse about the actor's favorite subject, the plight of the American Indian ("that's not something I can be flippant about"). And he leads a twenty-one-year-old former Miss U.S.A. into a deliberation on juvenile delinquency. The most memorable example of this elevation tactic occurs in the only scene filmed outside of the hotel. Standing in front of a Central Park entrance, Brando fields a question from a French reporter about personal responsibility for social problems. Speaking in French (his words are translated on the soundtrack), Brando offers a thoughtful reply, then, upon noticing an African-American woman walking by, he stops and brings her into the discussion. He repeats that the French reporter had asked him if the American government is responsible for "the progress of Negroes" and then asks the woman for her response. She contends that every person must take responsibility for his or her own life. This interchange legitimizes Brando's position as a serious man whose interests go beyond acting and certainly beyond the kinds of trite conversation he had been enduring in the Hampshire House. The moment stands as one of those fortuitous spontaneous moments for which Albert patiently waited.

Maintaining a sense of an authentic self that is separate from one's celebrity persona seems to be as important to Brando as it was to the Beatles, and his attempts at resisting the hucksterism of film promotion make him a mostly sympathetic figure in the film. Brando bluntly acknowledges that his popularity is much like a "hula hoop" or a "flyswatter." Although he recognizes that he is a popular Hollywood commodity for now, he knows he has a limited shelf life. If he wishes to set himself apart at all, Brando wishes to do so based on his knowledge of what he deems are important issues (race relations, the plight of Native Americans, education). Thus, he attempts to direct the conversation away from his performance in *Morituri* to more immediate, real-life concerns. He tries to convince those interviewing him (and by extension the film audience) that "thumping the tub" for a Hollywood film is trivial and even spurious. "It's only the movies" is the film's subtext, and that Brando understands this alerts, with a knowing wink, the audience that Brando, like the Beatles, will never be totally subsumed by the business side of show business. Unlike Levine in *Showman*, Brando takes no pride in the buying and selling aspect of Hollywood. Indeed, Brando continually mocks the whole enterprise, sarcastically stating (in the film's final segment), "For God's sake, go see that [film], will you, because you really won't know how to proceed in life if you don't see *Morituri*." He also tries to reconnect with the general public when he suggests that "we are all actors." That he happens to be paid (and paid well) for being a professional actor does not mean that he is better than or wiser than others.

Still, Brando's position should not be lauded absolutely. Whatever deeply held convictions he espouses in the film, he seems to do under the duress of the moment, not solely because he wishes to seize the opportunity to promote social change or to overturn the commercialism of Hollywood. His is a spontaneous performance, often convincing but also at times stilted and inarticulate. Frequently he is profound and insightful; but nearly as often he is flippant and sarcastic merely for the sake of it. His treatment of the women reporters—all of whom became objects of his flirtations—is especially appalling and undermines his more serious points. His consistent references to their looks or their personal mannerisms taints the discussions. (Your voice is like "pulverized walnuts," he tells the Philadelphia reporter who has patiently listened to his less than convincing assessment of Leakey's findings on human aggression.) Even when he pulls aside the African-American woman to ask her opinion, he is also clearly attracted to her beauty.

Brando sees himself as trapped in a world he cannot escape—and hindsight allows us to see that his attempts to rise above it were then and later insubstantial. Like Levine, much of what Brando must do may be tiresome, but he continued to do it and did so until his death. Many years after this little film, Brando's career may be regarded as having been less encumbered than most stars by the double bind of celebrity—he remained a mostly private figure—but he never made his revelatory Native American film, nor did he find a convincing way to unmask the falseness of Hollywood.

Meet Marlon Brando, like most of the Maysles brothers' work, thus resists a clear reading. In the film, Brando comes across both heroically and pathetically. Robert Steele recognized the duality of the portrait when he observed in 1966, "Brando is free as an individual in the Maysles' film, but also shows he wear blinders" because he willingly allowed himself to be used as a promotional tool and accepted enormous payoffs for doing so.[28] Like the Beatles, Brando understood the nature of his dilemma, but he did not cast it off. Indeed, Brando blocked the film from having a wide release, even years after it had been made.

Although the Maysles brothers presented Brando as being wise to the celebrity game, they actually enhanced the star's image (as a difficult celebrity) and helped to promote the film Brando himself seems eager *not* to promote. For despite Brando's consistent downplaying, the Maysles brothers' film, had it been released more widely, would undoubtedly have created more, not less interest in *Morituri*. Those who have studied the phenomenon of celebrity have noticed that when audiences are provided glimpses into what purports to be the authentic individual behind the façade of celebrity, the result is generally *greater* interest in the celebrity and his or her work.[29] Certainly, many viewers would have wanted to see if Brando's lack of support for *Morituri* was justified. Then, if that film proved to be "just another product" as Brando alludes, his authenticity would only have increased in his fans' eyes. The Maysles brothers' critique of celebrity, rooted in a genuine humanistic philosophy, neglected to take this into account (and again they were limited by the scope of this project). They would need to profile a different kind of celebrity in order to avoid this dilemma in the future.

WITH LOVE FROM TRUMAN

In the mid-1960s, National Educational Television (a forerunner of the Public Broadcasting Service) commissioned a series of films on novelists and their work. The producers contacted the Maysles brothers and asked them if they would be interested in making a film on an author. Given the option to choose whomever they pleased, the brothers selected Truman Capote because of the perceived parallels in artistic approach, a perception that was certainly borne out. Although initially Capote was reluctant to be filmed (this reluctance is evident in the early part of the film), he eventually acquiesced.[30]

The resulting film serves as an exploration of a contemporary author's quest for his own method of achieving authenticity. Capote's *In Cold Blood* had just been released to critical and popular acclaim in 1966. The book takes as its subject the brutal 1959 murders in Holcomb, Kansas, of four members of the Clutter family, then traces the investigation, trial, and subsequent capital punishment of the two convicted killers. Riding high on that success, Capote had begun to think that his nonfiction-novel concept might revolutionize the way fact and fiction could be intertwined in prose. Within the film, he asserts, "Factual writing can reach the altitudes of poetry that poetry does. And at the same time it has the extraordinary extra dimension of being completely true." This poetic rendering of the truth made him an ideal subject for the Maysles brothers, two men who aspired to do much the same in their films.

Due in large part to NET constraints, the structure and content of the film are straightforward. Over the course of the twenty-nine minutes, Capote discusses his work, particularly *In Cold Blood*, and relates some of his thoughts about the writer's craft in general. Rather than interview him themselves, the Maysles brothers had other people (primarily *Newsweek*'s Karen Denison) perform that task. Unlike the filmed reporters in *Showman*, *What's Happening!*, and especially *Meet Marlon Brando*, however, Denison is never even implicitly ridiculed for her questioning, nor does she steer the interview towards promotion for herself or any product. Competent and trustworthy throughout, she also appears for the most part comfortable on camera, and there are only a few apparent awkward moments in which either she or Capote self-consciously performs.

Several different filmed scenes constitute this film, providing a less claustrophobic environment than in the Brando film. First, Capote is seen at a restaurant speaking to an unidentified reporter, explaining how he takes a dispassionate approach to writing for the sake of the product. He speaks about wanting to convey an emotional quality to an audience without being too caught up in the emotion himself: "You know if you can reproduce [the feeling], you can make it have exactly the same effect on someone else." Immediately, then, the Maysles brothers give voice to one of Capote's and their own philosophical tenets. An honest and direct reproduction of material obtained from real life *can* have an emotional impact on the audience. Like the Maysles brothers, Capote entrusts his audience to understand and appreciate this material without having to be manipulated.

From the restaurant, the film cuts to Capote in his publisher's office signing a copy of *In Cold Blood*. The camera provides a close-up of the book's title page whereupon Capote has written, "With Love from Truman." Soon after, Denison appears (Capote introduces her self-consciously to the camera); the film cuts to Capote and Denison riding in the back seat of a car. They are traveling, he announces, to Capote's Long Island studio. The car shot, one of the staples of direct cinema filming, is in this case both authentic and stilted. While Capote seizes the opportunity to discuss his new form of writing, he is less articulate than usual. Of course, even Albert's ostensibly unobtrusive equipment would affect such a situation. The brothers have frequently relied on inside-a-car footage, most famously in *Salesman*, and the effect is generally the same in the Capote film: The subject in a trapped environment performs more self-consciously than usual albeit generally in an interesting and self-revelatory way.

Capote seems much more at ease in the next fifteen minutes of the film, which takes place inside his Long Island studio. Perhaps the Bloody Marys Capote prepares help to relax him, or perhaps it is the reassurance of his own interior; in any event, the Capote of this series of scenes is amusing and secure and far more articulate about his new aesthetic. When the conversation turns to the particulars of his new book, Capote speaks with pride in his accomplishment and with fondness for those whose lives he encountered in writing the book. Like the Maysles brothers, who have always maintained positive feelings towards the people in their films, Capote recalls his relationship with both Richard Hickock (one of the murderers) and with Alvin Dewey (the detective in charge of the case) as meaningful to him. His technique for making them comfortable with him once again parallels the Maysles brothers' strategies: "I would never insist on any subject [of conversation] because then it would make them become self-conscious. So I'd have to wait two months between having discussed it once. . . . Then every time we'd go through it again, and they would begin to elaborate on it more. And bit by bit I got . . . everything I needed for it." The gradual accretion of information under the watchful eye of the nonintervening artist produces what is believed to be a more authentic text.

As in the previous three Maysles brothers' works, this film allows Capote to present himself to the viewing audience, speaking on his own behalf and displaying his personality. Still, this portrait is not without its manipulative qualities. Albert and David take more liberties with their editing in this film, exercising a crosscutting technique they had not used before. For example, as Capote shows Denison photographs of Dewey, Hickock, and other principals of the finished book, the soundtrack shifts to voice-overs of Capote reading selections from his book. Obviously, the sound and the image on screen are not in synch. Although the manipulation of the two serves the finished product and does not misrepresent Capote or his work, the use of nonsynchronized sound violates one of the practices of direct cinema. The Maysles brothers described wanting to bring some "film quality" to the "basically static situation [of] Truman in his house"; the editing choice served that particular need.[31] Such a deviation from pure direct cinema technique would become a hallmark of the Maysles brothers' style (described earlier as an ad hoc approach). The deviations were few in the first four films but would become more numerous with each subsequent film.

Crosscutting is employed even more strikingly towards the end of the Capote film. The author mentions that he and Dewey (and Dewey's wife, Marie) formed a friendship as a result of the writing of the book. As the camera holds on a photograph of Dewey, Capote recalls that the Deweys visited him in New York City. As he says, "the first time they'd been to New York," the film cuts to Alvin Dewey, wearing an overcoat and hat, standing in Rockefeller Plaza, looking around admiringly. The next series of scenes shows the Deweys in New York: at Random House looking at proofs of *In Cold Blood*, window-shopping with Capote, walking in and out of Tiffany's (in delighted reference to Capote's *Breakfast at Tiffany's*), visiting the author's city apartment, then, finally, on a ferry looking out at the Statue of Liberty. The whole sequence provides some visual relief from the interior of Capote's studio, but it is rather superficially rendered. The familiar story of Midwesterners in the big city relies on a clichéd stereotyping of character that the Maysles generally avoided. Despite the ungainly imposition of these scenes, the sequence does underscore Capote's connection to his subjects (again, the similarity to the Maysles brothers' approach to filmmaking) and also sets up a later juxtaposition (described below) that *is* quite effective.

Back in his studio, Capote looks through letters he exchanged with the convicted men. The film cuts to a melancholy Capote lying on a chaise lounge, discussing a telegram he received shortly before one of the accused men was hanged. As he speaks, the film cuts to photographs of the two killers; the camera zooms in on their faces. In voice-over, Capote mentions that he was present at the executions, but in his book, he chose to present the scene through Detective Dewey's perspective. The film cuts to a close-up of Dewey in an unidentified setting. In a rare use of the close-up device, Albert freezes on Dewey's face. Capote's voice-over continues, this time as he reads from the last page of *In Cold Blood*. When he reaches a passage about a meeting in the cemetery, the film cuts to the actual Clutter family grave site from a distance. The camera pans to a group of barren trees, around the graveyard, back to the headstones, then zooms in on the headstone of Nancy Clutter, the mother. The film cuts back to Capote in an armchair, reading from the end of the novel. The camera holds on his face briefly after he says, "the end." This series of cuts and juxtapositions, one of the most complex series of edits in a Maysles brothers film, successfully connects all the key figures in the story. The film achieves a poignancy that would not have come about without the editing choices.

In the end, both the Capote concept of the nonfiction novel, as realized in *In Cold Blood*, and the Maysles brothers' film about him offer a possible remedy to the celebrity fixation and mass merchandising of popular entertainment. In their work, Capote and the Maysles brothers strive for what David describes as "poetry that comes out of nonfiction." Recognizing a kindred spirit, David further stated, "Truman Capote's book is the closest thing to our own work we have ever come across. What we are doing is in direct parallel in motion picture form to what Capote is doing in the literary form." In addition, the brothers admired the way Capote had "work[ed] to establish a balanced human relationship before" he had started writing, just as the brothers tried "to get the complete trust of the person" they were filming.[32] The connection between subject and filmmaker would be a staple of all of the Maysles brothers' projects.

A PARADOXICAL POSITION

In the Beatles, Brando, and Capote films, the Maysles brothers looked at the subject of celebrity from a unique and paradoxical perspective. Although the artists in these films are human products in the entertainment business, they verify their own authenticity through their implicit and explicit critiques of the celebrity process. The Maysles brothers thereby advanced their own opinion that to be a celebrity who derides or mocks celebrity is to reclaim authenticity. When Brando mockingly offers a sales pitch for Optima Cigars, or when John Lennon and George Harrison pretend to hawk Marlboro cigarettes, they are proving that they see through the blatant commercialism and hucksterism. Brando especially seems to understand that a staged interview in order to promote a film is a pseudo-event designed merely to sell a product that, he believes, has no real intrinsic value. He rejects the framework of the pseudo-event to the extent that, in the footage of this film anyway, he never discusses *Morituri* at all. Similarly, the Beatles dodge some of the questions presented to them at their press conference, not in an "uncooperative" way as one interviewer labels Brando's methods but with the confidence and clever banter of a group of young men who want to demonstrate that they can play the game of meet-the-press and win. They refuse to be overwhelmed by the process.

In the construction as well as in the sympathetic treatment afforded the subjects, the Maysles brothers' films of Brando and the Beatles show that these performers understand they are being marketed as what's happening and as fads. As the films highlight, these celebrities resist such marketing in small but meaningful ways. Still, the Beatles' and Brando's resistance are only partial. Although they deride or mock, they also participate—and profit. Because they perform in popular-culture media, they are inherently part of a materialistic and commercial business. Even self-aware celebrities may become trapped in a vicious circle, just as Levine cannot seem to break out of his tiresome life.

The answer must lie outside of these realms. More than any of the other figures in the early films, Capote provides a possible alternative or at least a means of circumventing the celebrity dilemma. Because an author is required less often to appear in the public eye, the work may speak for itself. Capote's aims for his art were, ostensibly, loftier: To be a writer who rejects standard forms of popular writing is also to be authentic. Thus, the Capote film serves as a mediated manifesto of the Maysles brothers' own ambitions. The sympathetic and respectful attitude toward Capote in the film about him (enhanced, admittedly, by the commissioned nature of the film) indicates that his approach towards his craft provided a model for the filmmakers, one that they had already begun to develop and that they would take to an even more advanced stage with their next effort. Although the modernist aesthetic is not yet evident, the attitude that art in and of itself provides a remedy for the inauthentic—specifically, the commercial products of culture that saturate the market—foreshadows the full-fledged modernism that would appear in their later films.

What the films do not outwardly acknowledge, perhaps because the brothers did not completely understand this idea themselves, is that they serve the same process they criticize. Unwittingly or not, both Brando and the Beatles benefitted professionally and therefore commercially in presenting themselves the way they did. Rather than turn people away from celebrity, their self-awareness and hip deflection of the media foster greater popularity. The Maysles brothers' early films therefore possess a critical blind spot regarding the complexity of celebrity commodification. They do not account for the notion that a celebrity's public resistance to being treated as an object may ironically only increase the inevitability of his or her being treated as such. Essential to this lack of understanding is the brothers' failure to consider that a celebrity's supporters may be willing and aware of the filmmakers' complicity. Postmodern theory has provided new ways of understanding fame and celebrity, and cultural historians have begun to examine audience reception and impact, recognizing that there is a dialectical relationship between the producers and receivers of celebrity commodification. Meanwhile, celebrities and their fans alike are now more conscious of the process as well. Madonna, for instance, has allowed her observers to see that she manipulates her image; in turn, the observers' inside knowledge of Madonna's manipulations makes them feel more powerful and more aware of the machinations of the celebrity business and encourages them to buy even more Madonna product.[33] The Maysles brothers, confined in part by the nonintervening style of direct cinema, failed to appreciate fully the audience as willing and complex agents of participation.

One other related problem plagued the Maysles brothers during these early years. Although all four of these films met with critical acclaim—especially from European filmmakers and critics like Jean-Luc Godard, Ian Cameron, and Marcorelles—none of them reached a significant audience. *Showman* ran in limited engagements in Paris, London, and New York and then disappeared. Levine himself authorized that it could be shown in the United States only as a one-time special on a television network. Given the limited success of the Drew Associates films, no network was eager at the time to broadcast that film or any other direct cinema product. *What's Happening!* was shown as scheduled on British television and also received an edited airing in the United States on CBS (with narration by comedienne Carol Burnett inserted). The Beatles themselves did not want the film to interfere with their fictional release *A Hard Day's Night*. After that, the brothers' film appeared only in New York film festivals or in Maysles brothers retrospectives. (It has since been repackaged and redistributed as *The Beatles! The First U.S. Visit* (1991) and now features the famous performances on the *Ed Sullivan Show*.) *Meet Marlon Brando* never found an audience, either on television or in theaters, a victim of its brief length and Brando's own detachment from it. It appeared briefly in Boston and New York, sharing the bill with other short films. *With Love from Truman* played once on public television and resurfaced only sporadically.[34]

Although the lack of national distribution did not seem to faze the brothers nor prevent them from taking on subsequent projects, it did mean that direct cinema remained to a large degree an intellectual, artistic phenomenon, based almost exclusively in New York, Paris, and London. Television's decision to turn away from Drew Associates–style films exacerbated the lack of exposure. As a result, only a small percentage of moviegoers actually saw the direct cinema films of the mid-1960s. In turn, this meant that direct cinema remained an isolated enclave of dedicated professionals whose own view of celebrity was paradoxical, at times even callow. The lack of connectedness to a larger audience and the concomitant failure to understand the sociology behind celebrity led to their less sophisticated, more idealized view of what an audience could and should be.

If in the final analysis the Maysles brothers' celebrity-related films seem tame and their uncovered truths less profound given today's level of sophistication on the subject, they should be understood in the context of their era. When the brothers created their first four films, there was an earnest concern that an overzealous attitude toward celebrity was ushering in an age obsessed with "a new kind of eminence" in which "new-model 'heroes' are receptacles into which we pour our own purposelessness."[35] Many believed, as Brando asserts in the film, that Americans needed to take a look at how and why they were being manipulated. Political activists like Hayden even feared for the future of participatory democracy. Forces greater than any one person threatened the ability to live an authentic life, regardless of how one wished to define authenticity. In a halting way, with plenty of trial and error in technique and style, these early Maysles films also make their point about the inauthentic, and the brothers' critique of a celebrity-crazed culture helped them define what they would strive to do in their own films.

Filmmakers David and Albert Maysles, circa 1985. Photofest.

Albert Maysles working on his camera during the shooting of Jean-Luc Godard's *Paris vu Par,* for which Al shot one episode in 1965. French support for the Maysles brothers was very strong during the 1960s, and Godard recognized Maysles as one of the best cinematographers in the world. Photofest.

Paul Brennan wooing a prospective buyer in *Salesman* (1968). David Maysles said of
Brennan, "He wants to make a warm pitch, not a cold one." Photofest.

Left to right: David Maysles, Charlotte Zwerin, and Albert Maysles in 1969 during the making
of *Gimme Shelter*. The unique level of collaboration has benefited the Maysles Films
productions. Photofest.

Mick Jagger in performance in *Gimme Shelter* (1970). The concert footage of the film stirred audiences but was overshadowed by a spectator's stabbing death. Photofest.

Christo holding a sketch of his *Running Fence* at one of the many public hearings on the matter. For Christo and Jeanne-Claude, these meetings are as much a part of the art as the fabric and fence poles. Photo by Gianfranco Gorgoni. Photofest.

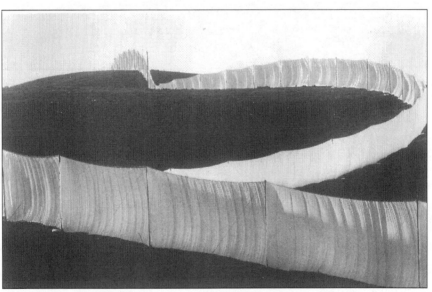

The constructed *Running Fence* (1975) as it undulates toward the sea. Photo by Wolfgang Volz. Photofest.

Little Edie Beale appearing in costume at a door. Doorways provide a key motif in *Grey Gardens* (1976). Photofest.

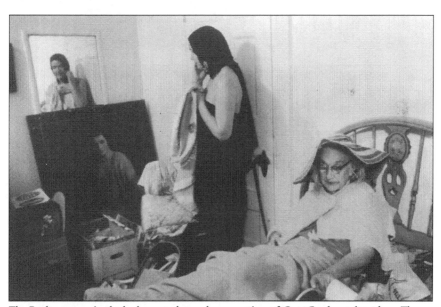

The Beale women in the bedroom where a large portion of *Grey Gardens* takes place. The claustrophobic, chaotic feel of the room is emblematic of the women's lives. Photofest.

Albert Maysles in 1994, still actively working as a cinematographer for Maysles Films, Inc., which is now in its fifth decade. Photofest.

3

Salesman and the Limits of Language

Soon after they completed *With Love from Truman: A Visit with Truman Capote*, the Maysles brothers began exploring the possibility of achieving in film what Truman Capote had done in literature: They wanted to create a nonfiction narrative that would resemble fiction in its dramatic structure and emphasis on character, but that would be rooted in real-life events captured spontaneously on camera. All they needed was a suitable topic, a story line that would lend itself to an interesting, even provocative film, just as the Clutter murders had been the impetus for *In Cold Blood*. The brothers solicited various suggestions from friends and associates, but Albert and David returned consistently to ideas involving people who have seen the world and who are enthusiastic about telling their own stories. David particularly admired a certain kind of restless dreamer, typified in the works of Eugene O'Neill and James Joyce, and he wanted to find a modern-day setting in which that kind of person might still exist.[1]

In 1966, Capote's Random House publisher, Joe Fox, suggested to David the idea of filming a traveling salesman. The brothers were intrigued by this notion—in part because both had been employed in door-to-door encyclopedia selling for brief stretches in their young adulthood—but they concluded that the product being sold would need to have "greater metaphorical overtones" to elicit a sympathetic audience reaction. After a series of false starts involving various other kinds of traveling sales, the brothers decided on Bible selling, which they believed represented a "metaphor of our time" with "ramifications reaching to every avenue of our culture." Soliciting several companies, they finally obtained permission from the

Mid-American Bible Company of Chicago and were allowed to follow a team of four salesmen on their rounds over a six-week period in the winter of 1966–1967. They received permission as well from the customers; when the filmmakers arrived at the door, they simply stated that they were filming a human-interest story. They even offered the potential Bible buyers a one-dollar gratuity for signing a consent release.[2]

The Maysles brothers' thematic agenda for this film was to show the ways in which materialism had saturated even the religious sector—and how stealthily it had done so, as neither seller nor buyer was fully aware of the problematic nature of the relationship. Albert explained further that "a Bible represents an ideology that is supposed to be American. The film is a collision between that ideology and our materialistic way of life. This collision is not enough to stop the Bible salesmen from selling their wares. That the purchasers do not see it as a collision is the story of our times."[3] Having found a topic of general interest that was also imbued with greater depth and dimension, they would advance the critique of materialism that they had offered in their first four films but which had been exclusively focused on the entertainment industry.

In addition, *Salesman* moved forward the modernist aesthetic that the Maysles brothers had started to develop within direct cinema. In 1962, as Albert and David were launching their solo careers, linguist and critic Walker Gibson compiled a thin volume of essays entitled *The Limits of Language*, "a book about some difficulties and peculiarities of using language in our time."[4] Gibson, having collected the written work of scientists, philosophers, and authors as diverse as Jean-Paul Sartre, William James, James Conant, and Gertrude Stein, submits in his own contribution to the book that "our modern relativistic ideas about the impossibility of determining any 'standard dialect' for expressing Truth in all its forms" had created something of a communication crisis in contemporary society.[5] *Salesman*, with its emphasis on the dysfunctional and dehumanizing language of the sale, concurs. Further, the Maysles brothers wished to explore the limits of language out of a modernist desire "to know 'reality' in all its depths and complexity, no matter how incomplete and paradoxical that knowledge might be, and no matter how painful."[6] This kind of exploration does not lead necessarily to definitive answers; indeed, easy answers should be regarded with suspicion.

Offering a modernist theme within an unconventional documentary, Albert and David alerted their audience that their aims were more artistic, even literary. Like Ernest Hemingway, one of their acknowledged influences, the brothers trusted they could "chronicle the disintegration of modern society and culture" but then somehow "make the world re-cohere" through their art.[7] While this is an ambitious and elusive goal, it remained part of their filmmaking blueprint at least through the creation of *Grey Gardens*. At the heart of this aim was not, as some of their detractors have suggested, a condescending attitude towards the people in their films but rather an idealistic one. They reveal the limits of a salesman's language, not to mock the salesmen or their customers but to reawaken them (and of course the film audience) to more personalized and meaningful modes of speech. This humanistic approach—using the "camera with love" in Al's words— also meant that, like Capote, they would form personal relationships with their filmed subjects.[8] In *Salesman*, the filmmakers connected strongly with all the salesmen, especially Paul Brennan, who reminded the brothers of their father, Philip. Not only had Brennan and Philip Maysles both lived their adult lives in the Boston area, they each defied cultural convention in their work lives. The elder Maysles, who died in 1945, eschewed a salesman's life (where the majority of first-generation Jews found employment in Boston) and instead had become a postal clerk. Similarly, Paul Brennan the Irishman entered the sales world, typically the domain of Jewish Bostonians. There were other less tangible connections as well. "Like my father, [Brennan's] a guy who has a soul," Albert said. "But he's never really found a way to put it into his work."[9] For David, that Brennan has a soul ultimately means "he can't be a salesman. He wants to make a warm pitch, not a cold one."[10] Thus, *Salesman* is in large measure about the need for people to make a warm pitch in a world in which only cold, calculating ones seem to be rewarded.

The Maysles brothers' modernist leanings also signaled their willingness to extend the parameters of direct cinema, and with *Salesman* they did move further away from the modus operandi of the Drew Associates films. From the onset, this film was to be a testing ground for what their ad hoc direct cinema could do. Since the early 1960s, they had looked for a way to make "a film that couldn't be classified," to use real-life actors to tell a story "that nobody knows anything about."[11] They looked to stretch the boundaries of the mode of representation they helped create. Due to the enormity of the task and because of their increased demands in the world of commercial advertising (which after all, was a steadier source of income than their feature-length films would ever be), the brothers sought a collaborator. They turned to Charlotte Zwerin, a young woman from Detroit, who had been earning a modest living in New York as an editor on a variety of small film projects. Zwerin's contribution to the completed

Salesman was extensive indeed. As the sole editor, Zwerin had creative control of the project. Sifting through nearly one hundred hours of filmed footage, Zwerin's task, with David's supervision, would be to craft a coherent narrative structure and to shape the material into something more meaningful and interesting. It is the combined vision of all three filmmakers that has made *Salesman* one of the most important American documentaries ever made.[12]

Before turning to the film itself, some historical context is vital to understanding the presentation of the salesmen in the film. Having found little to redeem their own door-to-door sales careers, the brothers wished to expose the negative aspects of the business, but they also wanted to understand what kinds of men would willingly engage in such an occupation. Judging by the popular culture of the 1950s and 1960s, one might assume that the traveling salesman was merely a relic of the past, the legacy of the American drummer who had long since faded away. Had not modern advertising and mass communication joined forces to make door-to-door selling an anachronism? The notion of a lost occupation, often called the vanishing salesman, had been around since the early twentieth century, reified in numerous short stories, movies, and jokes.[13] In 1949, Arthur Miller presented his ominously titled *Death of a Salesman* and killed off Willy Loman, the every-salesman symbol of the twentieth century. In 1962, E. B. Weiss, one of the leading business analysts of his day, seemingly pronounced the last rites: In his *The Vanishing Salesman*, he predicted the salesman's imminent obsolescence due primarily to the modern desire to maximize efficiency and minimize cost.[14]

Despite these gloomy assertions, the traveling salesman continued not only to survive but to thrive in many kinds of businesses. A 1972 report calculated that there were at that time, two million people engaged in door-to-door selling, working for more than sixty-six thousand companies and generating about $4 billion worth of sales.[15] Another study indicated that door-to-door selling was succeeding very well for the distribution of products as diverse as encyclopedias, tea and coffee, household cleaning products, major appliances, and aluminum siding. The Avon Company, for example, sold over $47 million dollars in cosmetics in an average mid-century sales year.[16] Even if "Nobody likes door-to-door selling, and nobody needs it," the traveling salesman was not a relic of the past; he was a ubiquitous presence on the American street.

Still, by the time the Maysles brothers made *Salesman*, Americans seemed undecided as to how they should feel about traveling salesmen. Stereotypi-

cal images depicted the salesman as either a comic figure—a crude, las-
civious, plaid-sports-coat–clad goof—or as a stoic and lonely one, a shining example of American individualism and entrepreneurial fortitude.[17]
Both stereotypes distorted the reality of the modern salesman's life, which,
as *Salesman* shows, was more mundane and more depersonalized. Cover-
ing hundreds of miles, trying to survive the vicissitudes of the marketplace,
the traveling salesman faced enormous personal and business pressures,
including a generally indifferent or even hostile buying public, local ordi-
nances, and federal regulation restricting where he could go and how he
could sell and zealous sales managers who, armed with the latest scientific
research from business gurus, cajoled and browbeat their sales force into
higher production. Turnover rates, not surprisingly, were high.[18] Equally
significant were the pressures imposed by the American obsession with the
individual work ethic. Espoused in a plethora of inspirational and how-to
books, the work ethic particular to salesmen demanded much from every
individual and was perhaps best exemplified in the "Salesman's Creed." As
strict and self-denying as Benjamin Franklin's list of virtues, the "Salesman's
Creed" was the brainchild of the National Sales Executives of New York
City and featured such promises as: "To look upon my work as opportunity to be seized with joy and made the most of and not as painful drudgery to be reluctantly endured" and "To remember that success lies within
myself, in my own brain, my own ambition, my own courage and determination."[19] The creed placed the bulk of responsibility on the individual
salesman's shoulders; there were no extenuating circumstances for failure
and no external factors that could be considered. As the men in the film
say, "It's not the bum territory, it's the bum in the territory."[20] Depicting
the exploits of four men of the road, *Salesman* illustrates what happens
when men internalize the self-abnegating language of the creed.

MISSED COMMUNICATIONS

In *Salesman*, the Maysles brothers and Zwerin turned their attention to the
unusual combination—or "collision" as Albert called it—of religion and
business. The film's opening scene establishes the religion-business connection and introduces the filmmakers' subtle but consistent point of view on
the matter. The first visual image in *Salesman* is an extreme close-up of a
Bible. The shot reveals the lower half of the oversized edition, which appears
to be white and on which the words *Holy Bible* are visible in elaborate em-
bossed lettering. A hand turns the cover, as a voice begins: "The bestseller
in the world is the Bible, for one reason: It's the greatest piece of literature

of all time." The hand continues to turn pages slowly, the close-up maintained, as we hear the words. After about ten seconds, the film cuts to a three-shot, in which at center is a woman seated in a rocking chair, looking down at the Bible in the speaker's lap to her right. A child, a girl of about four, stands behind what appears to be her mother, who is also looking in the general direction of the Bible in the lap. No one makes eye contact with anyone else; all gazes continue to be on the Bible. The speaker, now understood to be a salesman, continues to describe the various illustrations within. Finally, after offering, "So you can see how this would be an inspiration in the home," he turns to the child, "You like that, honey? What's your name?" He is told she is Christine, to which he responds, "She's pretty like her mother" and asks her to guess his name. She says nothing. "Paul," he informs her. "Paul, you know? Paul." The little girl, silent, clings to her mother. Meaningful human interaction appears to be difficult in these strained circumstances.

Returning to his sales pitch, the salesman begins to enumerate the various payment plans for the $49.95 Bible, which include choice C, "a little Catholic honor plan." He asks the woman which plan "would be the best" for her. Albert has positioned his camera so that both adults receive equal importance in the shot: Brennan, seated with his legs crossed, is at the left, and the woman, rocking with her daughter draped over her, is down-camera from him to the right. As of now no one has the upper hand; the transaction's outcome is still undetermined. But immediately after, the rejection begins. The woman demurely states that she is not interested until she can speak it over with her husband, and the film cuts to a profile close-up of her, holding her child. Even as the salesman counters that the book would be a "lovely gift" as a surprise for her husband, it is clear the woman is going to resist the pitch; the camera's unshifting focus is as much a signal as the salesman's more desperate tone. The film then cuts to the little girl plunking keys on the piano, as the woman says she cannot afford the Bible now on account of being "swamped with medical bills." The piano music, random single keys played on a descending scale, makes a clumsy but expressive accompaniment for the next image: the salesman's face, in close-up, looking pained, beaten, dejected. He gazes downward, again avoiding eye contact. Suddenly, a title appears on-screen to the right of his face, introducing him: PAUL BRENNAN, then, underneath, comes his nickname: THE BADGER. The nickname defines his sales strategy in this scene but also makes an ironic counterpoint to his clear defeat in this case.

In about ninety seconds, the film has laid out its basic scenario: a man in a suburban home attempts to place a Bible into that home, through a combination of pleasant banter and persuasive words concerning the advantages of his product. This short segment also introduces Brennan, who will prove to be a focal point in the nonfiction film, and quickly establishes the way he takes rejection personally. The look on his face and his tone throughout the scene suggest he is struggling with the game in which he is engaged. The scene also presents the kind of tension that pervades the film. An unmistakable discomfort is created here, familiar to anyone who has ever interacted with a salesman of any kind. It is a familiar capitalist dance, one that few people truly enjoy and made all the more awkward by the product being pitched in this case. No editorial or narrative comment is necessary to make the point; as is their custom, the filmmakers allow the viewer to come to his or her own conclusion.

Over the next minute of film, the filmmakers introduce three other salesman—Charles McDevitt, "the Gipper"; James Baker, "the Rabbit"; and Raymond Martos, "the Bull"—and take the audience through three typical traveling salesman moments, each one building on the last. First, McDevitt stands outside a front door, then begins speaking to a woman at the door while a dog barks persistently off-camera. Next, Baker makes his sales pitch inside a suburban home, narrating as he flips through some of his Bible's pictures, sharing interesting facts about the Vatican ("The [Vatican] guards are not Italian, they're Swiss. You know why? They're six feet"), and pointing out other attractive features of the book. Finally, the film cuts to Martos, at night, emerging from a house, closing the door as he says, "Good night, darlin', thanks for the order," apparently having successfully negotiated a sale. The film then cuts to him driving. In all, the three short sequences illustrate a salesman's routine: the approach, the pitch, the departure, the drive back to home base. The sequence concludes with the title credit, "The Maysles Brothers' *Salesman*" as Martos returns to the Pleasant Valley Motor Lodge where he and the others are staying.

The next several segments, totaling about seventeen minutes of film time, maintain this general overview of the world of Bible selling. That the film steers clear of becoming personality-oriented reflects the brothers' stated desire to accomplish something different than they had in their previous four films. The filmmakers achieved for the first time a final product that superseded the day-in-the-life format. Even when the film shifts from being the story of four salesmen to focusing primarily on Brennan's downward spiral, it still does not elevate this one salesman to a traditional main-character role. There are great limits on what is shown of Brennan's personal life, for instance, and his character does not develop in any conventional sense. There is no build-up to a climactic scene, and there is only an implicit conflict (Brennan's developing frustration and ambivalence toward his job). Many key scenes do not involve Brennan at all, or he is involved only peripherally. If Brennan may be set apart from the others at all, he may be recognized as the only salesman who seeks association with other people on a deeper or other-than-buying-and-selling level. To borrow an overused phrase, Brennan reaches out to other people. That his efforts are rarely reciprocated adds a degree of pathos to the film, but it does not totally transform the film into a modern tragedy in which he is the star. Brennan remains a type, an *example* of how the salesman's life can be a desperate and unpleasant one.[21]

Instead, the film's central concern involves the way language is manipulated, even abused, in the sales process and the erosion of human connectedness that results. The filmmakers show the limits of language, including its frequent breakdown in the competitive, depersonalized milieu of door-to-door Bible selling. Brennan is an important figure insofar as he is the person who appears most ill at ease with the misuse of language and the one who frequently attempts (albeit awkwardly and vainly) to refocus human communication in a more personalized, less materially oriented direction. His failure to do so is poignant partly because he recognizes the failure. (Significantly, he never says he recognizes this failure; it must be inferred from his facial expressions and increasingly desperate sales pitching.) But Brennan, an inconsistent man, also uses manipulative language; he, too, wishes to be successful at selling Bibles and is not above lying or being deceitful to do so. The theme transcends any one man's experience; rather, it implicates *all* people who appear in the film. For the first twenty minutes, the filmmakers begin building a case for what will ultimately prove to be the film's chief revelation: that meaningful human communication is thwarted in this environment.

The first sales meeting, at which sales manager Ken Turner implores the men to sell more and behave better, provides an important early scene. Within his lengthy address, Turner browbeats the men, relying on individual work ethic language: "All I can say to people who aren't makin' the money—it's their fault. Just keep that in mind, the money's out there, and go out and get it. I for one am sick and tired of hagglin' with you people and pleadin' with you to get you to do what's good for you. And what's good for us." His is the language of manipulation, designed to shame the men into higher sales. Moreover, his language is freighted with power. After suggesting later, in an unintentionally ironic phrase, that "maybe you see some missing faces here," Turner announces that the departure of those men was "a question of the sour apple spoilin' the barrel. Certain guys have a habit of gettin' a couple of beers and flyin' off the handle, and bashin' people around, and throwin' their weight around. I want to go on record, and I want to tell you all, the next man that gets off base with me I'm going to tag him out. The ball game's over." Replete with colloquialisms, Turner's speech is also unmistakably clear. He is the boss who, as he tells an associate, is "sick and tired of bein' sick and tired" and is not afraid to back up his words with physical force. To him, the men are "full of alibis and excuses." He has no time nor the desire to foster a personally enriching work environment. Perhaps he has read carefully the "Salesman's Creed:" He is convinced that the men's self-worth comes only through higher sales.

In the several scenes in which he appears, Turner manipulates his men, pretending one minute he is on friendly terms with them, strong-arming them the next. Oily and self-important, full of disingenuous jocularity, Turner epitomizes what makes this particular business unpleasant and depersonalized. He seems to have no sense that he is doing anything for which he ought to be ashamed; indeed, his company agreed to be filmed, and he knew he would be a significant part of the finished film. Worse yet, the men outwardly express no disagreement or discomfort with what he says to them. Perhaps they are afraid to express what they really think on camera—they do want to keep their jobs, after all. But even Brennan, ostensibly at the end of his rope by film's end, only internalizes his dismay. All four men seem to have accepted what Turner tells the assembled throng at the second sales meeting in Chicago: "If a guy's not a success, he's got nobody to blame but hisself." Brennan and the other salesmen never fault Turner or the company for creating an environment that tries to chide them into becoming selling machines, that erodes their humanity, and that forces them into situations in which cajoling and even deceiving customers is "good for them and good for the company."

Meanwhile, in nearly every scene, the salesmen and the buying public struggle to communicate. In one scene, Brennan tramps through the snow, briefcase in hand, following up one of his leads. Upon reaching the back door of a modest home, Brennan enters and finds himself in a dimly lit stairway. A man accosts him there, and the film records the conversation in media res:

MAN: Yeah, well, what the hell is it all about?
BRENNAN: Yeah, well, we have a display at the church, Mr. McDonald . . .
MAN: Yeah.

BRENNAN: And she gave me your name, and that's why I'm here, see.
MAN: She gave her your name?
BRENNAN: She gave me her name.
MAN: Yeah.
BRENNAN: And I'm here because she gave me your name, see. 'Cause we're visiting all the families in there that gave their names, you know, at the church . . .
MAN: Yeah.
BRENNAN: See, like if you're at the church, and you see the display, you say, okay, and you give me your name. See, I come to see you, see?
MAN: Yeah.
BRENNAN: This is . . .
(A woman's voice from above is heard: "What are you, sellin' something?")
MAN: No, no, I don't know what the hell . . .
BRENNAN: Lookit, tell her I was here, will ya?
MAN: Yeah, all right, I'll ask her. I don't know.
BRENNAN: Yeah. Okay.
MAN: Hope you got the right McDonald, that's all.
BRENNAN: Yeah. All right, sir. *(He leaves, heading back to his car, singing, "I wisht I was a rich man.")*

This exchange, absurdly comic in the way neither man makes headway with the other, typifies the dialogue in the film. Rarely does anyone express him or herself clearly; even more rarely does anyone listen carefully to another. The (mis)communication between people in the film exists on a painfully superficial and ineffectual level.

Other characters encounter similarly difficult moments. Baker and McDevitt's visit to a mother and daughter elicits a hilarious and typically inarticulate conversation. At one point, McDevitt jokingly refers to Baker as a mooch, presumably because Baker is tagging along with him on this sales run. The daughter's lack of familiarity with that term leads to a rapid and baffling dialogue:

DAUGHTER: What's a mooch?
BAKER: *(to McDevitt)* What do you mean?
MCDEVITT: A mooch. Book mooch, book mooch.
MOTHER: Easy, easy to talk into—
DAUGHTER: Oh, really?
MCDEVITT: Book mooch. No, people that read a lot and appreciate books.
DAUGHTER: Yeah.
MCDEVITT: Don't tell me you don't. I know you do.
DAUGHTER: *(motioning)* Well, these aren't the books I read.
MCDEVITT: Who was readin' this? *(points to a book on the coffee table)*
MOTHER: She—me! She don't read. I'm the one that reads.

The utter incomprehensibility of most of this segment humorously under-scores what will become more poignant later in the film: The false and forced scenario of buyer and seller not only produces inane dialogue, it fosters poor communication. What exactly does McDevitt mean by a "book mooch"? He seems to be equating the phrase with "avid reader," whereas the mother tries to explain it as something approximating *gullible*. The daughter's quizzi-cal expression throughout indicates she has not been enlightened. The mother's incorrect definition, as well as her assertion that her daughter "don't read" but she does, suggests she is less informed than she believes. (In response to her daughter's sarcastic inquiry, "You mean to say you don't think he [McDevitt] is an honest man, Mother, just by looking at him?", the mother answers, "You're not literal like I am.")

Later in the same segment, the daughter has the mistaken impression that these men are "on their own, doing things." She congratulates them for working at a job where they "get away from people over you." Coming on the heels of Turner's fiery sales meeting speech, her words are particu-larly ironic. Yet, Baker only encourages her, supplying her with the word *independent* when she struggles to finish her description of their situation. Perhaps Baker, operating under the necessary self-delusion of a traveling salesman, truly thinks of himself as independent, or perhaps he is merely agreeing with the daughter in order to keep the sale moving along smoothly. Either way, the moment illustrates perfectly that direct and sincere human interaction cannot exist under these conditions.

While many of these early sequences evoke laughter, several of the film's initial scenes also depict how language is misused in a negative way. All of the salesmen rely on ethnic stereotypes, both as a means of explaining and satirizing their customers' behavior and as a means of ingratiating them-selves with their potential buyers. When offering a pitch to a different Mr. and Mrs. McDonald, Baker tells a joke in which the punch line assumes Scots are miserly, especially in their associations with the Irish. Martos makes fun of the way his Irish customers say "ye" instead of you. And throughout the film, Irish people (the men's steadiest customers) are deni-grated as "Micks."

Brennan frequently resorts to ethnic stereotypes, especially those involv-ing Irish-Americans. Of Irish heritage himself, Brennan slips into a brogue easily and without hesitation, often relating the story of the Irishman "on the force. He gets a pension. It's a good job. He's a fine workin' boy, Pat. Puts in a lot of time. But he gets his reward—he'll get his reward on the other end." Brennan mocks the traditional path followed by the South

Boston Irishmen he knows well—the ones who join the police force, work hard for many years, and then retire with a pension. The irony that he is quick to point out is that many of these men die soon after retirement, so worn out are they by the years of hard work. Brennan loathes this kind of blind allegiance to stultifying work that leads only to the grave. His choice of the salesman's life reveals his attempt—perhaps a woefully misguided one—to escape that fate. What becomes clear over the course of the film, however, is that the brogue also provides Brennan with an outlet for his frustration—with himself and his growing failure in a depersonalizing occupation. For Brennan, using the brogue is at once a statement of independence and a self-deprecating defense mechanism.

For the first twenty minutes of the film, *Salesman* establishes the way language works in this environment. At its best, communication is shown to be comically inept, and at its worst, its breakdown is the reason for a lack of understanding and connection among people. All of the scenes are shadowed by the very real pressures that Turner (representing the company) exerts on the salesmen via his own kind of coercive language.

Brennan's particular struggle to maintain success as a salesman serves to dramatize the corrosive effects of this way of life and its negative effects on human connection. As Brennan, lost in thought, rides a train to Chicago, Turner's voice on the soundtrack implores the men once again: "What everybody's got to do is quit making alibis and excuses and accept the responsibility of success or failure." The film then cuts to the Chicago convention itself where salesmen, starting with McDevitt, offer confident projections of their sales for next year. Between each testimonial, the film cuts back to a pensive Brennan on the train, suggesting through the editing that his slump and negativity are in contrast to his zealous coworkers. Direct cinema filmmakers generally avoided such crosscutting because, they feared, it was an inauthentic presentation of material. The Maysles brothers and their coeditors used the technique sparingly but did not hesitate, as here or in the Capote film, to rely on it if it served the thematic concerns of the film. The manipulated juxtaposition of Brennan and the sales conference is meant to suggest that he is less sure of himself and his occupation and more alienated from the rest of the men engaged in the endeavor.[22]

Still, the extent to which Brennan recognizes, or is beginning to recognize, the absurdity of his situation and the falseness of the speeches is in many ways superfluous. More important to the film, the viewer—with subtle clues initially and the less subtle crosscut manipulation later—recognizes it. After all, the testimonials are not reports of actual results; they are predictions and optimistic ones at that. Another salesman, who has been with the company only three months, "expect[s] to make fifty thousand [dollars]" over the next year. "Or better." The language in this scene reflects the lies the salesmen believe about themselves and their jobs; they have been successfully indoctrinated into the system, as their speeches make clear. All three men who offer testimonials (and, of course, Turner as well) absolutely accept the "Salesman's Creed." They must maintain this blind optimism, but to the film viewer, who has already witnessed several examples of the day-to-day drudgery these salesmen endure, it smacks of self-deception. When a salesman announces that his "wife has just talked me into buyin' a big house. And she wants to have a few more kids and all this kind of rot," his reasons for self-deception are made manifest. It is a classic American middle-class paradigm: He must work harder to support an already overextended financial situation.

The testimonials are followed by the most ironic and telling speech in the film. The Mid-American Bible Company's "designer and theological consultant," Dr. Melbourne I. Feltman, addresses the salesmen. His lengthy speech/sermon concludes,

> Some of you, at one time or another, may or may not have had a higher income, but you have never held a higher position of esteem in the minds of the world, or in your own self-satisfaction, than you now hold, knowing what you are doing about your Father's business. Hold your heads very high. Be very proud of your position. Stop thinking in terms of Bible peddling, because I am confident that once you realize what you are doing for others, you in your own esteem will rise so high, not with conceit, but in humility, knowing that you have the privilege and the power to be of service to others. And with all my heart, for the coming year and for many years to come, God grant you an abundant harvest. Thank you.

In all, the speech stands as one of the most remarkable and revelatory moments in direct cinema history. Like many such moments, it nearly crosses the line of parody. (One can imagine a contemporary filmmaker like Michael Moore having a field day with this footage.) But Feltman's unwavering earnestness in the scene and the salesmen's rapt attention ward off laughter. Moreover, because the filmmakers have already (through their recent illustration of Brennan's point of view) begun to question the motives and consequences of this speech, Feltman's manipulation through language emerges that much more strongly. The parallel he draws between Bible selling and some form of holy work ("Father's business") reflects on the curious combination of religion and business that so fascinated Albert. Moreover, Feltman

reinforces the salesman's work ethic, infusing it with a spiritual significance. According to Feltman, the men should think of themselves as something akin to evangelicals, whose "privilege" it is to sell Bibles for $49.95.
Should their holy purpose result in "an abundant harvest," they need not
have any misgivings; God approves, even encourages, their good work.

Feltman serves the role of cheerleader in this scene, a function that has
been described as integral to 1960s sales management strategies. The cheerleader's job was to "rekindle" the spirit of the salesman, to reenergize him
for a few months—until the next convention at least.[23] Thus, when Brennan
and the other three salesmen hit the road for Miami soon after, they take
with them a revitalized sense of purpose and optimism, laden with religious
overtones. That renewed sense of devotion to the job receives another boost
from Turner. At a Miami motel, he leads the men through a practice selling
session in which Baker plays the customer. Throughout Turner's demon-
stration, his language is direct, forceful, polished, and even aggressive at
times; his no-nonsense approach to the sale differs from anything seen thus
far. He assures his customer that his Bible is "published by the Catholic
Press" (a misleading label) and that in "buying anything Catholic, you will
look for the imprimatur. It's your assurance that, of course, it's approved."
Role-playing Baker stammers through a few objections, primarily centered
on the fact that his wife is not Catholic and might object to the Bible, but
Turner bulldozes right through these paper-thin concerns. At the end of
his pitch, he asks:

> TURNER: Do you want it?
> BAKER: I do.
> TURNER: Well, then quit making excuses and sign right here.
> BAKER: Okay, I'll go along with it, because I'm trying to figure—
> TURNER: Quit figuring and start writing, Mr. Baker. *(Turner chuckles.)*

The power dynamics illustrated in this sequence reveal a great deal about
the nature of selling. Turner's strategy, which presumably is indeed the one
he employs when he sells, consists of treating as inferiors the middle- and
lower-middle class, mostly Catholic customers with whom he is interacting. Depersonalized, they are people to be bullied, much as he bullies his
sales force. The language remains the same, too: "Quit making excuses,"
he tells the prospective buyer. Again, his manipulative use of language
forces his customers into sales they would probably not make otherwise.

Baker's behavior reflects both what he would like to see from his own
customers—that is, offering only token resistance to the sale—and his own

fear of refusing Turner, who after all is more than a pretend Bible sales-man; he is, as ever, Baker's boss. One wonders just how useful this exer-cise really is as a training tool. Turner's unqualified success in the dem-onstration ostensibly teaches the men something about being forceful, sure, and even dishonest as needed. But its other, unspoken value for Mid-Ameri-can is that it reinforces Turner's authority over the other men. Albert's cam-era work in the scene attempts to mitigate Turner's power. He does not privilege Turner; only twice does Albert frame him in close-up, despite that Turner does most of the speaking. Instead, Albert scans the room, not only showing Turner and Baker in their role-play but also the other men, who are attentive and serious. Their reactions become as important as Turner's words. Nonetheless, Turner's technique and use of language cast a long shadow over the remaining scenes of the film, much as his opening speech served the first part. His success and polish also provide counterpoints for the continued misfires that the others make in the scenes that follow. To be sure, their situations are never so contrived.

No scene more humorously illustrates the real challenges these sales-men face—and the limitations of the selling process language—than Baker's attempt to sell a Bible to a Cuban housewife. Seated together at a table in one of the better-furnished homes in the film, Baker and Mrs. Pages, for whom English is a second language, engage in a kind of linguis-tic tango. The English-Spanish language discrepancy is exacerbated by the heightened artificiality of Baker's language and his thick Boston ac-cent. The woman, in a housecoat and hair curlers, keeps her son in her lap during the first part of the conversation, as Baker good-naturedly begins his pitch.

WOMAN: I don't understand very well English.
BAKER: You don't un—
WOMAN: You know, I know the basic things, the principles. I understand you, but I miss many things.
BAKER: Right. That's why I . . . spake [*sic*]—if you noticed—very, very . . .
WOMAN: Yes.
BAKER: . . . slow.
WOMAN: Yes.
BAKER: *(resumes his usual speech speed, which is rapid)* Could you see where this would help the family? I mean, honestly, I mean could you see where this would help the children and Frank and yourself? Could you see—I mean, see what I'm tryin' to explain, Mrs. Pages, could you see where this would be of *value* in the home, a gain to you? Could you see where the, a Bible as nice as this—

Try though he may, no amount of restating the question seems to help Baker. With his thick accent, *value* and *gain* are barely discernible to someone for whom English is a first language. And his choice of the archaic *spake* (on which he pauses for emphasis) compounds the problem. Later, his use of *orders* really confuses his customer, inasmuch as the word comes out "ahduhs."

> BAKER: We do take orders. Wait until you hear this, you're gonna be very enthused. Wait'll you hear this.
> WOMAN: But what?
> BAKER: We do take orders, and you're gonna be enthused. We take orders.
> WOMAN: What?
> BAKER: Orders.
> WOMAN: What's that?
> BAKER: *(smiling)* We take orders on the new missal.
> WOMAN: *(saying the word as he does)* Orders?
> BAKER: You know Mass?
> WOMAN: Yes.
> BAKER: We have one, finally. With all the changes. Do you understand my point?
> WOMAN: No.

Baker does not give up yet. Trying a different tack, he adds more hand signals and holds a book up. Finally, the woman seems to understand, but despite Baker's enthusiastic assertion that "all the ecumenical changes" are in the new missal, she declines buying one. The scene is as exhausting as it is humorous, an absurdist comedy even Samuel Beckett could not script. Once again, the film shows up this ludicrous process for what it is. Remarkably, Baker remains the epitome of patience and resilience throughout, only betraying a ray of frustration at the very end. Albert must have found this remarkable, too, for he holds the camera position on Baker during the extent of the second half of the conversation, as the Rabbit unflinchingly tries again and again to explain the new missal on which "we take orders."

While this scene plays out humorously, the segment in which McDevitt takes advantage of a young couple does not. Brennan comments that his coworker is an "extremely effective" salesman "because he knows how to take advantage of everything in any circumstances." As if to prove Brennan right, the film cuts to McDevitt verbally maneuvering his way toward a sale. He is politely relentless, finally convincing the couple, who are obviously struggling to make ends meet, to pay their down payment on a Bible later in the week. He tells them he will "send one of the men from the Catholic Press and—you'll like this fellow—Mr. Brennan, Paul R. Brennan," who,

McDevitt assures, is "a very devout Catholic [who] feels that, that every Catholic family should have this." In this scene, the use (or misuse) of language leads to the couple agreeing to buy what they cannot afford, primarily because they are too meek to refuse the persuasive McDevitt. The obviously deceptive language receives no judgment from the camera movement. Albert simply observes the various people in the room, usually in close-up, and trusts the viewers to decide for themselves how to feel about what transpires.

Brennan partakes in this scheme as well. Three days later, it is "Paul R. Brennan" who returns to the house to collect the down payment. From her front doorway, the woman squints at Brennan, who never removes his sunglasses. Misrepresenting himself as a district manager, Brennan plays his role with a series of lies. He tells the woman that he's already mailed in her order. Next, if she changes her mind, he will have to charge Mr. McDevitt a penalty for "the cost of the mailing and the handling and everything, plus the bookkeeping." Finally, he will not allow her to call him later, after she has had a chance to discuss it with her husband, because he will have traveled to Jacksonville. Worn down, the woman disappears into the house to retrieve the cash.

Brennan also sells two Bibles in scenes immediately preceding this one. First, he sweet-talks an elderly woman. Barely letting her say more than "uh-huh," Brennan barrels through the transaction. When she offers meekly, "Well, I don't know how many years I have to read the Bible," he simply ignores the point and changes the subject. He mentions more than once that "it's very enjoyable talkin' to you." And indeed he is talking *to* her and not with her; the conversation is heavily one-sided and, despite his assertion otherwise, full of Irish blarney. The profile close-up of the woman shows that she does not make eye contact with him; instead, she shyly gazes down at the open Bible. Duped or not, the woman does seem to appreciate the attention, as she admits she is all alone. Her most meaningful human contact that day may well be a bastardized dialogue with a disingenuous Bible salesman.

Next, the film cuts to Brennan chatting with a middle-aged couple. The sale has been made, but now Brennan slips into nervous chatter, perhaps, in good salesman method, to keep the customers from second-guessing their decision. The man and woman sit on a sofa, arms crossed, looking fairly uncomfortable as if they were anxious to be done with the whole process. Brennan and the woman engage in an odd dialogue about how much their parents used to beat them and then discover they both hail from Massachusetts. After a minute or two of this banter, Brennan shakes the man's hand, to which the man observes, "He's gonna wear that hand out. He should have been a Protestant preacher." Understanding the artificial nature of Brennan's language and demeanor, the man recognizes Brennan for what he is—or what he has become.

Thus, Brennan enjoys brief success again when he is willing and able to use language as a means of manipulating his customers. He flatters and fawns his way through two sales and participates in outright deception to obtain another. Yet, it soon becomes clear that despite the change of luck and concomitant lack of conscience, Brennan's fortunes are not necessarily on the upswing. Again, a careful look at his language in these scenes illustrates that while the results may be more profitable, his communication prowess continues to decline. Brennan is amazingly inarticulate in the two scenes in which he makes sales, babbling nervously, changing topics rapidly, rarely finishing sentences. In conversation with the elderly woman, he offers, "Well, let me say this. I told this one woman—she said—she said, believe you me, Paul, she said, well, I mean, most of the time they call me Paul. I mean, it's Mr. Brennan, but to me I don't think a title 'Mister' means anything, but . . . what is your first name, Mrs. Gorman?" If Turner epitomizes the smooth-talking salesman, Brennan is at the opposite end of the spectrum. This lack of eloquence underscores his decline as a salesman. A leading how-to guide of the 1960s devoted two chapters to the centrality of language in a salesman's life: "How the [salesman] uses language in his selling will, in great measure, determine how his client will perceive him and his product or service. Therefore, one of the most powerful persuasive tools the salesman can hope to acquire is effective language."[24]

The film further indicates that Brennan's difficulty in expressing himself in the sales pitch reveals a growing disillusionment with his occupation. Even when reporting a sale to Turner, he complains that it was a strain: He gave the "old romance" to a "Mickey" customer, but she "didn't go for it." Whatever spark Brennan may have once possessed seems to be flickering out. Parallel to Brennan's inarticulateness as a salesman is an increased desire to talk about matters outside of business. In the midst of both of his successful sales pitches, he recalls some painful memories about his family. First, he remembers that his older brother, the successful MIT graduate he has mentioned before, set such a high standard in school that people asked, "Where did you come from, Paul?" The comparison meant that he "kind of got an inferiority complex. And, of course when I got married, that made it worse." He and the woman, the wife of the sanitation department employee, engage in a discussion about their parents, which includes Brennan's revelation that "my father never hit me in his life" but "my mother clobbered me."

Brennan's last two filmed interactions with customers confirm his downward spiral. In one of the sales calls, Brennan's conversation with his customer Mrs. O'Connor is so strained that it is the most difficult segment to watch in the film. Her face, captured repeatedly in close-up, suggests a tiredness that extends beyond this moment in time. Clearly, she wants nothing more than for this salesman to leave her alone. Yet, she cannot muster the courage nor find the appropriate words to make him leave. She rarely glances at him, instead holding her gaze sternly straight ahead. Brennan presses her, eager to reverse his recent ineffectiveness; for the first time, he truly seems deserving of his *badger* moniker. When Mrs. O'Connor assures him that the family already has a Bible, an heirloom in fact, Brennan tries to downplay the sentimental value: "I bet it's over two hundred years old or something?" Family relationships do matter to Brennan, as he has spoken repeatedly of his own, yet he is forced to dismiss this woman's sentimental attachment for the sake of a sale. He also must resort to salesman double-talk that sounds (and reads) ludicrous: "As they say, it's the only thing that I know that you secure in a lifetime that doesn't depreciate. A car after three years is worth nothing. A Bible like that is really something that will really build up a heritage in the home. . . . It's like a good wine, with age it improves."

Then, in one of those fortuitous juxtapositions that the Maysles brothers always sought, the voice of a young woman, whom Mrs. O'Connor later refers to as Maureen, on the telephone somewhere in another part of the house, adds an extra layer of tension to this scene, as the background buzz from her conversation imposes itself on the other dialogue. Maureen's casual and conversational tone highlights the difference between meaningful and enjoyable human communication and the kind of strained communication being played out in front of the camera. Mrs. O'Connor pauses, searching for words and seemingly listening to Maureen for a moment. Eventually the strain overwhelms her, "All right, Maureen, you've been on that phone long enough," she calls out sharply. Maureen continues to speak on the telephone.

Brennan, too, looks and sounds like a desperate man. Having tried several other tactics, Brennan attempts the "old Mickey stuff" but makes the mistaken assumption that Mrs. O'Connor is Irish. Upon learning that she is Polish, he tries to recover but does so badly: "I know a lot of good Polish people. They're very devout Catholics, too. . . . But I, as I said before, don't, don't think—in Worcester, I had quite a—all the Polish section there. Believe you me, we placed more Bibles than you could shake a stick at." Whatever linguistic skills Brennan once possessed are failing him, and as the close-ups reveal, he seems self-consciously aware that he is failing. With visible strain, he presses on in vain, becoming increasingly shrill. She continues to resist. Nearly mocking the woman as he stands to leave, he asks, "Is it the dollar a week that's holding you up, Mrs. O'Connor? I mean, I don't understand. Really, honest to God, I've been selling Bibles for ten years. I don't understand a dollar a week." Albert's camera is as relentless as Brennan's sales pitch in this sequence: He maintains a close-up on her face, even as a long silence follows. Her discomfort is in full view. Finally, she thanks him for his time. "That's all right. That's my job," replies Brennan with a discernible amount of dismay.

His decline continues in the scene in which he accompanies McDevitt on a sales call. The men visit a middle-class home where a husband and wife query the salesmen about the usefulness of the Catholic encyclopedia they offer. Their three children move about the room. Demoted to the role of observer, Brennan sits to the side of the action, engaging one of the children in a bit of play with a toy car but otherwise looking bored and ashamed. After McDevitt struggles to convince the couple, Brennan suddenly pipes up. Spewing out a series of salesman's cliches, sprinkled with references to the popular press, Brennan launches into an aggressive sales pitch.

> BRENNAN: May I interject to say one thing? The hand that rocks the cradle rules the world. Is that right? The woman behind every great man— there's a good woman. Now she spends, according to the *Reader's Digest*, about eighty-five percent with the children. Now whatever she is and whatever she imparts to them is how those children are going to grow up, and this is the age when they need it. Because if your house doesn't have a foundation, you've got no kind of a house. Does that make sense?
> MAN: That's just, well—
> BRENNAN: *(interrupting)* There we are. There we are.
> MAN: That's exactly what—
> BRENNAN: There we are! And we have that in white and red. And we can give it in any color that you might like. And that's another thing, too: The Bible is the heritage of life. And so, when you come right down, I know the price is something that doesn't enter in at all. It's the utility of it. And believe you me, I think you both have to agree that you have the utility there. Is that true or isn't it?
> WOMAN: Well . . .
> BRENNAN: That's all we have to say.

Never leaving his seat, the Badger has tried to command the room with words alone and has failed miserably. His speech is the epitome of nonsense, and it is delivered with an almost drunken urgency, in a more mean-spirited and cynical fashion than any of the salesmen have used so far. Invested with desperation and self-pity, Brennan's "That's all we have to say" serves as a fitting epitaph for his career.

Indeed, Brennan has very little left to say in this film. Back at the hotel room, he packs up his belongings so that he may return to Boston. As he sits, contemplative, the others avert their eyes. Against the blank white hotel-room wall, Brennan repeats his Irish story. But this time, the words take on a new poignancy. Rather than mocking the safe choice many of his fellow Irishmen made, he now expresses regret that his path—supposedly a more independent route—has led him to this moment of disappointment. "He's all set for life," concludes Brennan in his brogue, his voice quavering, referring to the man who opted for a pension. After that, he is silent. The closing image, a shot of Brennan framed in a doorway, looking out, speaks eloquently.

In the end, the film implies, the language of selling is a corruption of language; it hinders rather than helps human communication and connection. Albert's comments support this reading: "One thing is sure, that no matter where you are involved with the selling process, you cannot have a really free or candid expression of feeling." He also acknowledges that when he worked for a short time as an encyclopedia salesman, he "discovered the whole canned speech that they used for their customers. I believed every bit of it, and it took me a week or two before I began to see that there was a basic deception involved in that kind of selling."[25] The film rejects "canned speech" and its deceptive qualities; the problem is, as the film illustrates, a salesman who struggles to communicate beyond the parameters of canned speech has difficulty surviving in the business. The language of selling *is* the language of manipulation and self-deceit.

The last two filmed interactions with other salesmen also point out how painfully ill-equipt the others are to help Brennan in his plight. Martos says nothing when Brennan, at the end of his rope, articulates how hard the last few days have been for him. Instead, he lies on the bed next to Brennan, sorting through his call slips and book orders. He cannot find the words to respond to a man with whom he has worked and shared hotel rooms for years. At one point, he yawns and looks at his watch; for the sake of his own self-preservation, he must repress Brennan's struggles. Martos's insensitivity pales in comparison to McDevitt's in the penultimate scene in which

Brennan concludes, "We have nothing more to say." As they prepare to leave the house, McDevitt explains that he's brought Brennan along to help "give him a spark" because Brennan's sales have slumped so drastically. Adding public humiliation to Brennan's already overwhelming sense of personal disappointment, McDevitt shows that he is not worthy of the praise Brennan bestowed on him earlier in the film when he referred to McDevitt as "extremely effective" and "a wonderful guy." He has clearly lost touch (if he was ever in touch) with Brennan's feelings as a human being; alas, the "Salesman's Creed" says nothing about how one should treat a fellow salesman.

Albert once described *Salesman* as "basically a tragedy of a system that divides us one from another. . . . This film is a story of disconnectedness; people without a hope of ever making a connection with one another."[26] Brennan's inability to forge "connectedness" with people, as well as his understanding on some level of the harmful aspects of language, pushes him from being a struggling salesman to a desperate one. No longer in league with the other salesmen, he may not be entirely capable of fitting in anywhere else. The last scene, in which he stands alone, silent, powerfully underscores the message.

CRITICAL RESPONSE TO *SALESMAN*

When Zwerin's editing was complete and the film was ready to be released in 1968, Albert believed *Salesman* was so revolutionary that it would land the filmmakers on the cover of *Time* magazine.[27] The brothers touted *Salesman* as the most complete and authentic product thus far of their particular style of filmmaking. It would, they believed, "prove to everybody . . . that you could take someone from everyday life and make a film about him."[28] Ever optimistic, the brothers believed the film would create a whole new popular demand for nonfiction film. The realities of the film industry certainly hindered the brothers' ambitions, however; *Salesman*, like the vast majority of nonfiction films, then and now, received a limited national release in 1968. Even so, the film generated lively and mixed critical response and attracted substantial audiences in the art houses where it was shown. In New York, for instance, John Craddock reported that box-office receipts netted $12,000 in the first week, "with a house record set on the first Saturday."[29] Several national magazines reviewed the film, as did all the major New York-based publications, *Variety*, and major newspapers in Chicago, San Francisco, Los Angeles, and Washington. For the first time, both the popular press as well as the film-oriented publications weighed in. The brothers' high expectations of the film and an aggressive marketing campaign encouraged close attention, and in many ways, *Salesman* became a major test both for the Maysles brothers and direct cinema overall. Thus, while a few critics inevitably compared the film to Miller's well-known play, the vast majority used their discussion of *Salesman* as a springboard for a more general consideration of either the merits or drawbacks of direct cinema.[30] *Salesman*'s status as a lightning rod should come as no surprise. Direct cinema was at that time almost a decade old, and its aims and stylistic tendencies had been scrutinized carefully all along. But the product, so plentiful in the early 1960s, had tapered off significantly, especially now that television expressed less interest in vérité documentary, and most of the photographers for Drew Associates had gone their separate ways.[31] Many of the technical innovations had become more commonplace and accessible; some of the stylistic elements, such as extended tracking shots, were already bordering on cliché.

Therefore, those already prone to dismiss direct cinema's claims of artistry and authenticity were eager to find fault in *Salesman*. The criticisms primarily pointed to two perceived weaknesses in the film: first, a lack of structure and clear point of view, which in turn led to an overwhelming ambiguity; and second, a condescending approach to the salesmen that bordered on the unethical. On the film's unapparent point of view, film critic John Simon was particularly outraged. In the *New Leader*, he inquired, "How does the filmmaker, in a situation like this, avoid having a pronounced view on the subject, and how, having such a view, can he still appear impartial? And if he succeeds in *looking* impartial, how can he avoid being either wishy-washy or a hypocrite? It seems inconceivable to me that he could simply say: 'This just happens; it's just there.'" A lack of clear perspective, Simon argued, leads to "a certain moral ambiguity, a slipperiness based as much on fuzzy thinking as on wanting to have it both ways, comes to light. The film tries to be at once tough and sentimental, mocking and sympathetic." According to Simon, the advertisement for this film epitomized this ambiguity. (In it, a walking figure, identifiable as Jesus, carries a salesman's case in each hand.) The advertisement's association of religion and commercialism troubled Simon inasmuch as it admitted no point of view. "Are we debunking religion or apotheosizing that quintessential American, the salesman?" He wanted the Maysles brothers to announce openly where they stood on the issue without "getting away with statements about how they really 'like' these salesmen."[32]

Stanley Kauffmann, film critic for the *New Republic*, echoed Simon's concerns. "[T]he film's viewpoint is unclear. Does it mock the commercialization of religion? No. . . . Is the film an indictment of sales as the absolutely central American profession? No. . . . Do they attack selling as corrosive of individuality? No. . . . Insofar as it is focused, it's a portrait of a man in the wrong vocation. . . ." What Kauffmann later described as a "fuzziness of viewpoint" undermines, he felt, the dramatic impact of the film. Likewise, Ernest Callenbach, writing for *Film Quarterly*, faulted the lack of a clear "organizing principle" in *Salesman*. Although he appreciated that the film was an "honest document," he felt the "lack of interest inherent in the material" did not justify a ninety-minute film.[33]

Frequently, the concern over point of view also led to charges of condescension. *Variety*'s critic, for example, complained, "The contradiction between God's word and the selling of same constitutes a child's perception—but the Maysles [*sic*] milk it to death via 90 minutes which can only seek to foster snobbism on the part of spectators whose talents have led them to ostensibly 'purer' careers. . . . [The film has a] superior, condescending air" that could find an audience "if there are enough liberal intellectuals around who consider themselves above 'the type of thing' shown" in the film. John Simon concurred: The film generates an easy sense of superiority in the viewers, he believed. A New York newspaper critic thought that "the film seems to encourage condescension on the part of the audience." And, much to the Maysles brothers' dismay, those, like critic Judith Crist, who believed the film to be condescending often castigated the brothers for their unethical behavior, accusing them of "patronization and exploitation" or of "pot-shotting at sitting ducks."[34]

While these assessments of *Salesman* raised legitimate concerns about the overriding philosophy of direct cinema, many reviewers betrayed their implicit distrust of the people within the film. Many of the film critics asserted that the subjects had been duped or manipulated unfairly. But Brennan and the others signed releases after having seen the finished film. For his part, Brennan reportedly said, "This is one part I will always be proud of."[35] Yet, his acceptance and support of the film were not always heeded. (An even more vehement argument would be made "on behalf of" the Beales of *Grey Gardens* who, it was condescendingly assumed, could never judge for themselves whether the film was fair to them or if it used their eccentric lives as voyeuristic exploitation.) In *Salesman*, everyone who behaves badly is ultimately exposed only for being human, for falling victim to a materialistic system that often brings out the worst in everyone. With the possible exception of Turner, every person featured in *Salesman* also has redeeming qualities. All of the men demonstrate resiliency in the face of hard work, and each has a sense of humor that is frequently self-effacing. Brennan especially emerges as a noble if humanly flawed man.

Some critics at the time did defend the Maysles brothers against the charge of condescension. To say that *Salesman* is "condescending in its treatment of its subjects," responded John Craddock, " . . . misses the compassion and understanding with which the filmmakers have imbued the film. We are all salesmen in some aspect of our lives, and we have all been sold once too often. The truths of this film affect us all." After three screenings, Vincent Canby was especially impressed with "what I can only describe as the decency of [their] point of view. . . . [E]veryone in the movie seems to be touched by the Maysles's compassion. . . . *Salesman* somehow transcends such surface mockery, partly, I think, because the salesmen really are no less vulnerable than their customers."[36] The Maysles brothers' genuine interest in and compassion for the people they filmed meant that they were unafraid to show these people as complex and, at times, not particularly likable. No one is admirable all the time, the filmmakers understood, and to pretend otherwise would be a misrepresentation. Albert reasoned that the film "shows us the difficulties of our lives through witnessing people who are nice guys doing bad things."[37] Zwerin thought that it was a "staggering portrait of the American dream, and the kind of shabby things people give themselves to so completely and totally."[38] The filmmakers wanted their audience to judge the activity of door-to-door Bible selling, not the people doing the buying and selling.

David once responded that the critics who cried condescension were "the condescending ones. The ones who never admit anyone exists below the middle class. Somehow they think it's condescension to show some of the supposedly foolish or outrageous or otherwise damaging things we showed."[39] In other words, some critics had mistaken their own discomfort with the filmed situations as proof that the film mocks the people living out those situations. But what makes a viewer uncomfortable is the recognition of one's own weaknesses and vulnerabilities as others engage in awkward, even demeaning situations. (Here again the Maysles brothers' hard truths connect them to John Cassavetes's pragmatic modernism.) Everyone has, at some point, been a buyer and, in some context, a seller. The difficulties with language and the struggle to communicate and to find human connection are therefore familiar dilemmas.

Moreover, the ambiguity that worried many critics was, of course, intrinsic to the filmmakers' project. They did not wish to provide pat answers or for that matter represent any problem as clear-cut. In *Salesman*, the collision of business and religion is accurately portrayed as a complicated matter. Religion and the pursuit of material gain have, like Jesus with the briefcases, walked hand-in-hand consistently and curiously in the United States since the nineteenth century.[40] A salesman charged with the responsibility and burden of doing his "Father's business" is therefore given a unique and paradoxical task, and the film's ambiguity reflects most Americans' mixed and mixed-up values. The negative reviews, however, seemed to regard ambiguity as "slipperiness" and "fuzziness," as if no filmmaker would willingly leave it in a film, particularly because it allows for a latitude of interpretations. Yet, ambiguity has always been essential to direct cinema. Frederick Wiseman has explained, "Since the reality is complex, contradictory, and ambiguous, people with different values or experience respond differently. I think that there should be enough room in the film for people to find support for their views while understanding what mine are. Otherwise I'd be in the propaganda business."[41] A Maysles Brothers film, too, provides "enough room," again underscoring an inherent trust in the audience. The ambiguity should not be confused with a fuzzy sense of purpose; it is part of the modernist aesthetic.

In showing the limits of language, the filmmakers not only explored a modernist theme, they also extended direct cinema into new territory. Compared to any direct cinema film that had come before it, *Salesman* was a bold manipulation of the form. Many film critics and historians did recognize its import and praised the film at the time of its release. Hollis Alpert of the *Saturday Review* reported that the Maysles brothers had "converted" him to the merits of cinéma vérité, which Alpert "used to regard with skepticism." He contended that they "have come into their own with *Salesman*, which strikes me as one of the most important American films ever made." Bob Sitton called *Salesman* "a milestone in film making." Stephen Mamber concurred: "*Salesman* is the Maysles' most ambitious work to date and in many ways the most important product of American cinéma vérité." Erik Barnouw's extensive history of documentary film, first published in 1973, devotes four pages to *Salesman*, a sizable chunk in that text. Barnouw's text claims that with this film "the Maysles moved into a very different world, and gave direct cinema an unexpected dimension."[42]

Since its original release, the film has indeed earned its place among the most important and skillfully made nonfiction films. Its strength lies in its ability to tell a true story authentically with all the plangency of a fictional work. The "unexpected dimension" to which Barnouw alluded, however, failed to impress some viewers and the criticisms it received bespoke a more widespread turn away from direct cinema. This backlash would reach its zenith in the mid-1970s—around the time *Grey Gardens*, the next Maysles film taken from everyday life, appeared in theaters.

In summarizing both his negative reactions to the filmmakers' process and to the feelings the film elicited in him, John Simon offered that the Maysles brothers have "stumbled on to something much bigger than they realize: a condemnation—however fragmented, fortuitous, and even inept—of the human condition, of man himself; but also of society plagued by superstition, idiot competitiveness, and stultifying materialism."[43] While Zwerin and the Maysles brothers would probably not have objected to the word "stumbled" here—suggesting as it does a completely spontaneous capturing of something—nor would they have disagreed with Simon's assessment of what plagues society, they *would* have absolutely refuted having condemned the human condition. *Salesman* uncovers a painfully dehumanizing process but does not condemn the people engaged in it. The filmmakers respect the humanity of the men and their customers while showing the appalling nature of the activity of door-to-door Bible selling. Seeking authenticity, they also confronted the inevitable breakdowns of modern communication.

4

Can We See How They Look?: Observing the Rolling Stones in *Gimme Shelter*

The Maysles brothers' next project took them in a new direction. In early 1969, the Rolling Stones, already one of rock music's most successful and recognizable acts, launched an extended American tour in support of their album *Let It Bleed*. Interested in having their New York City appearance at Madison Square Garden filmed, the Stones contacted cinematographer and filmmaker Haskell Wexler, whose documentary-like fiction film *Medium Cool* had recently earned high praise. After a brief consultation, however, the band and Wexler recognized that their concepts of the potential film differed. Wexler referred them to his friends Albert and David Maysles, who were looking for a potential means of recouping some of the expenses of *Salesman*, which despite respectable showings at art houses across the country had lost money.[1] The brothers agreed to film and record the Stones concert, but at that time, they had no preconception as to whether the project could evolve into a feature-length film. Once engaged in the project, however, they became intrigued by the personalities of the Stones members, especially Mick Jagger, and the commotion the group provoked at every public appearance. According to Albert, the brothers followed a "hunch that we would make a film story of more than just rock concerts. . . . [W]e wouldn't make just a concert film if there weren't other elements, beside the spectacle, which attracted us."[2]

With some initial financial backing from the Stones but mostly at the brothers' own expense, Albert and David continued filming the band as it completed its American tour that year. The film would prove to be the brothers' most ambitious undertaking, a "collaboration on a grand scale," according to codirector Charlotte Zwerin, who was brought on board to give structure to the raw material and to supervise the massive editing process. The final credits note twenty-two different camera operators (in addition to Albert), fourteen sound recorders (in addition to David), four film editors, and three assistant film editors.[3]

Just as the brothers' "hunch" about a Joseph E. Levine film proved well-founded, so, too, did their assumption about a Rolling Stones film although partly due to circumstances no one could have foretold. This particular Stones tour culminated on 7 December 1969, with the now infamous free concert at Altamont Speedway near San Francisco. The Altamont concert, which was supposed to be the Woodstock of the West, was held four months after the Woodstock, New York, event, which had been a large-scale, outdoor festival of peace, love, and rock and roll. Altamont was attended by more than three hundred thousand people—and it turned into a disaster.[4] The concert suffered from poor planning, horrendous traffic snarls, inadequate sanitary facilities, an excess of potent hallucinogenic drugs, limited medical aid, the violent participation of the Hell's Angels motorcycle gang, and most infamously, the stabbing death of a spectator. The victim, a man named Meredith Hunter, was knifed in self-defense by a member of the Hell's Angels, who collectively had been hired (reportedly for $500 worth of beer) to protect the musicians from overzealous or overdrugged audience members. Greed and poor planning turned Altamont into a theater of the absurd; the Maysles brothers' film captured the event for perpetuity.[5]

Gimme Shelter is an important historical artifact, spotlighting a particular and notorious moment in time. Altamont marked for many the event at which the hopefulness of Woodstock dissolved, replaced by drug-laden cynicism and frequent senseless violence. Days after the concert, Todd Gitlin, who attended many of the numerous outdoor festivals that summer, including both Woodstock and Altamont, lamented the close of a promising era and chastised those who had turned the counterculture into just another culture of consumption. Years later, Gitlin maintained his original view, recalling how Altamont "felt like death" and had taken much of the life out of the counterculture. The day following the concert, the Berkeley *Tribe* concurred; a headline read: "Stones Concert Ends It—America Now Up for Grabs."[6] The counterculture's attempt to provide an alternative to the dominant culture's values, epitomized by the spirit of cooperation at Woodstock, had seemingly vanished with the death of Hunter. A

few other outdoor festivals followed (they were, after all, extremely profitable), but none of them could offset the tarnished image.[7]

Still, even if Altamont is designated the nadir of massive outdoor concerts, too many accounts of the event have overstated its broader import and
oversimplified the context in which the concert occurred. Altamont should
be remembered as one in a series of contentious incidents that marked 1969,
including the trial of the Chicago Seven, ongoing student unrest at various
colleges and universities, and the deaths of two Black Panthers members at
the hands of the police. Other events of the preceding year—race riots in
several major U.S. cities, the police/protestor showdown at the Chicago
Democratic convention, the assassinations of Robert Kennedy and Martin Luther King Jr.—and the ever-present specter of the Viet Nam conflict,
simultaneously reduce Altamont's significance and make the concert appear to be a far more logical expression of the troubled times than the
comparatively benign Woodstock. Many other factors contributed more
profoundly, if also less conspicuously, to the demise of Woodstock nation
and its concomitant politics of authenticity.

This exaggerated historical emphasis on Altamont has also meant that
Gimme Shelter has generally been treated simply as a documentary of the
"death knell of the counterculture." Such a view does the film a disservice.
Although the brothers did not have the same degree of creative freedom
they had enjoyed with *Salesman*, they and codirector Zwerin did have
enough free rein to once again stretch the parameters of nonfiction filmmaking. Rather than report on a rock-music phenomenon or a particular historical event, the filmmakers produced a film that had more in common with literary models like *In Cold Blood*, just as they had done with
Salesman. In discussing *Gimme Shelter*, they reiterated their "interest . . .
in making films as one would write a novel or do a painting or even compose a song. . . . *Gimme Shelter* and *Salesman* are unique [in that regard]."[8]
Accordingly, the filmmakers rely in *Gimme Shelter* on such literary devices
as out-of-order chronology and self-reflexivity, and the film once again
moves forward many of the Maysles brothers' modernist impulses.

Thematically, they contemplate within the film the limited possibility
of understanding and seeing reality. Just as modernists have realized that
language in contemporary society can be a barrier rather than a means to
human communication, so, too, have they understood that seeing can be
deceptive and may in fact lead to less rather than more knowledge. In his
classic 1972 text on the subject, John Berger postulates that "the relation
between what we see and what we know is never settled." The interaction

and frequent discrepancy between sight and "truth" are openly acknowledged and become a matter for exploration in a modernist text. Seeing may lead to believing, but modernist filmmakers frequently ask their viewers to reconsider what they believe and assume, especially when such beliefs and assumptions are based solely on what is visible. In so doing, modernists can, in the words of Gilberto Perez, "make us notice what we are *not* seeing and lead us to recognize the inescapable limitation of our view." Moreover, the modernists point out, what *is* visible is often a manipulated or reproduced image that may or may not be authentic.[9]

In *Gimme Shelter*, the filmmakers created a work that *rejects* the possibility of seeing chaotic moments in time—such as the Altamont concert—as coherent and easily understandable. The filmmakers refused to simplify this historical event. If anything, *Gimme Shelter* exacerbates the confusion. Zwerin's decision to show the Rolling Stones watching footage of concerts and Altamont backroom negotiations, listening to various reports of the aftermath, and viewing the murder scene adds one more layer to the already complex story. This film within a film motif creates additional distance between the events and the viewing audience.

Although many people at the time hoped that the film would provide some answers to the Altamont debacle, the filmmakers resisted that assignment, shaking off what they believed were burdensome expectations that their film would address the question "Why did this happen?" Albert recognized that easy answers were not available, even if they had wished to make a problem-and-solution kind of film: "We all seek answers: It was the Angels or the Stones, money or the 'superstar trip' which was responsible for the stabbing. But it was really much more complicated than that. We think the film shows just how complex it was."[10] They also correctly observed that the particular historical context in which the film was released affected the way people saw it: "Right now, the rock scene being what it is, people may just think that *Gimme Shelter* is the voice of doom. Six months ago it might have been different."[11] Later, in response to film critic Pauline Kael's negative (and grossly inaccurate) review, the three filmmakers stated even more concisely, "Rather than give the audience what it wants to believe, the film forces it to see things as they are."[12] And "things as they are" do not necessarily cohere; the world as it is, according to the Maysles brothers' pragmatic modernism, is an uncertain place where knowing and seeing are elusive goals.

In addition to this modernist response, the brothers returned to an idea they had already explored thoroughly. In all their films up to this point, they consistently expressed dismay at the way materialism and celebrity fixation have infected American culture. They again show in *Gimme Shelter* that too much concern with what celebrities say and do and with making money in the celebrity/entertainment business leads to any number of negative consequences, including a lack of concern for other human beings. More than previous films, however, *Gimme Shelter* depicts how that process may spiral out of control, rendering everyone involved powerless. Whereas there was an innocence to the celebrity obsession in *What's Happening!*, *Gimme Shelter* reveals the dark side of this compulsion. Albert and David followed a hunch and found a more contemplative story than they had envisioned.[13]

"IT'S REALLY HARD TO SEE THIS TOGETHER"

The structure of *Gimme Shelter* is highly complex, reflecting the difficulty of getting at the truth, of seeing complicated circumstances clearly. In a culture in which celebrity, materialism, and media coalesce into an amorphous mass, blame for any disaster spawned by an entertainment event becomes nearly impossible to assign absolutely, especially in a case like the Altamont concert where so many people with so many different motives were brought together. An extensive *Rolling Stone* article of January, 1970, features more than twenty observers each offering their own assessment of what they saw, what they believe went wrong, and who was to blame. Carlos Santana, whose newly formed band played at Altamont, cited not only the Angels' aggression but also a potent combination of "reds [hallucinogenics] and liquor." Under the influence, "you lose control of respect for yourself, and you lose control of respect for anybody else." Captain William Bradshaw of the California Highway Patrol faulted the lack of preparation time and a generally hostile crowd. David Crosby, whose band did not attend the concert, defended the Hell's Angels based on the their past effectiveness as security guards, then surmised: "Blame is the dumbest trip there is; there isn't any blame."[14] Many people may take part in an event, and everyone relies on his or her own limited perspective of that event as the truth. A film, too, has limited sight in that it can only show what a particular camera operator was able to see through his or her lens at a given moment. Rather than hold itself out as a definitive source, *Gimme Shelter* asserts that it cannot be the true measure of seeing the Rolling Stones and the Altamont concert.

At the same time, the film illustrates that the Rolling Stones exert a great deal of effort controlling and manipulating the way they are seen. They had, from their earliest days as a performing group, cultivated an image as a more aggressive, more sexually adventurous alternative to the Beatles.[15] Jagger particularly had dedicated himself to the task of creating an image as a petulant, androgynous rock star. In *Gimme Shelter*, the filmmakers question Jagger's naivete (which is possibly feigned anyway) as well as the "problem of Jagger's double self."[16] The lead singer presents himself as a nearly out-of-control, sexually predatory "street-fighting man" onstage; he frequently reins in and manages his image in an almost workmanlike manner offstage. When Zwerin decided to show Jagger and the other Stones watching film footage and listening to news reports, she turned the band members into observers and listeners, an important role-reversal. Stripped temporarily of their power to manipulate an audience, the Stones are thrust into a position of passivity; as viewers, they are put on an equal basis with all other observers of their act. In the process, the band is implicated—after all, they are the ones whom people wanted to see in the first place and they could have behaved more responsibly, knowing (and to a great extent promulgating) how they were being seen.

Yet, *Gimme Shelter* also forgives the Stones; the film implies they cannot be held accountable for everything an audience does. The behavior of an audience engaged in celebrity-watching of any kind is far from rational and predictable; the Stones like any other performing entity cannot possibly monitor every person who watches them. The film shows that the band cannot dictate how they are managed either. As one part of an enormous Rolling Stones quasi-corporation, they must leave this business to other people, most of whom engage in backroom negotiations and intentionally shield them from the kinds of logistical issues that exploded at Altamont. Within the story of the film, Jagger and the rest of the group are shown to be no more or less guilty of the subsequent Altamont fiasco than are attorney Melvin Belli, manager Sam Cutler, concert organizer John Roberts, speedway owner Dick Carter, Hell's Angels leader Sonny Barger and his men, or even the spaced-out audience members, all of whom played their parts in the real-life drama. Altamont was a collective mess; the film indicates that all the players involved ought to examine their roles in contributing to it.[17]

The opening scene of *Gimme Shelter* establishes several key motifs. From the outset, direct cinema convention is violated: The soundtrack initially is not in synch with the images on the screen. The film starts in darkness; nothing is visible, and what can be heard initially comes from a distinct but thus far invisible source. Against the black screen, crowd noises are audible, then comes high-pitched feedback from a microphone, then a British-accented voice, unrecognizable, announcing: "For the first time in three years, the greatest rock-and-roll band in the world: the Rolling Stones!" As soon as the name of the band is delivered, the film offers the first visual image, but rather than providing what might be expected—namely, a visual representation of what we have begun to hear—the directors instead cut to a bizarre image of a man (the Stones's drummer, Charlie Watts), dressed outlandishly in a long white cape, bright red scarf and an armored helmet, atop a burro, brandishing a rifle. The frame freezes momentarily, as if to signal that the image of the man is being shot by a photographer, then cuts to the same man, in a head-and-shoulders shot, now wearing a trench coat and an Uncle Sam–style, red-white-and-blue hat. All the while, the soundtrack has not changed; the concert sounds continue, and the next voice, recognizable as Jagger's, addresses the boisterous crowd: "Let's have a look at ya. We're gonna see how beautiful you are." He repeats the sentence, in an apparent attempt to turn the tables on the spectators: He wants to see the crowd, who of course are there to see him. Meanwhile, the filmmakers continue to show footage of the Stones at their unusual photo shoot. Standing by the side of a highway, Jagger seems to be directing Watts who, in his outrageous Uncle Sam garb (actually Jagger's standard costume for the Stones's American tour), cavorts with the burro. A photographer takes pictures at the scene. Jagger's "Let's have a look at ya" may also be directed not only at the as-yet-unseen concert crowd but also at his band mate. In all, the filmmakers present a highly convoluted situation in which they have filmed someone else photographing the Stones while we hear Jagger on stage asking to look at his audience.

It is an appropriately complex scenario in a film that wishes to illustrate the complicated nature of observing and being observed, of controlled and uncontrolled spectacle. The photographer in this segment, as a recorder of images that will in turn become permanent things to be viewed (and that will adorn commodities that will be bought and sold), plays a vexed role in the whole process. He is at once a chronicler of real events as they happen but also a participant in a profit-driven falsification that seeks to make lasting images out of fleeting moments. (The filmmakers also reveal themselves to be a knowing part of this process.) Jagger, as the director of this scene within a scene, demonstrates that he understands the process and helps foster it. The film immediately establishes that the Rolling Stones are objects to be seen and frequently also directors of their own image-making.

At the photo shoot, Jagger takes the Uncle Sam hat away from Watts, then the film quickly cuts to Jagger holding a similar hat at the concert from which his voice-over originated. The hat serves as a visual link between these two scenes, which are really, the film indicates, intricately connected. Without the created and manipulated spectacle epitomized in the photo shoot, there might not be an audience paying to see the live spectacle. On stage, Jagger calls one last time: "New York City, let's get a look at you." But as the band launches into "Jumping Jack Flash," it is he who really "gets looked at." Fully realizing all eyes are upon him, Jagger plays his role as lead singer and agent provocateur of the Rolling Stones. The chief spectacle at the Stones's concerts, he dances, prances, preens, and generally demands attention—"strutting and grinding like a cockatoo that got into the Benzedrine," one critic wryly observed.[18] Albert complies with Jagger's (and presumably the film audience's) wishes, fixing his camera on Jagger almost exclusively in the opening number. On the few occasions when the film cuts to the audience, they are shown either in rapturous gaze (staring at Jagger, too) or, ironically, with binoculars or cameras, the better to see and capture the spectacle they have paid to see with their own eyes.

As the song ends, the film cuts to a brief shot of band member Keith Richards trading one guitar for another on stage, then there is a cut to the same image on a monitor in a studio. The image that just moments before had filled the screen now only occupies a small portion, as the monitor in the next segment is shown. Sitting atop an editing table in a studio, it appears quite small. Then, directly underneath the image of the monitor, the first credit appears on the screen: THE ROLLING STONES. It is a significant moment at which to present the band's name. Because the title appears on a monitor that is a small part of the larger movie screen, it takes up a relatively small portion of the total frame. Lest the audience think it might gain some privileged access to the Stones or to some kind of unvarnished truth, the monitor image underscores how difficult, perhaps impossible, that may be. This image suggests the best any spectator may be able to do is to see already viewed and possibly restructured pieces of the Stones from a distance; the filmviewer is, after all, only watching a film, not experiencing anything first-hand. The truth, the actuality of lived experience, is only possible for those who were actually there—and even they can only understand a limited amount of what transpired from their own limited individual perspective. The film makes this point consistently and continuously: We cannot see everything we might need to see in order to fully understand any complex situation, and what we *do* see is so laden with culturally inscribed motifs of performance that we may actually be led in the wrong direction. The segments of the film that follow maintain this position.

The Stones themselves are introduced by name as they are shown watching themselves on editing monitors. (The images they are seeing are not revealed; the camera remains fixed on their watching and their reactions.) One by one, their names are revealed; they watch themselves perform and give faintly smiling approval. Meanwhile, Jagger's voice-over from the concert is heard again: "I think you really dressed up tonight, and I think we'd like to see how you look. Can we see how they look? Let's have a look how they look. . . . Ah, we're starting to see how they look. Ah, we couldn't see you." His desire to have the lights turned up on the audience so that he might "see how they look" parallels the filmviewer's desire to see how the Rolling Stones look. Yet, neither desire is fulfilled here. The film does not visually represent what Jagger asks to see and apparently does see (the audience), nor does the film ever really show the film-viewing audience how the Stones look either. The best that can be done is to show the Stones watching themselves; only then do they seem to be conscious of themselves as performers and only then—perhaps—do they stop performing.[19]

A question from Watts in the editing room continues the seeing motif and immediately introduces the next segment: "It's really hard to see this together, isn't it?" he asks as he watches David and Zwerin edit the film. Watts's statement marks the fifteenth time already in the film that the words *look* or *see* have been used, an astonishing number that when quantified suggests overkill on the part of the filmmakers. Yet, the repetition is scarcely noticeable because of the way it is edited into the flow of the visual images. The seductive quality of observing, the allure of voyeurism, draws viewers in (thereby implicating them in the process), yet so subtle are the forces that shape the way we observe that we may not even know what we are doing. In this case, viewer responses are further colored by the celebrity of the people being observed. In his history of fame, Leo Braudy relates the complex relationship between audience and performer:

> In show business the audience watches and thereby possesses the performer as an aspect of itself. . . . The eye appropriates what it sees. Normally, objects remain separate from us, but those images we see on the screen or on the page are continuous with our imagination of what they are 'really' like. Because our imagination participates in their creation, it is difficult to separate who sees from what is seen. . . .[20]

This blurring of the lines between one who sees and what is seen permeates *Gimme Shelter*.

Unwittingly, Watts's question also announces the overarching trouble with the Stones's tour, the climactic appearance at Altamont, the subsequent search for answers and scapegoats, and, even, the attempt to encapsulate the entire experience into a film. It *will* be hard to see this (the film) together; it will be difficult to take in all the visual images, to listen to the music and dialogue, then to draw clear conclusions, or to grasp fully what lessons may be learned. Just as salesman language presented an impediment to effective understanding and communication in *Salesman*, the overwhelming complexity of this film, coupled with the inability of some of the main figures to cease performing, frustrates anyone's ability to say definitively why Altamont ended in tragedy.

The ensuing conversation between Watts and an onscreen David Maysles takes on even greater significance:

MAYSLES: It'll take time.
WATTS: What?
MAYSLES: Eight weeks.
WATTS: Eight weeks. You think you can do it that quick?
MAYSLES: This gives us the freedom. All you guys watching it. We may only be on you a minute. Then go to almost anything.

This admission of the film's subjectivity is crucial to understanding *Gimme Shelter* and to dealing with it on its own terms. David acknowledges that *Gimme Shelter* will not present a step-by-step account of the Rolling Stones 1969 tour. It will instead present a disjointed series of scenes, all of which defy easy interpretation and thwart the viewer who wishes to lay blame for the Altamont debacle, including the killing of Hunter. The filmmakers may "go to almost anything" rather than build a case in some kind of linear fashion toward one right interpretation. David announces the arbitrarily constructed quality of the film and thereby inscribes it as a modernist text. Like a John Cassavetes film or a Bertolt Brecht play, *Gimme Shelter* seeks to challenge the viewer's assumptions about the nature of seeing with one's own eyes.

The filmmakers also permit the audience to see how *they* look in this sequence, a rare event in a Maysles brothers' film and rarer still in direct cinema. David's and Zwerin's appearances further erode the distinction between observer and observed. As in many modernist films, the viewer is reminded that he is watching an edited visual document, which is necessarily different than that which we see in person. The film provides *one possible* way of seeing, not the only way of seeing. This would seem to be an unusual admission to make as it amounts to an acknowledgment of the limitations of film in general, including direct cinema. Indeed, both the lack of chronology and the on-camera appearances are on one level stunning compromises of direct cinema's precepts. Again, however, one principle consistently governed the brothers' filmmaking and defined direct cinema Maysles-style: The process of editing for them and their collaborators meant finding an appropriate organizing principle for the filmed footage and coordinating the content to that form. If, as in this case, the principle that made the most artistic sense also violated some generally held conventions of direct cinema, the best interests of the final product were nevertheless served.

The freedom to which David refers when answering Watts in *Gimme Shelter* remains ambiguous and appropriately so given the theme of the film. Freedom to do what? To cut back and forth without respect to chronological order? To connect the Stones's responses to filmed footage of key events to the events themselves? To find fault with the band's behavior without overtly blaming them? All of these freedoms *are* exercised in the film. Yet, when the filmmakers present themselves openly as creators of a film about a rock-and-roll band that has already created a particular and well-defined image, they also implicate the entire image-making process. The freedom to which David refers might well be a freedom to expose this process and the materialism that supports it in its true light. The Maysles brothers had been consistent critics of anything that in their view deterred authentic human communication and connection. Or, possibly, it is the freedom *from* something that David espouses. He and Zwerin were free from having to establish a problem-solution format; from offering explanations for the events that occurred—from being cultural historians instead of nonfiction filmmakers. They never sought the role of historian and bristled at those who wanted to impose it on them, especially in light of the Altamont fiasco.

As if to demonstrate the advantages of editing freedom, the film cuts immediately to Jagger and Watts listening to a recorded tape of a San Francisco–based radio call-in show. The program, originally broadcast 8 December 1969, centers on the Altamont concert, marking the first time in the film it has been mentioned. The announcer from KSAN radio reports that a man was apparently murdered but concludes: "We were there. We didn't see it. But we did see a lot. We want to know now what you saw." Again, the emphasis on seeing and its limitations returns. It is possible to see a lot and still miss something, even a murder. The radio show's listeners will offer other viewpoints but never the definitive, omniscient one.

Meanwhile, that the film presents the death out of chronological order simultaneously emphasizes and de-emphasizes it. The filmmakers were faced with a dilemma: how to deal with an event about which, by the time the film was released, everyone knew and held opinions. How to be sure that Hunter's death does not somehow overshadow the entire film? Their strategy was to introduce and acknowledge the shadow from the outset, thereby reducing the tension of building toward it (the audience need not wonder "What about the stabbing?"). Yet, this also privileged the murder as the defining event of the entire tour. It was a conundrum the codirectors could not entirely resolve.

The radio show introduces some of the key supporting figures as well. Hell's Angels leader Barger calls into the program, railing at Jagger, who, he says, "played us for dupes." On film, Jagger reacts with mild surprise at the accusation. Watts is more thoughtful: "Well done, Sonny," he says wistfully at the end of Barger's tirade. Then, Watts acknowledges the power and impressiveness of the Angels as he saw them, especially the way they cleared a path with their motorcycles when the performers emerged to take the stage. Making an impressive entrance had long been a staple of the Stones's concert appearances, and the spectacle of this moment had impressed even the laid-back Watts. "Did you see them do that?" he asks David, who replies, "I was there, yeah," knowing full well that being there means seeing a lot but not seeing it all. "Oh, dear, what a shame," Watts concludes, his remorse seemingly genuine and loaded with powerlessness.

Jagger seems less affected by what he hears and sees. If one of the film's intentions is to explore the ways in which Jagger has been moved by the experience at Altamont, it thus far reveals only inconclusive evidence. Having explored the matter briefly and inconclusively, the film cuts to a concert performance of "Satisfaction." As Jagger sings the sexually charged lyrics, he struts to the driving bass of the song. Immediately following, the film switches to a press conference, at which Jagger coyly discusses the ways he is and is not satisfied—"sexually satisfied, financially unsatisfied, philosophically trying." He is the epitome of the self-assured rocker in this segment, clear-eyed (rare in the film), and confident, playing the press as he does the concert audience. The juxtaposition of the concert and the press conference highlights that in both situations, Jagger performs skillfully; the editing links the appearances as two aspects of the same image-making game. Although Jagger does not seem to question the connection, he nevertheless criticizes his performance at the press conference. Upon watching this footage of himself, he responds, "Rubbish." It is difficult to interpret his reaction, however. Is he acknowledging the frivolous nature of his answer, the absurd press conference in general, or critiquing his own performance in this setting? How *aware* is he? Unlike the Beatles and Brando films, *Gimme Shelter* continually clouds the viewer's ability to feel sympathy for Jagger because Jagger's degree of self-consciousness is much harder to determine.

Immediately after Jagger's self-critique, the film returns to the press conference. Here Jagger introduces the idea of a free concert. His motivations sound idealistic, as he is interested in "creating a sort of microcosmic society . . . which sets an example to the rest of America as to how one can behave in large gatherings." With the shadow of the stabbing death already cast, Jagger's prediction reads ironically, of course, but his statement also underscores his naive approach to the concert. Never worried about legal or logistical complications, Jagger can perform a role as the benevolent bad boy, generously participating in a counterculture experience that he elsewhere in the film calls "an excuse for everyone to get together . . . and get very stoned." That the concert may well be better described as an excuse for the performers to get together and get a great deal of publicity—which, despite the free admission, refuels the money-making endeavors of all those interested in becoming more "financially satisfied"—is left unsaid. Those who remain behind the scenes, offstage and unseen by the public, negotiate the details, leaving Jagger to perform his public acts unencumbered.

The film does reveal some of these usually unseen moments. Intercut with Jagger's rosy predictions and the group's concert footage are three scenes in attorney Belli's San Francisco office. Belli, one of the country's most prominent lawyers at the time (he had, for instance, defended Jack Ruby in the Lee Harvey Oswald shooting), had been retained in order to help secure a site for the free concert. In three different segments, Belli attempts to pave the way for the festival, and he performs the role of a lawyer as much as Jagger performs the part of a free-spirited lead singer. Frequently jocular, Belli confidently negotiates with concert promoters and raceway owners. Using his speakerphone like a microphone, he dominates his office as a singer might command a stage. In one scene he even jokes: "I'm practicing. I'm going on before the Stones." An annoyed local sheriff finally asks Belli to pick up the phone, in effect taking the mike away and disarming him of one of his most powerful performance tools.

For all his skill at playing an attorney, however, Belli has no more grasp on the big picture than does anyone else in the film. When one of the

Stones's managers describes what might happen at Altamont, Belli appears genuinely surprised. "You have no idea what goes on here," a promoter tells Belli. "It's an amazing phenomena. It's like lemmings to the sea." The prescient quality of the statement notwithstanding, a major point of this and the other juxtaposed office scenes is to demonstrate how ineffectual any one person can be in the face of a human event on the scale of Altamont. Belli may wield influence in the legal community, but amidst these overwhelming cultural and financial forces, he is out of his league. The last shot of Belli in the film shows him speechless, stymied by the parking problem he has just been discussing. He looks down to avoid the camera's gaze. The other men in these segments—including the band's promoter Ron Schneider and concert organizer Roberts—attempt to shape order out of chaos, but it is clear that the unpredictability of the situation exceeds any of their expertise.[21]

From the first office scene, the film cuts to a surprised Jagger, watching the taped footage on the monitor, his raised eyebrows again illustrating his distance from negotiations in his name. The film never shows Jagger or any other member of the Rolling Stones interacting directly with Belli; the attorney admits to another caller that he has not met personally with anyone in the group. The Stones's distance from such things is again mirrored by the device of the film within the film.

Perhaps more illustrative of the Stones's disconnectedness is the behind-the-scenes glimpses of the group. Whether in the studio, hotel room, or backstage, the film also reveals the group to be surprisingly distanced from their own music. In passive roles as listeners and observers, they are generally transfixed by their own performances, listening intently, sometimes mouthing the words, or dancing a little. Only briefly, in a scene at the Muscle Shoals Recording Studio in Alabama does Jagger suggest how to edit a song; grinning foolishly, he punctuates his direction with a swig from a liquor bottle. Another musician-based direct cinema film, D. A. Pennebaker's *Dont Look Back* (1966), contrasts sharply. In that film, Bob Dylan works consistently at his music, whether typing up lyrics, trying out new blues songs on a back-stage piano, or rehearsing already written songs. There is a clear sense that Pennebaker's and Dylan's presentations of Bob Dylan the performer onstage reflect only a small percentage of the passion and commitment he feels as a songwriter and musician. The members of the Rolling Stones, on the other hand, in their pursuit of building image, seem to have removed themselves not only from what happens in front of them at their concerts but also from their own talents as musicmakers. Other than the scenes at the Steenbeck editing machine, *Gimme Shelter* shows the Stones in performance mode only.

Almost precisely halfway through the ninety-minute film, the scene shifts to the actual Altamont concert. In the initial series of images, there are numerous signs that the concert site is a chaotic one: A helicopter shot from above Altamont Speedway shows what appears to be a miles-long traffic jam; workers frantically set up a haphazard stage and sound system in the dark; three men urinate against a drainage pipe; a man sells LSD and other narcotics; naked people wander aimlessly; one teenage girl remarks, "I've been falling a lot lately"; and numerous people appear to be suffering unpleasant results from hallucinogens. Even liberated sex, so gently depicted in two contemporary festival films (*Monterey Pop* and *Woodstock*), comes off as awkward and unappealing, as two people are shown fumbling with each other, while their dog, attached to them by a short leash, strains to get away. Another woman struggles against two men trying to escort her away from the stage area; "I want to see Mick Jagger, damn it," she cries, spontaneously articulating one of the film's central issues. All this before anyone takes the stage to play music.

Seeing Jagger will be a challenge. The Stones are shown arriving via helicopter, and immediately, a crowd surrounds the band. One person pushes through the mob and strikes Jagger; warily, the singer completes the journey to his trailer and closes the door.[22] Before the Stones's set, Jagger emerges only briefly from his trailer. Blurry-eyed, he signs a few albums and mingles with a small gathering of fans. When asked what he has seen thus far, he confesses he has been in seclusion all day: "I can't get very far." Trapped by the celebrity he has so carefully created, Jagger is literally unable to see what is happening in the microcosmic society he has helped to build. This scene, juxtaposed with a scuffle between two concertgoers, emphasizes his isolation.

Those in charge of setting up the stage and preparing the sound system struggle in the early hours of the festival. Manager Cutler is uptight and unfriendly, barking at various people or hustling strangers away from the stage. Trying to maintain order, he asks a few attendees to dismount the scaffolding: "If we could have some sort of reason, whatever that might be," he says into the microphone, barely disguising his exasperation. He even expresses disdain for a medical professional who would like to make an announcement about those needing attention: "I'm not gonna lay bum trips on this crowd." The medic's feeble reply, "At Woodstock this was done," falls on deaf ears. For the film audience, all of whom are familiar with the quite different outcomes of the two concerts being compared, the irony of the medic's statement rings loudly.

Along with these scenes, however, there are also a few peaceful and amusing images that foretell no disaster: A flower child distributes roses to other people; a white woman asks for contributions to the Black Panther Defense Fund, chirping, "After all, they're just Negroes, you know"; a happily tripped out man embraces a member of the film crew; someone reports, "A chick's having a baby." (Confirming this last piece of news, irrepressible speedway owner Carter insists that any announcements about the birth refer to his place as *Dick Carter's* Altamont Speedway.) Thus, when the Flying Burrito Brothers, a country-rock band, take the stage first and energize the crowd with "Six Days on the Road," the initial tumult of Altamont seems to be yielding to dancing, bubble-blowing, and general festiveness. Cutler's wishful announcement that this could be "the greatest party of 1969" seems to be coming true. Although a small scuffle between a Hell's Angel and a spectator follows the first song, it is quickly resolved. The filmmakers emphasize in these scenes that Altamont was a complex social event; these visuals suggest that the concert was not just "Thanatos unleashed" (as historian Allen J. Matusow has referred to it), but, in part, a gathering of "gentle people" much like those seen in *Monterey Pop* or *Woodstock*.[23]

The tone does shift, however, during the Jefferson Airplane's set. As the San Francisco band plays "The Other Side of This Life," the Hell's Angels have begun to pummel an audience member whom they believe has gotten too close to the stage. Airplane singer Marty Balin jumps into the crowd and is promptly knocked unconscious. Most of this commotion remains unfilmed, however; Albert's steady camera remains focused on the band, in the midst of an extended guitar solo. Finally realizing what has happened, lead singer Grace Slick attempts to restore calm, repeating "Easy, easy" into the microphone in her most soothing tones. But like the pleas Jagger will make later, Slick's are completely ineffectual, and the scuffles continue. Onstage, Airplane guitarist Paul Kanter takes the microphone to announce gruffly, "The Hell's Angels have just smashed Marty Balin in the face. I'd like to thank them for that." What follows is almost comical: An Angel leaps to the stage, grabs a different microphone, and confronts Kanter. Although the two men stand only feet apart, they communicate not directly but via the microphones. "If you're talking to me, I'm talking to you," says the man. "Let me tell you what's happening. We're partying like you people." This brief exchange, strange and ironic, is one of those spontaneous eruptions Albert and David maintained could not be scripted, only captured. The scene also typifies the kind of communication barrier that the brothers find troubling. Without personal, face-to-face interaction, free of techno-logical and cultural impediments, human beings are doomed to flounder in a materialistic, narcissistic society, devoid of meaningful connection.

Later, after Balin has been removed, and the band is ready to continue, Slick tries to summarize what has happened. In narrator-like fashion, she announces into the microphone: "You gotta keep your bodies off each other unless you intend love. People get weird, and you need people like the Angels to keep people in line.... But you don't bust people in the head for nothing. So both sides are fucking up temporarily. Let's not keep fucking up!" Her desire to salvage the festival may be admirable, but again, knowing the outcome of the concert, the optimism of her admonition sounds hope-lessly naive. This segment actually marks one of the few moments in the film in which the motives and practices of the counterculture in general are questioned; the desire to bring diverse elements together is shown to be unworkable and overly idealistic. Uniting Hell's Angels, well-paid rock bands, and middle-class hippies may seem like the key to a better society, but as this festival made manifest, such diverse groups have little in com-mon other than a nebulous distrust of authority and a fondness for mind-altering chemicals. Here, the Airplane and the Angels seem miles apart philosophically if not geographically; their only common ground would seem to be partying, very broadly defined.

Shortly after Altamont, Craig McGregor tried to dispel this we-are-one myth in an article written for the *New York Times*: "The lesson the counter-culture(s), hopefully, will carry away from Altamont is that deluding our-selves we are One [*sic*] is a surrogate for working out how to deal with the fact we are not." The same dilemma faced the New Left and other authen-ticity-seeking entities of the late 1960s; theory and practice were decidedly more difficult to combine when human beings were involved. Nowhere is that more clear than in the Jefferson Airplane segment of *Gimme Shel-ter*. On one hand, the Rolling Stones, who were not Americans, had nur-tured a kind of outsider image for many years; their sudden attempt to become one with the American counterculture would always smack of expedience. But the Jefferson Airplane, like the Grateful Dead, was a group that emerged from Northern California, the very heart of the American counterculture movement. When things fall apart on their watch, the ide-alism that they espouse is cast in a harsh light. They are powerless to unite the crowd: Kanter reverts to passive confrontation via his microphone,

Slick's words sound forced and disingenuous, and one of the concert organizers can only mumble, "It's really weird, man, it's really weird," in response to the Angels-Airplane showdown.[24]

If the Airplane's set marks the point at which uncontrolled and uncontrollable behavior gains the upper hand at Altamont, the Stones's arrival, behind the escort of the Angels on their bikes, precipitates an even stronger shift. After the dramatic procession, the band takes the stage. "There's so many of you," Jagger remarks as he scans the crowd. Then the band launches into "Sympathy for the Devil," which, appropriately enough, provides the musical impetus for a disturbance: Angels wielding pool cues assault a rowdy spectator. Jagger tries to calm the crowd and quips, "Something very funny happens when we start that number." His absurd innocence rings hollow; his casual attitude betrays a total lack of understanding for the seriousness of the situation developing in front of his eyes. The song resumes, touting the devil as a misunderstood historical figure. At one point, a concerned fan shakes his head and looks pleadingly at Jagger, imploring the singer to take some action against the violence all around. Jagger pauses but then struts away and tries to lose himself in the music. The film seems eager to lose itself, too; the camera maintains tight close-ups on Jagger, then Watts, even as more serious altercations take place in the audience below. This was a practical matter as well. By the time the Stones took the stage, the audience area was in near-complete darkness. Any photographed images would have been obscured by darkness, but the effect is to underline an abortive and futile attempt on the part of all—Rolling Stones, filmmakers, and audience—to escape into a more sedate world.

Soon after, another scuffle in front of the stage halts a song. "Why are we fighting?" Mick then asks the audience, genuinely puzzled, despite having already acknowledged the power of his band's music to create "funny" responses. "I cannot see what's going on," he admits, and then he implores,

> All I can ask you, San Francisco is, like, the whole thing, like this could be the most beautiful evening we've had for this winter. Let's get it together. I can't do anymore than just ask you, to beg you, just to keep it together. You can do it. It's within your power, everyone. Hell's Angels, everybody. Let's just keep ourselves together. You know, if we *are* all one, let's show we're all one.

This last comment, which echoes Grace Slick's "Let's not keep fucking up!", receives a cynical reply of "Preach it, brother," from one of the crowd. Few people seem willing to listen to Jagger's plea very seriously, as another fight ensues shortly after the Stones resume playing. Although he makes an appeal to keep a Woodstock-polished image of the counterculture alive,

Jagger's words fall flat, not only on the crowd but on the film audience as well. Trying to control what he does not fully understand and what he literally and figuratively cannot see, the Jagger of *Gimme Shelter* seems ill-equipped to handle the responsibility of the role in which he has cast himself. Having presented the complexity of the cultural milieu in which such violence could occur, *Gimme Shelter* implicates the Rolling Stones and especially Mick Jagger as if not instigators of the disturbances, at least ineffective leaders against it. Jagger's pathetic plea to the Altamont crowd serves as a memorable example.

If the lyrics to "Sympathy for the Devil" provide an appropriate background to the events that accompany them, then the words to the band's next song, "Under My Thumb," bring ironic counterpoint. While Jagger sings of regaining control within a relationship, the concert falls into deeper chaos. What transpires in the crowd just beyond the stage is obscured in darkness and impossible to see clearly. Instead, the camera focuses on a man just in front of Jagger and the stage. Obviously under the thumb of a powerful hallucinogen, the man moves very slowly, rolling his eyes and his head. At one point, Jagger's profile occupies half the screen while the tripping man occupies the other half. The light and dark of the outdoor festival receive full visual illustration. Eventually, two Angels pull the man away. Then, just after Jagger sings the phrases "It's all right" and "I pray that it's all right," the band concludes "Under My Thumb," and the killing of Hunter occurs. Again, the unintended juxtaposition of Jagger's lyrics with a situation clearly not all right nor under his thumb makes for chilling irony.

The film captures the stabbing, but it is initially at regular speed and without explanation, underscoring how difficult it was to observe what was happening. Only when we go back to the editing table, and the same images are displayed in slow motion, do they become clearer. The film abruptly cuts to Jagger in front of the monitor: "Can you roll back on that, David?" As he does, David asks Jagger, "Could you see what was happening?" Jagger replies, "No, you couldn't see anything. It was another scuffle." At this moment anyway, Jagger's inability to see is borne out by the film. Even in slow motion, the events are difficult to discern; the gun Hunter holds is merely a shadow against his girlfriend's crocheted dress and the Angel's knife a glimmer of steel. By this time, the air had become so thick with a "rancid combination of fog, dust, smoke and glare" that the "squinty, grey light made everything hard to look at," let alone capture on film.[25]

Should Jagger be blamed for something he could not see? Or, like some modern day Greek tragic hero, did his hubris prevent him from seeing what should have been obvious all along: that the band instigates violence, that their willy-nilly decisions regarding a free outdoor concert bred disaster, that the combination of factors working together at Altamont was a volatile mix? The next moment would seem to be crucial; Jagger's reaction to the stabbing might indicate he has learned something or that he accepts at least some responsibility. "It's so horrible," he says, sounding sincere. But before the believability of Jagger's comment might be determined, the film cuts back to the concert, to a segment in which Hunter's body is readied for a helicopter ride to the coroner's office. As the helicopter takes off, the concert soundtrack overlaps with the noise of the rotor blades. The song is "Street Fighting Man," the inclusion of which at this point renders moot the answer to the question of Jagger's sincerity. At Altamont and during all of their performances, the Stones tacitly encouraged violence, and when that violence turned real and reached its grimmest possible outcome, they played on, not necessarily out of callous disregard but because, according to their own accounting of the event, they did not know what had actually happened in the darkness before them and, further, they did not know what else to do.[26] They could not rewind, as a film can, and regain control of a moment after control had been lost. Instead, they concluded this concert the same way they had concluded all their American appearances: with a song that glorifies a figure who has learned to fight his way up from the mean streets of London. Jagger's "Why are we fighting?" becomes a rhetorical question.

The film then cuts to the Stones piling into another helicopter, making their exit from Altamont. Within the time of the film, their helicopter ride follows Hunter's by only a minute; the film manufactures a juxtaposition that shows how easily the Stones may leave behind the chaos—specifically, the Hunter killing—they have helped create. Even more striking is the next image. As the helicopter exits into the darkness, the soundtrack falls silent. On screen, silhouetted figures scramble down a hill. The only light—possibly the headlight of the helicopter—occupies the right-hand part of the screen. Blinding in its intensity, it backlights the scene without illuminating any of the figures clearly. This combination of darkness, bright light, and flailing human shadows, almost grotesque in appearance, is one of the most powerful visual images in any Maysles brothers' film. It is the dark side of the Altamont experience in abstract visual form.

The film immediately returns to Jagger, staring at the monitor, his head on his hand. He has just watched the same images the film audience has watched, so his response is eagerly anticipated. What has he *seen*? He stands up, stretches, then begins to leave, uttering only a brief, "All right, see y'all." He takes one step, and the film freezes on him. His face conveys little other than weariness, marking Jagger as inscrutable as ever; whatever he may or may not have learned remains, appropriately enough, impossible to see. The camera zooms closer on his face, but rather than providing greater clarity, the zoom makes the image fuzzier; we are closer but see less well. It is a suitably ambiguous image on which to leave Jagger.[27]

Originally, the filmmakers had decided to end the film on the Jagger close-up. After consulting among themselves and with some input from Jagger, they decided this ending was "too much of a down" and put too much of the blame on the Stones. Zwerin, for one, did not want the "finger pointing [so] squarely at [Jagger's] nose" inasmuch as there was plenty of fault to be distributed widely. Instead, the film ends with a Jagger-less, ambiguous scene that serves the film's overall goals much better.[28] With the song "Gimme Shelter" playing on the soundtrack, the film shows images of concertgoers walking across the barren fields outside the Altamont Speedway. It is bright daylight, but it is not clear whether these people are coming to the concert or leaving it the next morning. They carry bags, blankets, flags, beer bottles; some are smiling, others are expressionless. They move almost mechanically, "like lemmings to the sea," while Jagger sings about the need to have some sort of shelter from the chaos of the world. Toward the end of this series of images, the camera holds on the horizon, where the sun blazes toward the lens. Appropriately, this shot makes the images difficult to see; the blinding light in this scene renders fruitless the ability to discern. As Richards's guitar becomes more frantic, the sun continues to blind. Only as the song reaches its climax does the film cut to a softer image of the horizon, the sun just below it, with three Altamont attendees walking across, and then disappearing from the screen.

At least one critic objected strongly to this ending, arguing that "it would seem to betray a fundamental misunderstanding on the part of the filmmakers of the very film they have created."[29] Having implicated the Stones up to that point, the writer believed "giving them shelter" was going too far. To the contrary, this ending is much more in keeping with the film's previous ninety minutes than a freeze-frame ending would have been. This conclusion extends culpability beyond Jagger and the Rolling Stones, as it should. After all, the Stones could not exist without their audience and vice versa; it is a dialectical relationship. The final image in which the sun blinds the viewer parallels the film's opening image of darkness. In both cases, one's vision is blocked; literally speaking, nothing is seeable. As pragmatic modernists, the Maysles brothers emphasize that understanding the world means coping with the fact that much of the world is beyond understanding; an informed confusion may be the best we can hope for. Moreover, the film suggests, the power and authority of the image called "The Rolling Stones" is ultimately quite shallow. *Gimme Shelter* demonstrates the impossibility of being able to see how the Rolling Stones look and questions the desire to do so in the first place.

SPONTANEITY UNCONTROLLED

Coming at the end of a divisive decade, the spectacle at Altamont seemed a neatly packaged culmination of many things troubling the United States at the time. The concert attained a notoriety and significance that elevated the Maysles-Zwerin film beyond the observational–human-interest level at which their other films resided. As creators of the film "of record" for the concert, the filmmakers were saddled with high expectations as well as the ongoing popular response to Altamont even as they edited the film that would eventually become *Gimme Shelter*. Although there were some delays in getting the film distributed, eventually it did earn wide release, which, in turn, brought even more attention to it.[30]

In response, however, the filmmakers resisted providing explanations, just as they had refused to do in their previous films. Instead, *Gimme Shelter*, through its complicated structure, confusing chronology, and refusal to assign blame, intentionally frustrates those who want it to offer answers. Writing for the *Film Society Review* at the time, critic Patrick MacFadden applauded the ambiguity, noting the filmmakers instead have "resolutely refused to provide a pinch of psychic absolution. . . . Not the least of their merits is to have understood the uneasy cohabitation at Altamont of both the significance and the total insignificance of the Hunter slaying, to have grasped the essential banality of this cut-rate Walpurgisnacht, to have pinned down the imbecility, not of the generation-culture gap, but of the star gap, to have shown a process, not an individual."[31] The Maysles brothers comprehended that people may be swept up in phenomena larger than any one individual can recognize, let alone alter, and that events are both more complex and simpler than they are generally portrayed. Ambiguity therefore reigns in *Gimme Shelter*, as befits both the event and a modernist text.

Nevertheless, finding villains amidst the complicated tragic events at Altamont quickly became paramount, as if, as one film critic noted, "the harmony of our situation could be restored [and] life would attain once again its manageable shape."[32] *Rolling Stone's* reviewer Michael Goodwin praised the film for its complexity and refusal to grant easy answers but nevertheless wanted the film to carry a heavy burden: "We blew it at Altamont. . . . *Gimme Shelter* lets us watch ourselves blowing it, and makes us understand how and why." Later, Goodwin pushes the psychotherapeutic import of the film even further: "No purpose will be served by pretending Altamont didn't happen—the only way to salvage it is to work it through, encompass it, and transform it. That's what *Gimme Shelter* is for."[33]

Thus, the film engendered lively critical response, once again coming from a wide range of sources, both academic and popular. The reactions to *Gimme Shelter* often reflected the particular viewer's desire for more definitive answers and greater clarity. It was clear that the film would not and could not please everyone. Some, for instance, believed the Maysles brothers had been too forgiving of the Stones and their role in the unfortunate events at Altamont. Albert Goldman, in a lengthy early-1971 article in the *New York Times*, saw *Gimme Shelter* "as a piece of special pleading on behalf of the Stones" and a "whitewash" of Jagger especially. Goldman held that blame was placed on too easy a target: the Hell's Angels. "The most unruly generation in American history is demanding—and receiving—punishment by big father figures with ogre faces, beer bellies and the humorless promptness of dragons rising to the provocation of young, twerpy hippies." Likewise, in a terse review, the *New Leader's* John Simon observed: "Jagger and his henchmen emerge as archetypal creeps to me (just as to the young they appear to be archetypal demigods), but the nature and background of their quiddity is not even cursorily examined." Joel Haycock of *Film Quarterly* objected to those who had elevated the Altamont concert to an inflated symbolic significance, but he nevertheless criticized the Maysles brothers for their "self-serving obtuseness" about the situation and faulted them for making the Angels the villains of the "melodrama."[34]

Others expressed concern about ethics, hypocrisy, and disclosure. *Variety's* reviewer spoke for a widespread point of view in regarding the film's inclusion of the stabbing-death scene as unethical: "Without the climactic bloodletting the Maysles would have had little or nothing on which to peg a documentary." Haycock believed that "like the Altamont myth on which it feeds [*Gimme Shelter*] . . . is the product of slick, tabloid sensibilities." Pauline Kael was especially dismissive of the film on these grounds. Her review in the *New Yorker* called the film "disingenuous moviemaking," and she encouraged the filmmakers to "drop the Miss Innocence act and tell us the straight story of the background to the events." Kael further insinuated that the Maysles brothers played a part in setting up the events at Altamont, and that much of what transpired was done for the sake of the camera. Finally, Kael criticized the "Maysles brothers' approach to moviemaking [as] much too callow to cope with the phenomenon of people who are drawn to Mick Jagger's music in order to lose control—except at the level of attracting them and then exploiting the disastrous consequences."[35]

Unfortunately, the filmmakers had left themselves open to this kind of attack. They were thwarted in their attempts to rebut certain reviews. The *New Yorker* at the time did not publish letters to the editor so Kael's accusations went unchallenged. The *New York Times* did print the filmmakers' reply to Goldman but shortened it by nearly one-third, denying the full opportunity of public defense.[36] More problematically, the film itself is not clear enough about its own contribution to the Altamont trouble. In the self-reflexive moments of *Gimme Shelter*, especially the onscreen appearances, the filmmakers seem willing to implicate themselves. These scenes indicate that they were grappling with issues of image-making and were attempting to come to grips with the ramifications of performance even within the more authentic direct cinema films. David is visible over Jagger's left shoulder in the final freeze-frame image; he seems to understand he is also part of the complex picture. Yet, without a more direct assessment of complicity, and with the seriousness of the slaying looming over the entire project, the brothers could have gone further. A simple expression of awareness does not sufficiently acknowledge the knotty aspects of any film about a celebrity. After all, even a celebrity-focused film that contains implicit criticisms still relies on the same celebrity value to attract an audience. Within the film itself, the Maysles brothers and Zwerin could have been even more explicit about their own roles in the making of the film and in any possible encouragement of the Stones to perform for the sake of the camera. There were claims that at Altamont, the Stones purposely delayed taking the stage because they wanted the film to capture them entering in darkness amidst floodlights and smoke. That delay would have exacerbated the problems of violence, fatigue, and drug-induced medical reactions among the crowd.[37] Everyone involved in making *Gimme Shelter* has steadfastly maintained this to be untrue, but somehow their voices were drowned out amidst the various conspiracy theories.

Moreover, the film implicitly criticizes the band but never explicitly questions whether the very fact of making a film in any way contributed to the way events transpired, which some claimed it did. To be fully candid, especially in light of the sensitive subject matter, the filmmakers could have admitted on camera and/or shown at least some of the ways their creative enterprise affected the event(s) filmed. After the film was complete, the codirectors could have included some mention of the troubles. Anything less invites misunderstanding and unfair criticism, as the filmmakers discovered. For *Gimme Shelter*, this would have meant a longer, probably even more complex film (further hampering the distribution woes), but whether the filmmakers liked it or not, the subject in this case demanded it.

In the film, one of the Altamont-concert organizers decides not to worry about the anticipated chaotic parking situation: "For once, we're gonna let it all happen, for experimental reasons if for nothing else." Letting it all happen in front of the camera had, of course, been the mantra for the Maysles brothers since their earliest work. Yet, in this case, just as Altamont was an experiment gone haywire, *Gimme Shelter* at times becomes overwhelmed by the unfolding events. In the end, the killing of Hunter proved to be a "spontaneous eruption" that in many ways superceded the workable format of the film. One essayist has described the concert as "an experiment with too many variables and not enough controls";[38] the same might be said of the Maysles-Zwerin film. Partly a traditional concert film, partly a sobering social document, partly an exploration into new ways of presenting direct cinema, the film attempts to juggle all these components—a difficult task indeed. That it succeeds at all is a testament to the skill and sensitivity of the filmmakers.

Albert and David themselves worried that they had created too somber a picture, one that provided no opportunity to celebrate humanity.[39] One of the contributing factors is that unlike *Salesman*, *Gimme Shelter* lacks a visible sympathy for the main figures in the film, showing instead a tangled web of celebrity, media, materialism, and mayhem. Film historian Stephen Mamber believed that the lack of connection between subject and filmmakers produced a weak film: "The Maysles' were almost like spectators at native tribal rites, but without the knowledge of their subjects so basic to ethnographic work. Lacking this foundation, they fell back on interests and methods developed in ten years of American cinéma vérité work, their own and others."[40] While this assessment is too dismissive—Mamber unfairly regards *Gimme Shelter* to be derivative of other films—it does recognize the value of a strong underlying sensitivity towards the subject in direct cinema. That kind of sensitivity would be a hallmark of their next three films (*Christo's Valley Curtain*, *Grey Gardens*, and *Running Fence*).

The Maysles brothers never again made a film about celebrities of the magnitude of the Beatles, Marlon Brando, or the Rolling Stones. Their subsequent films either featured noncelebrities or artists whose fame was distinctly more limited than the popular-culture icons they showed in their 1960s films. On several occasions, the brothers sought out or were hired by artists who believed, as they did, that art of all media should be focused on the exploration and, ultimately, the liberation of the human spirit, independent of material gain.

5

Working Within the Limitation of Reality: The Christo Films

In their next effort, Albert and David made a film under more controlled circumstances. Environmental artist Christo Javacheff, the subject of two of their next four films, was for the Maysles brothers a kindred spirit, a man whose dedication to the process as much as to the product of his art made him an ideal study for the Maysles brothers' direct cinema. "When you see [our] film[s] and get to know Christo," Albert told an interviewer in 1977, "you realize that as an artist, his style is in many ways similar to ours.... [H]e has a conception which is just a starting point, and then he goes to find a place for it."[1] In that way, "we each create art within the 'limitation' of reality."[2] Christo, who is generally known only by his first name, and his wife and artistic partner, Jeanne-Claude, have appreciated the similarities in approach: "Our works of art take place in real life and the films by Maysles, not just those about us, are real life, as it happens."[3]

The relationship between filmmakers and subject began many years before the first film. The Bulgarian-born Javacheff and Jeanne-Claude, the daughter of a French politician and aristocrat, met the brothers in 1962 at a midnight screening of *Showman* at the Paris Cinematheque. There was an immediate connection both personally and artistically to the extent that "it did not take us much time until we called Albert, David [and their mutual friend Dimiter (Mitko) Zagoroff] our brothers."[4] In 1974, when Christo and Jeanne-Claude needed someone to film the design and installation of *Valley Curtain in Rifle, Colorado*, they looked to the Maysles brothers; the immediate results were *Christo's Valley Curtain* (1974), a twenty-eight-minute film, and the fifty-eight-minute *Running Fence* (1978). Again, the brothers relied on the essential collaboration of Ellen Hovde (*Valley Curtain* codirector) and Charlotte Zwerin (*Running Fence* codirector).

Christo and Jeanne-Claude have argued that their projects should provoke and encourage spectators to re-examine old ways of seeing things, much as the Maysles brothers had hoped their films might engender new ideas about cinema. Both the filmmakers and the environmental artists hoped to "induce fresh ways of looking, feeling, thinking," of experiencing the world as if seeing it clearly for the first time.[5] Christo is, like Albert and David, an "ambiguous catalyst of unplanned moments and of unfolding layers of meaning";[6] as a catalyst, he believes his job is to set a process in motion and then stand back and observe, letting the process determine the course. For Christo (and the Maysles brothers), an authentic artist seeks out opportunities to face "real life, as it happens" and then reacts to it. Those reactions in turn become an essential ingredient of the art itself. A goal for the Christo projects is the promotion of greater intimacy between the art object and the viewer; similarly, the brothers hoped to create intimacy between their subjects and the viewing audience.

Equally important, the filmmakers and the environmental artist shared reservations about the commodification of modern society. Throughout his career, Christo has consistently and deliberately subverted the usual process of commodification in art. Instead of creating permanent pieces that can be bought and sold on the market, he has produced art that is purposely ephemeral, designed to be installed and in a relatively brief time removed. Only the by-products (including the films) and remnants are permanent, and these make money only to fund the next project. Christo does not reject the buying and selling of art outright; he is no Marxist (he fled Communist Bulgaria). He is not a pessimist either. Christo is interested in the interrelationship of art and the real world but not in the cynical way some postmodern artists are. Instead, his intention is to focus attention on what makes reality meaningful. Like the Maysles brothers, Christo believes "with a perfect faith that progress is the inevitable effect of heightened awareness."[7]

The Maysles brothers infused their Christo films with a high degree of self-reflexivity; the films' justification of Christo's process ultimately justifies the Maysles brothers' films as well, and the environmental artist becomes a kind of surrogate for the Maysles brothers' aesthetic views. Hanging an enormous orange curtain or constructing a twenty-four-mile-long nylon fence or draping a series of coastal islands in pink fabric is like making a documentary film with no preconceived notion of how the story will develop. Each is an "outrageous act of faith"—a favorite phrase of David's—that requires trust in a process that is often and by design out of the artist's control. In virtually every case, the self-reflexive moments of the Christo films are also self-affirming moments; each acknowledgment of the filmmaking process asserts that Maysles-style filmmaking brings people together and succeeds as art despite formidable financial and artistic obstacles. At times, the self-reflexivity gives way to self-aggrandizement, which has led to criticisms that the films are mere hagiography. While such a generalized dismissal overstates the matter, the symbiotic relationship of filmmakers and subject proved to be one of the many "limitations of reality" that, whether to the films' benefit or not, factored into the final product.

The Maysles brothers' paradoxical relationship to celebrity, manifested in their first four films and again in *Gimme Shelter*, resurfaces in the Christo films. While, on one hand, the brothers applaud Christo for avoiding the trap of celebrity and for willingly participating in a more democratic art form, they also hold up the environmental artist as an individual to be admired, thereby molding him into an artist-celebrity in his own right. Their enthusiastic support of Christo redirects the criticisms they had made in earlier films. Albert and David had objected to the construct of celebrity and applied that criticism liberally to popular entertainment (such as rock music and Hollywood movies) but found less to dislike about artists like Truman Capote and especially Christo, whose works they believed merited closer attention and broader audience support. Thus, they seemed to suggest that there was a right kind of celebrity, of which Christo (and by extension themselves) ideally fit the mold. Here the Maysles brothers connected to a long-standing tradition in the arts; the artist-as-protagonist has pervaded modern works from James Joyce's *Portrait of the Artist as a Young Man* to the films *Il Postino* and *Pollock*. In all cases, the character/artist's vision is treated as a means of transcending the everyday or, often, as a means of creating a new world order. Thus, the Maysles brothers' treatment of Christo reflects their pragmatic modernism.

While championing Christo, however, the filmmakers frequently also undercut his heroic stature. In *Valley Curtain* and especially in *Running Fence*, the brothers show how the success of the projects relies not just on one man but on many other people and on many factors outside the artist's control. Christo is heroic to be sure, but part of what makes him admirable, the films illustrate, is his willingness to work collaboratively and his ability to motivate other people to perform their own heroic deeds. He is a new kind of celebrity-hero, posited as a better alternative. Certainly, the brothers had long believed in a highly collaborative approach to filmmaking; again Christo's choices mirror their own.

It must be noted that the Christo films are not full-fledged modernist works; their more conventional form and structure demarcate them from the broader modernist ambitions of *Salesman* and *Grey Gardens*. Bearing witness to the highly unconventional Christo, these films proffer a more traditional format than much of the other Maysles brothers' work. Both Hovde and Zwerin employed a three-part structure in their editing of the first two Christo films. In the first phase of the films, Christo explains the project, either through voice-over or in front of a governmental body from which he needs permission to proceed. Second comes the introduction of conflict, in the form of individual opponents of the projects, wary governmental agencies, inclement weather and/or technical complications. The conflicts give the films a dramatic tension through manipulation of direct cinema's crisis structure and also allow for a Christo-versus-the-opposition showdown. In all the Maysles films about Christo, the artist, with the integral aid of his wife and supporters, eventually overcomes the obstacles before him. The third part of the structure may be called the admiration scenes. Christo, Jeanne-Claude, and others look out approvingly onto the completed project. The audience's view of the finished work is often a privileged one: overhead (via helicopter) or from angles not otherwise made available to the public. In all, the brothers allowed Christo's vision to dominate their films rather than imposing their own.

Still, the style and structure films do not recall the early days of direct cinema. There are moments in the Christo films in which direct cinema precepts are rejected, as the ad hoc nature of the Maysles Films aesthetic emerges. Whether manipulating the crisis structure (with Christo as an atypical crisis hero) using voice-over, crosscutting, music, or subtitles, the filmmakers strive to make the films more than straightforward reportage of the events. Indeed, these direct cinema violations mark some of the most compelling moments in the films as well as some of the most stylized. Sorting through the film footage, which had been shot over many months, required a high degree of flexibility including some blurring of the actual timeline. Codirector Hovde, assistant editor Susan Froemke, and the other assistant editors once again brought order to the chaos in a process nearly as complicated as the curtain project itself.

Finally, both *Christo's Valley Curtain* and *Running Fence* contain an additional, highly effective ingredient. In speaking of the second film, Albert has observed that *Running Fence* is "just a piece of nylon fabric and it's just two people, Christo and his wife, and there are plenty of usual people in that film. There are fifty-five farmers that Christo has to approach in order to get permission from them to use their land for the project. These are people who know very little about art. During the course of the film, however, these usual people become unusual."[8] The process by which "usual people become unusual" (and vice versa) has been part of earlier Maysles brothers' films—Paul Brennan, for instance, is particularized in *Salesman*. The reactions of these usual people also factor into the larger cultural question about the nature and definition of art. Christo's work has been a catalyst for discussions that transcend the actual projects at hand, leading almost inevitably to a what-is-art debate. The Christo projects have typically gained the approval and support of a surprising number of people who may claim to know nothing about art but nevertheless get caught up in Christo's work. Many of the hired workers, without whom the projects would have remained only extravagant ideas, come from this group. These average people, on camera quite often in the first two films, describe the projects as "nifty" or "beautiful" or a "vision," and their heartfelt reactions bring the films an added emotional dimension. (The absence of these workers' comments from the subsequent Christo film *Islands* (1986) is a weakness of that film.) Through Albert and David's sympathetic treatment of these people and of Christo and Jeanne-Claude, the filmmakers unashamedly align themselves with those who believe the projects are in fact artful expressions.

CHRISTO'S VALLEY CURTAIN

Christo's Valley Curtain opens with an extreme close-up of an orange curtain on a canvas. The image is highly ambiguous; at first, the object itself is indeterminable—only its orange color is evident. Ambiguity, so central to all of Christo's projects and so maddening to those who wish to categorize his works, is established from the outset. Quickly, the camera pulls back to reveal first the entire canvas, then two figures (Christo and Jeanne-Claude) on either side of it, trying to position the large canvas onto the wall. They step back to examine it, then Christo returns to it, coloring in more orange with a pencil.

The next cut exacerbates the sense of confusion. The people are seated on a leather couch, outwardly regarding (it appears) the canvas they have just hung. They exchange words in French, for which the film offers no subtitles. Another close-up of the canvas follows, then a cut to Christo again working on the canvas, adding still more orange. The next cut returns to Jeanne-Claude, still seated and looking. "It's a very different feeling," she says, this time in English, an observation that will prove to be as true of the project as the film about it.

The next frame is another extreme close-up, this time of Christo's bespectacled eyes. A voice-over begins, during which the artist, in his heavily accented and frequently broken English, explains his work, noting for instance, "For me the excitement, really the excitement begins when I leave the studio," and "What happens in the real world change [sic] my original idea and the drawings themselves. This is what I like." During the course of the monologue, the camera pans around the studio, showing drawings, sketches, and photographs of earlier projects, including the Wrapped Coast for Little Bay, Australia (1969) and the 5,600 Cubic Meter Package (1968), and moves to a series of specific planning sketches and blueprints of the Valley Curtain project, culminating with a long-distance rendition of the curtain between two craggy bluffs in Rifle, Colorado, as the voice-over ends. "This is what I like" accompanies the final image of the valley curtain. The next shot shows the interior of the artist's office. The camera pans slowly to show him working, hunched over a small table, adding charcoal to one of his drawings. Suddenly, the screen blacks out to show the only opening credit: Christo's Valley Curtain.

In just over one hundred seconds, the filmmakers take the viewer from confusion (What is this orange drawing? Who are these people? What did they say in French?) to at least partial clarity. They introduce Christo the artist and his collaborator, Jeanne-Claude; they allow Christo to deliver his manifesto; they briefly provide his curriculum vita; they heighten interest in the project at hand. The key to the success of this opening segment is the editing, most of which was done by Hovde. Quick cuts and an emphasis on close-up deliver a great deal of information and provide a sense of intimacy with the people on screen. The voice-over provides Christo an extended opportunity to state his position, a position celebrated in this film. The curtain project itself tests existing boundaries. The filmmakers approve and will do the same, not only because they believe Christo's process and product deserve approval in general but also because Christo's process is the Maysles brothers' process. Not surprisingly, many of the statements included in the film could just as easily apply to the Maysles brothers' film about the valley curtain as they do to the project itself. The filmmakers underscore the connection visually by including many shots of framed art (of Christo's work especially) within the movie frame and of the curtain itself. As Christo intended, the curtain is a highly suggestive symbol that connotes among other things the promise of the unexpected and the imaginative as does a drawn curtain before a staged performance.

Shortly after this opening segment, the film introduces a technique that will prove to be its defining motif. Like the use of voice-over, it will work against direct cinema convention in order to serve the aesthetic and thematic concerns of the filmmakers. Albert shows Christo working on a pencil sketch of the project. Christo's other hand holds a photograph of the site, using this picture as a reference for his drawing. The camera zooms in on the photograph, then the film quickly cuts to virtually the same image at the site itself. For the first time, the real outdoor canvas for Christo's artistic vision in Rifle, Colorado, appears. The use of crosscutting here and throughout the film creates what art historian Nancy Scott has referred to as "a series of fruitful juxtapositions" that help define and shape the nature of Christo's work, "emphasizing his goal of making art that bears a relation to the real world, and underlining the important interrelation of art, nature, and society. . . . The dialectical reference of Christo's art is thus powerfully evoked by the very structure of the film itself."[9]

For the filmmakers, the crosscutting serves three main purposes in this film: It heightens the sense of tension, as the crisis scenes are continually interrupted and therefore prolonged by cuts to Christo's studio; it establishes a nexus of artist-workers-golfers (the last group representing observers of the project) so essential to the process of Christo's work; and it affirms the link between what Christo does in his studio and on site. When he says, "It looks just like the model" near the film's end, he is merely voicing what the viewer has already come to appreciate.

Of course, life as it happens cannot exist for the same person in two different places and in two different times simultaneously. The meaning that may be inferred from the juxtapositions is meaning that would not exist independent of the filmmakers' editing strategy. Although Albert hoped that he could rely merely on "the benefit of spontaneous juxtapositions that occur in filming—in life itself,"[10] again the editing must help the viewer make these visual connections, much as it does in the Paul Brennan train-ride sequence in *Salesman*. Sometimes, the technique produces a humorous effect. A concerned Christo barks, "Don't cut the fabric!" at a worker struggling to unveil the curtain; the film moves to a scene of Christo carefully ironing orange fabric in his studio. Foreshadowing may also occur: A shot of the sketched image of the valley curtain in the studio prefigures the successful unveiling of the actual curtain in Rifle.

This editing technique is best illustrated early in the film, shortly after the first glimpse of the curtain site. With no explanation, the film cuts to a shot of a golfer, visible from the knees down, with his putter poised over a ball. The hole itself is visible, perhaps three feet away. The golfer sinks the ball and exclaims, "Ah, look at that putt, boy." The camera pulls back gradually to show the golfer reaching down for the ball, then it reveals his playing partner, then finally provides an explanation as to why the golfers are included in the film. Visible in the background is the cable for the valley curtain with some of the sheathed curtain suspended. The curtain site must therefore exist directly next to a golf course. In this case, Albert has his "spontaneous juxtaposition," as the coincidental propinquity of golf course and curtain site allows this unusual combination of images to "just happen."

At this point, the film cuts to a shot of a golfer from behind, leaning on his putter, gazing out (apparently) at the embryonic curtain in the distance. "That's something, isn't it?" he asks. Someone responds, "That's quite an idea there. I don't know whether it'll work or not." The film cuts to a woman on the putting green, facing the curtain. She says, "It's just something different. I think everybody can hardly wait to see what it's really going to look like." As if to let her know, the film cuts to Christo in his studio, filling in more sketches. The next cut returns to the ironworkers, high above the scene. Again, the lines in the sketch are repeated in the cable lines. David's onsite sound recording captures the ironworkers engaged in nervous banter. "Just as good as mother's arms," quips one worker as he embarks out onto the wire in a wobbly transporting cage. "You'd better hope you're in J. C.'s arms," responds another.

This series of three cuts connects the major players in the Christo project: golfers (who represent the viewing public), artist, and workers. All are vital to the process by which the art is produced. Moreover, in this film at least, all support the endeavor. There are no dubious town officials, no naysayers proclaiming, "This isn't art" as there will be in subsequent Christo films.

The golf course location provides more than just a handy site from which to film audience reactions to the project; it also suggests that certain accepted uses of the natural environment are no more or less legitimate than Christo's creations. Is playing golf any less absurd than hanging an enormous fabric? Is it a better appropriation of the natural world? While the film provides no firm answers, it does certainly support the Christo vision of the world. The self-reflexive mode of this film also emerges in the golf course scenes, which serve as a metaphor for the dichotomy between the riskier, orange-curtain world of the direct cinema filmmaker and the more conservative, golf course existence of traditional filmmaking, epitomized by Hollywood. The Maysles brothers have consistently argued the superiority of their kind of filmmaking, even vis-à-vis fictional productions. They believed that because their work required more human endurance and patience and involved unforeseen pitfalls, the end result was a more artistic and more authentic presentation of life than any mainstream film. Albert argued, "Essentially what I see as cinematic—because only films can do it—is catching hold of reality in a spontaneous way. . . . It seems to me that other films are departures from cinema, where we are right in the middle of what cinema really can do."[11] Similarly, in this film, the brothers show Christo right in the middle of an immense project, creating a new kind of order, reacting to what happens around him, much of which despite extensive testing and planning happens spontaneously. (The scene in which Christo places a high-velocity fan in front of a large-scale model to test the fabric's wind strength is particularly memorable in *Valley Curtain*.) The true measure of artists, the film suggests, is how well they deal with what happens all around them, and only the most talented and flexible artists are able to integrate those unfolding events into the art form itself.

In the process, Christo often faces what might be identified as crisis moments. When Robert L. Drew began making nonfiction films, he believed crisis moments would help reveal something profound about the film's principal, showing how that person would react under pressure and thereby illuminating what Drew believed would be the person's true character. In addition, Drew assumed the subjects would be preoccupied with the crisis at hand and thus less aware of the camera's presence; this lack of guardedness would in turn enhance the audience's glimpse into this authentic moment. In their own work, the Maysles brothers typically did not rely on a crisis structure; from *Showman* forward, the brothers worked against that mode of filmmaking. (Crisis is even de-emphasized in *Gimme Shelter*.) On the surface, however, the Christo films contain all the ingredients of a crisis-oriented film. Christo encounters at least one classic crisis situation, and the viewer witnesses his reactions to those situations. Moreover, the films help build the tension of these moments, often through the use of crosscutting, rapid scene shifts, excited dialogue, and music. Despite these connections to classic crisis-oriented direct cinema, however, the Christo films have a much different goal. The filmmakers instead wish to manipulate the crisis structure to reveal what is inherently laudable about Christo's process of art-making. Whereas a Drew-directed film might ask, "How will Christo hold up under the intense pressure of this situation?", the brothers' film asks, "How do these moments of crisis contribute to the process of Christo's art?"

Rather than shining through as a man of action, Christo emerges as a rather ineffectual figure during these difficult moments. He is virtually powerless; his project's fate rests in the hands of other people, those usual men and women who have no artistic training but who are nevertheless carrying out the designs. These crisis moments underscore the essential democratic nature of Christo's work and emphasize how the larger process, specifically the parts Christo can never imagine, goes well beyond one man and his individual vision. This is what the Maysles brothers admire most about the Christo projects—and why their films highlight these crisis moments.

The first crisis occurs approximately eight minutes into the film. After Christo, Jeanne-Claude, and the site engineers agree to unwrap the outer cocoon of the fabric, despite the potential for high winds in the area, the project literally hits a snag. Something is preventing the ironworkers and the men and women below from removing the sheath. The film moves through a series of nervous-making images. Anxious faces look upward. Christo paces the site and then shouts orders to unseen workers. An exasperated Jeanne-Claude admonishes and then is frightened by the high anxiety of an ironworker. An angry Christo threatens everyone that there will be "no lunch today" unless the problem is solved. One of the engineers reminds Christo and Jeanne-Claude, "We don't want to fly off the handle with a crackpot decision." On two occasions, the editors interrupt the drama with scenes of Christo's studio, the relative calm of his controlled environment starkly contrasting with the chaotic scene developing onsite. (Here again direct cinema convention is violated for effect; events are not presented in chronological order.)

During the four-minute segment, no explanation is given as to the exact nature of the problem. At this point, we can ascertain only that there is a hang-up on the line, but the specifics are not as important as the general fact that a problem exists and must be confronted. The process has reached one of its inevitable yet totally unpredictable moments. The crisis is averted when ironworker Don Jenkins (the man who scared Jeanne-Claude) unsnags the cocoon from high above the ground. If Christo were a quintessential Drew crisis hero and *Valley Curtain* a typical crisis structure film, Christo himself would resolve the issue. Christo would become a man of action facing a win-or-lose showdown. Yet, here the resolution is out of his hands; he must rely on another man to save the project. The film's ostensible hero, Christo, can only anxiously watch, then vigorously thank the actual man of action in this scene.

The second crisis scene in *Valley Curtain* echoes the first. As the curtain itself is dropping open, it gets caught on the cable that stretches between the mountains. One of the film's most remarkable images occurs during this sequence. From the perspective of the golf course is the sight of the curtain being unveiled and getting caught halfway through its release. From below, Christo hollers "Pull!" to the groundcrew. When it is apparent that no amount of pulling can untether the curtain, Christo scrambles around searching for a particular truck operator. "Get in the truck!" he shouts and begins cursing in another language. Here again, Christo must rely on others to rescue the execution of his artistic vision. His lack of control at this point is emphasized by his comment, "This is ridiculous watching." An ironic juxtaposition helps solidify the point. The film cuts to a woman on the golf course, looking out at the project. "Nobody thought he could get the job done," she says. "And after all he's an artist. One of these people who paints pictures. Well, he's an artist. And he's very well-educated." The next cut takes the viewer to the moment when the curtain is finally extricated, not because of anything Christo has done (unless one could somehow attribute the breakthrough to his verbal exhortations) but because of the courageous actions of the ironworkers. The film points out that Christo being "well-educated" is meaningless at those moments of crisis when his project is literally hanging in the balance. He must instead rely on the presumably *not* formally educated ironworkers. The woman on the golf course may not yet grasp what these environmental projects are all about—she still wants to promote Christo as the artist/individual, who can "get the job done" alone—but the filmmakers understand that without collaboration and cooperation, there is no *Valley Curtain*. The celebrations that ensue after the ironworkers free the curtain underscore the idea: An engineer hugs and kisses Jeanne-Claude, Christo embraces several different construction workers, and ironworkers whoop and holler and hug each other.

The closing series of images once again emphasizes the creative vision of the artist and the essential, even humorous ambiguity of the entire project. From medium distance, Christo is standing in front of the curtain. The camera pulls back to a distant shot of the curtain from the golf course point of view. The final image reveals the enormous curtain, hanging in the distance, and the golf course flag flapping in the breeze. Both fabrics coexist, each equally a part of the landscape, at least for now, neither one any more essential or permanent in comparison to the phenomenal natural landscape all around. The artist's work and the public's recreation share the final stage as the screen goes to black, and the brief list of closing credits roll.

In both its form and content, this film legitimates and supports Christo. The painstaking way in which Christo completes a project mirrors the careful, detailed approach of the Maysles brothers and their coeditors. One key difference is that Christo includes everything; he and Jeanne-Claude publish "complete texts" of their projects, which are like unedited reels of film. The film, on the other hand, never gives a sense of telling the whole story. Important information is not included, such as that in 1973, the first attempt to hang the fabric ended in failure when 150-mile-per-hour winds tore it apart even before it could be successfully unveiled. What appears in this film are several fragments of the whole picture, a few pieces of cloth out of the larger fabric. Moreover, that the film gives so much time to the workers' experience of the project substantiates Christo's work as a "democratic art form" (as it is described by an off-camera interviewer). In both crisis scenes, Christo's role as both hero of a crisis-oriented direct cinema film and "supreme master" of his art is de-emphasized. What is accentuated instead is Christo's earlier assertion that the real excitement begins outside of the studio as the real world transforms his original vision in ways he cannot imagine. In celebrating this approach to art, the film also champions its own existence and direct cinema in general.

The limited critical response at the time reflected the likable quality of the film. Vincent Canby of the *New York Times* wrote that *Christo's Valley Curtain* "is marvelous reportage of the sort the Maysles brothers do best." Calvin Tomkins wrote that *Christo's Valley Curtain* is "by far the finest film I have ever seen about an artist and his work." The film received an Academy Award nomination in the category of best documentary short subject.[12]

RUNNING FENCE

Running Fence contains a similar combination of direct cinema convention and rule-breaking in order to document Christo's 24.3-mile-long, eighteen-foot-high nylon fence, which ran through Sonoma and Marin Counties, California, for two weeks in September, 1976. It is a more complex project and a more complicated film, double the length of *Christo's Valley Curtain*. The film bears witness to several community council meetings, face-to-face appeals between Christo or Jeanne-Claude and the local ranchers, responses from the workers and ranchers, and segments in which some local townspeople express their disapproval of the project.

Like most of the Christo concepts, *Running Fence* defies pat interpretation. Just as the orange curtain suggested multiple meanings, none of them definitive, so, too, does a white fabric fence imply, connote, and allude. A fence divides a land; it pens in and keeps out; it crisscrosses the natural terrain in a way that seems simultaneously natural to and imposed on the environment. If extensive enough, a fence may be more reminiscent of a wall, a hard boundary between people. It may also suggest a frontier, which like all frontiers "is not static, but rather a *line* that *keeps changing places.*"[13] Thus, like *Valley Curtain* in Rifle, *Running Fence* transcended the usual reference points of art and architecture. Designed to be removed in a short amount of time, it blends elements of both the permanent and ephemeral. Christo himself often described the fence as a "ribbon of light."

Still, there is as much untold in this film as there is in *Valley Curtain*; ambiguity remains an essential ingredient of both the project and the film about it. Zwerin told an interviewer: "There are so many aspects of the process [intentionally] left unanswered in the film . . . yet you do not have to know all the details to understand the whole construction."[14] This elliptical strategy, in which a few parts speak for the whole, is a deliberate attempt to subvert the usual mode of expository filmmaking. Once again, form mirrors content in this film, as the unaccounted details echo the ambiguity of the fence and its creators' vision.

In the opening shot of the film, Christo opens the gate of a white picket fence on one of the many ranches he must traverse in order to construct his own less permanent fence; the shot immediately and effectively establishes the central image and character. He promptly asks a question that is suitably suggestive: "I can leave open?" Receiving an affirmative response, he walks through it. The film then cuts to Christo and Jeanne-Claude watching cowboys rope calves in a fenced arena. Their smiling admiration of this activity and their outward glances at the natural landscape establish their connection to this place, their approval of traditional Western activities and uses of nature. Within seconds, however, the film cuts to the first of many scenes at a county council meeting at which local politicians discuss the pending project. The juxtaposition of the two scenes emphasizes the connection between Christo's artistic vision and the more mundane but equally essential realities of "getting permission." Here the film also introduces Stephen Tennis, one of the attorneys for *Running Fence*, who emerges as an integral player. In this scene, Tennis acts as intervening narrator and provides the initial explanation of the project, verifying his importance in the process.

Describing the film's opening image, Albert observed that the "film opens with Christo opening a fence. Farmers open their fences every day, but there is something different about him, and there is something different about the way he cuts all that material."[15] As in *Christo's Valley Curtain,* where the actions of usual and unusual people intersect and contribute equally to the process, so, too, does *Running Fence* imply a link between the everyday and something different. As before, at the nexus of this link lies the kind of uncontrolled art that the Maysles brothers, and Christo and Jeanne-Claude advocate. Yet, there is something different about this opening sequence, too. Unlike any other Maysles brothers' film, *Running Fence* uses music on a soundtrack to help establish a mood. Again violating a direct cinema convention, the film places country-Western music in this and other sequences to signify the location in which the action takes place. The music also provides background for the numerous montage sequences in the film (another direct cinema violation). Additionally, the music establishes a classic Western movie motif for the film. Reviewer Denise Hare summed it up well: "[M]any of Christo's actions ha[ve] a curious kinship with that tradition [of a Western movie]: A stranger comes into the territory on some extraordinary errand. He must do what he has to do. A man of virtue, he is misunderstood. Sides are taken."[16] He is a stranger in a strange land, like Clint Eastwood's nameless character in several Italian-made Westerns. The initial scenes at the rodeo and the many interactions with rugged frontier ranchers support this reading of the film. So, too, does Christo's impassioned speech in front of the county commission (discussed in detail below). And certainly the scene in which workers carry out Christo's vision, pounding the fence's supporting steel poles into the ground as the soundtrack provides a country-Western version of the song "Take It to the Limit," posits a Christo-as-Western-hero idea.

Within the film, other people also attempt to fit Christo into this well-worn hero mold. Les Bruhn, a rancher who appears frequently in the film, serves as the voice of local wisdom. He advises the artist that there were two "things you had going against you" in dealing with the other ranchers: being a stranger to the area and choosing the wrong rancher (namely, a recalcitrant German immigrant named Harry Milden) with whom to lock horns. "You gotta overcome that," encourages Bruhn, the veteran rugged individualist who speaks from experience. Later, after Christo and

Jeanne-Claude do manage to win over the hearts (and land) of all the ranchers and successfully convince the Sonoma County board to approve the project, one of the supporters congratulates Christo: "You hung in there and got 'er." The contest does not end there, however. In order to avoid a court injunction, Christo and his crew must work feverishly to complete the installation of the fence's metal anchoring poles in a matter of hours.

Christo has also decided that the crew will build the final part of the fence that is designed to plunge into the ocean, despite a temporary restraining order against such an action. He will break what he considers an unfair law in the name of achieving his vision. The way the "plot" develops thus becomes classic Hollywood Western (albeit with a modern-art twist). Against all odds, taking the law into his own hands, Christo defeats the opposition by completing his fence; victorious, he rides off into the sunset. The film even concludes with Christo and Jeanne-Claude gazing out into the water where the fence meets the ocean; they sigh romantically as the sun sinks into the horizon. In this way, Christo achieves true heroic stature because he is an artist with a cause, a man whose noble artistic ambitions rise above the pedestrian rules and regulations of an unenlightened society. The filmmakers thereby rely on old notions of what a celebrity-hero should be.

Yet, the film also defies a formulaic reading. A classic Western hero (or a crisis-structure hero, for that matter) is not supposed to succeed merely through persistence. He is a man of action, who when taken to the limit, in a showdown situation rises to the challenge and defeats single-handedly his opponents. Instead, when Christo encounters obstacles—in the form of governmental agencies, skeptical ranchers, environmentalists, and disgruntled workers—he must consistently rely on others to support or stand in for him. His lawyers, for instance, must continually negotiate their way through the process, ultimately defeating a last-minute attempt by the California Coastal Zone Conservation Commission to stop the project. All the workers must band together to put in the fence posts ahead of the injunction. As in *Valley Curtain*, Christo turns to others to provide the heroic action necessary. The film therefore consistently undercuts Christo as hero, showing he is no more typical a Western hero than he is a crisis-structure hero. Both scenarios would require him to operate individually, to conquer the odds alone, which does not happen in *Running Fence* any more than it does in *Valley Curtain*.

What then is accomplished by this Western-hero motif? Most importantly, it reflects what British film critic Ian Christie noted as the "Maysles' need to use dramatic models and conventional ways of addressing their audience" in order to tell a compelling story.[17] David and Zwerin once again sought a suitable structure to match the filmed footage, just as they had done in previous efforts. The Western-hero elements, which presented themselves quite naturally due to the setting and the process Christo was obligated to follow, proved a ready-made narrative option, recalling again the anything-that-works philosophy. At the same time, the filmmakers could also highlight the democratic nature of Christo's process, subtly undercutting the heroic-Western ideal. Christo is no Clint Eastwood character here; he cannot simply impose his will on the people or the landscape. Again, other men and women, many of whom have no connection to the traditional art world, become instrumental in carrying out the design. For the most part, this gentle mocking of Christo as hero provides the film an appropriately light touch and a proper amount of narrative continuity. (One area in which the film overreaches on this front is in its use of music. Rather than provide ironic counterpoint, the music attempts too overtly to steer emotion, especially the song "Take It To the Limit," the lyrics of which include sentimental lines like "You know I've always been a dreamer."[18])

Christo and Jeanne-Claude's opponents also provide dramatic tension. This opposition, absent from the succinct *Valley Curtain*, is as vital a part of Christo's projects as is his studio time. As is evident in the films, Christo and Jeanne-Claude expect and accept, even invite, such opposition to all their endeavors, weaving the disapproval and skepticism into the working process. They have boasted, for instance, that they voluntarily commissioned environmental impact reports for both *Running Fence* and a later project *Surrounded Islands*. Those who have opposed *Running Fence* (and other Christo efforts) typically fall into one of three camps: those who believe Christo's work in general is a waste of money (all Christo projects are funded entirely by the artist and his wife through sales of project paintings, photographs, collages, and sculptures to museums, galleries, and private collectors); those who maintain that the projects are not art; and environmentalists who argue that the projects in some way harm the land on which they appear. In *Running Fence*, this opposition receives a significant portion of on-camera time, which in turn provides the film with dramatic tension and links to the crisis moments.

While the waste-of-money contingent does not appear in the film, the it's-not-art camp presents its argument in an early segment. The filmmakers offer a scene from a park in which a man proclaims that *Running Fence* is "stupid" and "not art" at all. He continues, even more vociferously: "What art is that, hanging a piece of rag up for fifty miles? I could hang a rag up. I'll bet he can't even paint a picture." Although the man's perspective is compromised by his clearly mugging for the camera, he nevertheless voices a concern many share: that anything so far removed from traditional art cannot be legitimate. Two speakers at a county-commission meeting support the man in the park's point more credibly (that is, less self-consciously), each asserting, "It isn't art. A curtain ten feet long and eighteen feet high is not art. And it's not art if it's twenty-four miles long." They also worry that anything designed to exist on such a short-term basis (two weeks only) cannot be considered art; to them, like many others, art should be permanent. Again, this argument against Christo's work has been a persistent one: The idea of an art form that lacks a transcendent object rankles many who focus on the commodifiable nature of art.[19]

Christo intentionally countermands this traditional notion of art's permanence: "[My work] challenges profoundly the idea of the art object that a very essential part of the aesthetic of *this* project is that . . . the work will be gone after three weeks. Today we are surrounded by repetitious experiences. We need something that happens once in a lifetime."[20] Not only does Christo believe great art can and should exist outside of museums, he has stated repeatedly that he wants to wrest art away from wealthy collectors in order to expose more people to it. He strives for what he believes is a more democratic art world. Like, for example, abstract expressionist Robert Rauschenberg, he has tried to de-emphasize the autobiographical or self-gratifying aspects of art so that his audience may understand it on their own terms. And like painter-sculptor Marcel Duchamp or pop artist Andy Warhol, Christo has attempted to make audiences look with fresh eyes at many of the everyday objects they take for granted. Wrapping the Pont Neuf in Paris is in essence quite similar to painting repetitious Coca-Cola bottles on a canvas; in both cases, the artist challenges the notion that some objects, whether as utilitarian as a bridge or as pedestrian as a Coke bottle, are outside the realm of art.

Moreover, in vigorously acknowledging that negative criticism is a vital part of his process, Christo has disarmed many of his critics. *New Yorker* critic-at-large Calvin Tomkins observed at the time, "Nothing infuriated the opponents of Christo's *Running Fence* more than the notion that they themselves, through their very opposition, had become participants in the work of art."[21] In response, Christo emphasized that many aspects of his projects are "not staged" or, like criticism, are unpredictable, yet he accepts even welcomes these aspects as part of what he calls his "expedition." French art critic Dominique G. Laporté observed, "To seek 'the involuntary beauty of the ephemeral' is to create the advent of surprise, to practice the art of the accident, as in those incomparable moments when an object, a landscape, an ordinary form appear suddenly for themselves alone."[22]

There is a political aspect to the art as well, a "kind of subversive dimension," according to Christo.[23] The 1960s art scene, from which Christo emerged, was rife with political statements, spontaneity, and surprise, much like the avant-garde of the 1910s and 1920s. Christo had been actively involved in a Paris-based art movement called *le nouveau realisme* in the early 1960s, which recalled the avant-garde and "had much in common with American and British Pop Art" in its use of common artifacts.[24] For Christo, although the simplicity of the original object remains (e.g., a fence is still simply a fence), it takes on a heightened, transcendent meaning when wrapped or extended or somehow re-presented.

Art critic Michele Cone made connections to other avant-garde movements when reviewing the *Running Fence* project: "In a Dada event, an Action painting, a Happening, chance enters the process and affects its ending. The *Fence*, in the course of becoming, encounters the unforeseen technical hurdles of its construction, the unpredictable resistance of individuals; it could stumble and be foiled on an environmental issue."[25] When the fence is made part of the landscape, the challenges continue. One rancher comments about the fence's presence in the water: "It's there. What can they do about it? I love it. It's happening." This rancher is "reminded of the '60s" when such happenings were more common; like many of the spontaneous gatherings of people in the San Francisco Bay Area during the late 1960s and early 1970s, *Running Fence*'s presence stakes its territory and dares its opponents to deal with it. Christo thereby elicits what Tomkins identified as "the rich contrasts of America in the 1970s." The *Running Fence* opponents spoke of protecting some lands as links to an agricultural past although many had previously supported other land use such as suburban developments and shopping plazas. While some celebrated the way the project defied authority, others feared the existence of *Running Fence* might lead, ironically, to "another Altamont."[26]

The Maysles brothers' obvious appreciation of Christo's philosophy means that they, too, were willing to weave the opposition into their film project. Still, the film's point of view is clear as it makes a distinction between those who get Christo's art and those who do not. Philistinism and an unconsidered rejection of a democratic artistic process will not triumph. In one of the film's most effective sequences—and a turning point moment in the story of this film—three county residents on whose land the Christo project will traverse for part of its course testify on the fence's behalf. Rancher Bruhn confesses that he is a sheep rancher who "don't know nothing about art," but he cannot see any good reason not to allow Christo access to his land, especially inasmuch as Bruhn and his fellow ranchers are being compensated ($250 plus the fabric and poles that will cover their respective lands). More persuasively, a woman identifying herself as Mrs. George Michelson steps to the microphone. She and her husband are supportive of the project, she says, and then she offers this insight: "There was one thing said about art being temporal. Some of the meals I prepare aren't much . . . but sometimes I go to a lot of work to prepare a meal that I think is art. It's a masterpiece. And what happens? It gets eaten up and disappears, and everybody forgets it." Like the ironworker in *Valley Curtain* who knows "It's not the erection of it, it's the thought," the ranchers understand better than skeptical people what Christo's projects are all about, even if they express themselves in everyday speech rather than in academic jargon. Mrs. Michelson's comparison of *Running Fence* to a well-prepared meal, like ironworker Jenkins' comparison of *Valley Curtain* to the Golden Gate Bridge, the Space Needle, and the Empire State Building, indicates that Christo's projects allow people to make sense of the work through their own frames of reference. Unconcerned with the issue of permanence (which after all may be more meaningful to someone who has the means to buy or possess fine art), these people connect to the process *and* the product and have been among Christo's most ardent supporters.

Finally, it is Christo's turn to testify. Just as he does in voice-over in *Valley Curtain*, Christo offers an explanation as to how process and art are synthesized in his projects:

> The work is not only the fabric, the steel poles, and the fence. The art project is right now here. Everyone here is part of my work—if they want, they don't want, anyway, they are part of the work. . . . They are an integral part of the process of making that project. I feel very strongly that twentieth-century art is not single, individualistic experience. It is the very deep, political, social, economical experience I live right now with everybody here. And it is nothing involved with make-believe. That appeal was not staged by me—that we have emotion and fear. But of course that is a part of my project. I like very much to live the real life—a little bit like expedition going to the Himalaya, New Guinea.

That the filmmakers would include such a lengthy speech makes sense on two levels. First, it provides Christo the opportunity to articulate his artistic philosophy, which, in its persuasiveness and in combination with the ranchers' testimony, sways the council into accepting the project. Second, it once again highlights the artistic philosophy espoused by Christo and the Maysles brothers. The implicit point of view in the film emerges even more strongly via the editing. The filmmakers choose to include the enthusiastic applause that punctuates each positive testimonial, whereas they cut quickly from the detractors' speeches.

Christo and company's effective testimony and eventual success lead to the admiration scenes that culminate all the Maysles-Christo films. In *Running Fence*, the ranchers' interaction with their newly fenced property supports Christo's claim that his fence will allow people to gain a renewed appreciation of their land. Bruhn silently looks on, admiring his land as his border collie ushers a herd of sheep through an opening in the fence. Here the music has not been added; as the fence undulates in ripples and waves in the wind, the soundtrack provides only the flapping of the fabric and the occasional mechanical "ching" of the fence's hooks and wires. Another rancher, after admiring the strength of the poles, proclaims that he will "sleep right up next to the fence" that night. The ranchers' awe, the striking visuals, and restrained audio combine to convince the viewer, too, that *Running Fence* is a beautiful and worthwhile albeit temporary addition to the landscape. The filmmakers provide further evidence with a series of overhead shots.

Nearly five minutes into this admiration segment of the film, Christo is shown observing his handiwork. He appears pleased and offers nearly an identical assessment as he made of *Valley Curtain*: "It looks like a giant-scale model." As the sun sets, Christo and Jeanne-Claude observe the fence as it disappears into the ocean. "It's ready to take the slightest wind," she says. "Okay," replies her husband, "okay, Mrs. Christo." For the first time, his voice registers calm. The closing image in the film consists of a long shot of the fence. Albert's camera is directly in front of a billowing section of the fabric. Eventually, the white of the fabric waves in front of the camera, turning the screen to black. The film ends there. The last few minutes of the film have been unchallenged admiration: workers, ranchers, artist and wife, filmmakers.

Like its immediate predecessor *Christo's Valley Curtain*, *Running Fence* went on to receive an Academy Award nomination. But with only a limited release in a few cities, the audience for the film was small, and there were significantly fewer reviews than there had been for *Salesman* or the controversial *Gimme Shelter*. Those who did see and review *Running Fence* felt positively about both the project and the film about it. (Those reactions may be inseparable.) Janet Maslin, in the *New York Times*, observed that the film "demonstrates wordlessly and at times almost magically, that what [the artist] hoped to accomplish was very like what he attained." Similarly, the *New Yorker's* Penelope Gilliatt praised the film for being "put together with impeccable honesty of moral intent, whatever one thinks of the value of Christo's work . . . and the unfaltering purpose of the Maysles brothers make the picture command attention." Content and form are joined in this film again, according to other viewers. The "expansive tone" of the film "reflects the expansive nature of the project," wrote one; the "provocative possibilities for [Christo's] art form . . . have been much enriched" by the films about it, noted another.[27]

Not everyone admired the project or the film, however. At least one important art critic, San Francisco's Alfred Frankenstein, believed the "illegal leap" into the ocean violated the ethos of the 1960s spirit on which it was based. While praising the "grandeur of the scheme and its heroic daring [that] took your breath away," Frankenstein condemned the "betrayal" of breaking the law. Christo's process being (supposedly) sacred warranted a continued and legal confrontation with the environmental board. "All the fine talk about process as superior to product was washed out with the tide."[28] Others lamented, "Christo is not an artist but an entrepreneur" and continued to see *Running Fence* as a money-generating enterprise.[29] The *Village Voice's* J. Hoberman criticized Christo as "obviously the businessman par-excellence" in *Running Fence*. No such criticism exists within the film itself, although the environmentalists' case is presented briefly in a nonjudgmental way. Christo defended his actions (off-camera) by stating it "is more important I cheat the law than I cheat my art. If I don't go to ocean I will be criticized for years, and rightly so."[30] In response to the Frankenstein criticism, Christo asserted, "I completely work within American system by being illegal, like everyone else—if there is no illegal part, the project is less reflective of the system. It's the subversive character of the system that makes it so exciting to live here—one reason, anyway."[31] Certainly, Christo's reply reads like a rationalization of his desire to complete his project regardless of ideals; the film avoids addressing the possible contradiction.

Hoberman's review also implicates the filmmakers as shameless and uncritical endorsers of Christo, not only "by making explicit the parallels between its construction and the making of a commercial film" but also through their careful omission of certain less pleasant aspects of the project: the "hordes of photographers, news crews, and art-world jet-setters" who overwhelmed the site; the ranchers' "lively selling and speculating on *Fence* memorabilia" after the fence had been removed; or Jeanne-Claude wheeling and dealing with museums and collectors to raise the necessary *Fence* fund. All of these aspects, Hoberman asserted, are as essential to the process as the "'naive' appreciation that the locals had" and the public-hearing showdowns. Not including them, he contended, makes *Running Fence* a sycophantic film ("laid-back reverential" in Hoberman's description) and reduces the self-reflexive elements to mere self-congratulations.[32] Christie, no great admirer of the Maysles brothers' work, also noted, "Christo's calculated post-modernism converges with the Maysles' more intuitive (and confused) approach to satisfy a mutual taste for social spectacle and justify a passion for provoking/recording it."[33]

These negative reviews raise important issues. The film *does* laud Christo, Jeanne-Claude, and the cooperative ranchers and purposefully overlooks or sidesteps the discreditable aspects of the enterprise. The montage scenes in the film especially push hard to underline the positive. In one two-minute sequence, punctuated with music, the film borrows many aspects of a commercial film: Christo and Jeanne-Claude making friends and holding farm animals, by turns negotiating and smiling, then negotiating and frowning; then, as smiling faces prevail, the film cuts to a close-up of one rancher's hand signing the permission form. The goal of the artist and his wife is never questioned, the objections of the hesitant ranchers barely articulated. The film condenses what was undoubtedly several weeks of door-to-door selling into this montage; as a result, they endorse Christo's vision without providing the audience much latitude in deciding if it should do the same. The lack of perspective undoubtedly grows out of what had become a strong personal connection. The relationship between subjects and filmmakers is best illustrated in a brief segment in which Christo and Jeanne-Claude make a frantic phone call to their lawyer. Both of them have squeezed into a glass telephone booth; Albert and his camera are visible in the reflection. The confined space and overlapping visual images not only underline Christo's difficult situation at this moment but also link all three of the people who are visible.

What is really absent from the film is any commentary about or acknowledgment of the film itself. While the film is self-reflexive insofar as it implicitly praises its own process of creation at the same time it celebrates Christo's, it is decidedly not self-conscious about the role it plays in the entire Christo production. A greater examination of the film's place within the larger Christo enterprise would actually strengthen the film, just as the filmmakers might have more thoroughly examined their contribution to the events that unfolded within *Gimme Shelter*.

In truth, the filmmakers were one part of an enormous undertaking that was partly about documentation and partly about publicity. Christo painstakingly includes every memo, every legal brief, even fabric samples in his project books; his official photographers (Wolfgang Volz and Gianfranco Gorgoni) take thousands of pictures of each event. When *Running Fence* made its debut, Albert and David were the official filming team, but there were scores of others from all over the globe. (By the time *Islands* was filmed in 1983, the Maysles brothers' film crew had to enhance its helicopter footage because news reports made such filming commonplace. They filmed Christo admiring the *Surrounded Islands* from within the helicopter.) All of these artifacts and the people producing them, including Maysles Films, feed into the publicity juggernaut that is Christo, Inc. They also help foster a cult of celebrity for Christo, Jeanne-Claude, and the projects. Indeed, construction manager Ted Dougherty apparently helped persuade "the skeptical ranchers" of the *Running Fence* project by showing them the film of *Valley Curtain*; the Maysles brothers were thus conscripted into the process as a "conversion" tactic.[34]

Every film and art critic recognized what the brothers themselves also understood but did not acknowledge within their film: *Running Fence* the film and the project are intimately entwined. Christo and Jeanne-Claude must continually think of future projects even as they complete the current one, for one project funds another. The films are one vehicle by which they fulfill this need. One potential problem, however, is that economic necessities will overtake artistic process. What if the quest for testing boundaries in art becomes merely a quest for financial backing? What if the chief limitation of reality is a financial one? In *Running Fence*, the filmmakers skirt the issue and thereby ran headlong into the criticism that followed.

Of course, the Christo films, like other commissions of celebrities and artists in action, feature inherent parameters. The artist's work, not the filmmakers', dominates the film, and in many cases, the producers' desire to cast the subject in a favorable light limits the creative freedom of the filmmakers. Certainly, the brothers had no objection to promoting the work of their fellow traveler in art. Christo has described many of his projects as "poetical gestures" while Albert Maysles similarly believes he has explored the "poetry of life" in his films.[35] While these films do not rise to the level of the Maysles brothers' more ambitious work, the Christo films do contain a certain number of spontaneous events—so that these films rise above the conventional biopic seen frequently today on commercial television. The Maysles-Christo films stand as permanent records of fleeting, significant events; they provide visual verification that Christo and Jeanne-Claude's monumental projects did in fact happen.

6

Looking into *Grey Gardens*

The Maysles brothers began working on their next project even as *Christo's Valley Curtain* was still being edited. In 1972, Lee Radziwill, sister of Jacqueline Bouvier Kennedy Onassis, contacted the brothers through their mutual friend Peter Beard. Radziwill wanted to commission a cinematic family album of her childhood, and she had compiled a list of people and places she thought could be filmed. Among the suggested sites was her aunt's ramshackle mansion, Grey Gardens, in East Hampton, Long Island, New York. Originally purchased by Phelan Beale, a brother-in-law of the Bouviers, the home was at that time occupied solely by Beale's widow and daughter, both named Edith Bouvier Beale. The elder woman, then in her late seventies, and the younger, fifty-six, had lived for many years in virtual isolation amidst squalid conditions. The house had long since fallen into disrepair and had nearly been condemned by the town in the late 1960s. (The Bouvier family, Jackie included, had rallied support to clean up the place in order to meet health standards.) Albert and David spent several days filming there as they accumulated footage of Radziwill's immediate and extended family. After seeing some of the initial, unedited film, however, Radziwill lost interest in the entire project, primarily because she recognized that a Maysles kind of film would not meet her expectations or desires. According to the filmmakers, she was also more than a little appalled by the notion that the viewing public would be witness to the conditions in which two of her relatives lived. But by then, the Maysles brothers themselves had become fascinated with the two women they had encountered at Grey Gardens.[1]

When the brothers decided to make a Beale-centered film at their own expense, they embarked on a project that would allow them more creative freedom than they had enjoyed since *Salesman*. They had no preconceived notion as to what kind of film they would have in the end; they knew only that these women intrigued them and, they believed, would captivate an audience as well. As it turned out, the finished film would be their most personal work and the finest example of their modernist aesthetic. *Grey Gardens* achieves an authenticity seldom seen in nonfiction film. The brothers were indeed truthful witnesses to the lives of two extraordinary women, whose humanity is on display in a film that details their eccentricities, regrets, humor, their contentious and loving relationship, and their desire to perform for an audience.

The structure and coherence of the film relies on a number of modernist characteristics, including the fragmentation of the narrative, blurring of time distinctions, repetition of language and image, and self-reflexivity. In short, the film marries the twin goals of authenticity (truthfulness) and artistry more completely than any other Maysles work. To achieve these goals, the brothers and their three codirectors and coeditors Ellen Hovde, Muffie Meyer, and Susan Froemke wove together direct cinema violations (e.g., a lack of chronology and the frequent appearances of the filmmakers) and compliances (no narration, no music, no enhanced photography). Skillful editing combined with sensitive photography ensured that although the filming was truly uncontrolled, the finished product speaks to the complexity of human relationships as few films before or since.

INSIDE A GREY WORLD

Grey Gardens integrates the three components of the Maysles brothers' work more successfully than any of their other films; the unusual interplay of their modernist tendencies, their use of an ad hoc direct cinema, and their desire to present their subjects' lives honestly (that is, authentically) reaches its zenith in this their most ambitious film. Although these three components work harmoniously in this film—indeed the success of *Grey Gardens* depends upon them doing so—I will deal with each of them primarily as separate entities. Casting light on the individual pieces shows that the complete product realizes, more fully than any of their other works, the brothers' goal of achieving a truly artistic nonfiction film, one that, more than any other, accomplishes their enduring desire to create "a film that couldn't be classified."

Two important points about collaboration must be made before turning to the film. First, the brothers benefitted greatly from the participation and on-screen presence of two women whose very natures made them ideal studies for this kind of filmmaking. At the time of the film, the Beale women were in actuality eccentric, even bizarre, women, but they were also natural performers; they were at ease in front of a camera and their comfort in turn infuses the film with spontaneity, humor, and nervous energy. Two handmade signs appear in the film: One identifies the mother, Edith, as "The World's Greatest Singer," and another labels the daughter, Edie, "The World's Greatest Dancer." These signs remind the audience that performing is at the center of these women's identities. Indeed, Edith and Edie have difficulty *not* performing; the camera's presence, not to mention the human companionship of the Maysles brothers, provided them a welcome audience, a friendly witness to the theatrics playing daily at Grey Gardens.

Second, the support and skill of the three directors, Hovde, Meyer, and Froemke, cannot be underestimated. As the primary editors, they transformed dozens of reels of raw footage into a coherent product. David supervised the process, and he and Albert had final say on the content, but the team of Hovde-Meyer-Froemke executed the intensive cutting and pasting. They made the majority of the difficult decisions as to what footage to include and in what order. The brothers' trust in their editors has been mentioned before, but in the case of this film, it was indeed an outrageous act of faith. The achievement of *Grey Gardens* must therefore be attributed to the joint efforts of seven people, not two.

The modernist qualities of this film are not difficult to identify, nor am I the first to point them out.[2] *Grey Gardens* tells its story through a highly fragmented, frequently repetitive narrative that recalls a cubist painting or a stream-of-consciousness novel. It is in many ways a self-contained, autonomous text; it eschews formulaic structures in an attempt to show that there is beauty and artistry in the commonplace lives of two isolated women who might be anyone living anywhere at any historical time. The particular and the universal are thereby united: The Beales' complex struggles and their small, human victories are uniquely their own, yet, paradoxically, their lives are profound because they are in many ways so ordinary. As a modernist text, the film is satisfied to explore the complexities of a mother-daughter relationship rather than offer definitive truths. *Grey Gardens* raises existential questions but avoids providing pat answers to them; the asking is what matters.[3]

As with most Maysles films, the opening frames provide a fruitful point of departure. In this film, the first image is a screen door. The camera is positioned back from the door so that it looks from within the dimly lit interior of a home, out through the doorway, and onto a porch. Like many of Albert's camera shots in the film, this one stresses a duality: It is both within (literally) and without (in its gaze), emphasizing the fluidity of these positions. The shot originates from an interior position yet looks out onto the exterior; the door thus serves as a suggestive boundary or gate, much like Christo's fence. Similarly, a home serves as a shelter from the outside world but may also be a sort of prison. For the Beales, especially the younger Edie, Grey Gardens is both at once. After a few seconds of silence, a voice, as yet unidentified, interrupts the quiet gaze: "What are you doing down there? Are you standing there?" As an opening line, it is both simple and evocative. The questioner interrogates not only an unidentified person in the house but also the camera and even, by extension, the audience. The voice asks the audience, too, "What are you doing there?"

The reply is even more significant because it comes from Albert: "I'm just filming the main room," he answers, marking a heretofore rare, audible moment for him in his films. From the outset of *Grey Gardens*, Albert is a featured part of the film, a character in the real-life play that unfolds before the audience. Editors Hovde, Meyer, and Froemke include the brothers and the filmmaking process as essential parts of the narrative, violating the usual direct cinema convention of the unseen (and unheard) cameraman. The editors expand this aspect of the film shortly thereafter. Having shown a series of newspaper articles and still photographs of the Grey Gardens–East Hampton Board of Health controversy, they conclude the sequence with a clipping about the pending film project and present a black-and-white picture of the Maysles brothers, showing Albert with his camera and David with his sound equipment. If Al's voice was heard only once, if he was never visible on camera as he is later in the film, perhaps one could dismiss the appearances as mere "accidents of the moment," as one critic charged.[4] But the photograph signifies that this will be a different kind of direct cinema product, one in which the brothers themselves are prominently on-screen. Indeed, their interaction with the subjects is a vital part of the film's story, making it the most self-reflexive of all the Maysles Brothers films. The photograph of the brothers, juxtaposed as it is with the Beales-related newspaper stories, clearly links them to the Beales; these four lives, the montage suggests, are about to intersect, and the film we are about to see is the result.[5]

As the camera holds on the brothers' photograph, another woman's voice proclaims, "It's the Maysles." Unseen, David replies, "Hi, Edie. It's the gentlemen callers." The brothers announce their entrance into the lives of the Beales and thereby establish themselves as both filmmakers and characters within the film they are making. Through this and other conceits, the film consistently acknowledges and even flaunts its own creation. The self-referential *Grey Gardens* constantly reminds its viewers that they are watching a film and that although the people on screen are real and their lives are being presented honestly, the medium through which they are seen is an artificial construct. This kind of artistic tension informs many modernist texts, allowing for what Gilberto Perez has identified as "a pull to involvement, an aroused impulse to empathy, and a concomitant push holding back that impulse and keeping us, not at an equable, comfortable aesthetic distance, but in an unsettled position both involved and estranged." *Grey Gardens* does pull in the viewer: The Beales' humor and individualism cause the audience to wonder, "Who are these women? What has happened in their lives?" But then the film pushes back, disallowing complete comfort. The filthy conditions of the home, the raccoons in the attic, the absurd conversations and behaviors, the fits of temper—in short, the unpredictability of the characters' behaviors as well as the nonlinear narrative structure—leave the viewer in an "unsettled position."[6]

Similarly, modernists keep audiences and readers off-balance through the blurring of time distinctions. Modernists have recognized the artificial nature of time as a construct but have been equally fascinated with the fluidity with which it works in the human mind. The past-present-future continuum is therefore compressed or even reconfigured in many modernist texts. As it does in several of William Faulkner's novels, for instance, the past continually impinges on the present in *Grey Gardens*. The filmmakers repeatedly pan over old still photographs of the two women and their families. They suggest that time has in many ways stood still for both the women. Although their bodies have aged, their minds remain rooted in the past, and Grey Gardens has become a land that time has forgotten. Accordingly, the two women reminisce constantly, recalling past glories both as performers and as the objects of men's affection. For Edie, especially, time distinctions seem to have lost their meaning. Shortly after the newspaper clipping montage, Edie states matter-of-factly that it is "very difficult to keep the line between the past and the present." Her pronouncement is verified at several points in the film: Edie never knows what time it is, does not answer her mother's inquiry about the date, and recalls an incident when her father chided her for being "five minutes late" to a job. Although she seems perpetually in motion, she cannot move forward in time; rather, she spins in place, repeating the same sentences and singing the same songs.

At the root of Edie's time problem are her complicated and frustrating relationships with men. The ghostly presences of several men of her past—namely, her father, Phelan; her mother's accompanist (and presumably lover), Mr. Gould; Tom Logan, the live-in handyman whom Edie believed wanted to marry her; Eugene Jiskevich, Edie's suitor whom Edith rejected as an inappropriate match—haunt her and the narrative. They are the figures around which all her regrets revolve. Logan, the erstwhile handyman who came for one night and stayed ten years, provides an ever-present reminder of Edie's missed opportunities as well as Edith's reliance on men to take care of her. Edie spins tales of each of these men to the extent that their stories meld together, much as they obviously do in Edie's memory: "I could have married Eugene, but mother didn't think he was good enough. She sent him away." Whether or not this actually happened as Edie remembers is impossible to say, but clearly she feels the power of the past and believes in the accuracy of her questionable memory.

In the film, the new handyman Jerry conjures up these past failures, but for Edie, he is also a reminder of the terrifying realities of the present and the uncertainty of the future. "He's going to be here for years and years," worries Edie after Jerry brings a used washing machine to Grey Gardens. Edie seems to regard Jerry as a continuation of the men who have wronged her before; she even calls him the "Marble Faun," connecting him to a nineteenth-century Nathaniel Hawthorne novel that features a highly eroticized sculpted symbol of the even more distant past. At some point in her past, Edie has read the novel, and whether or not she remembers it correctly matters little; for her, it is a "very deep" expression of the unknowable nature of romantic love. Thus, in yet-another duality, Edie is simultaneously fascinated with the idea that Jerry might want to have sex with her ("But he's not gonna get it, I'll tell you that right now") and "pulverized" when she believes "the Marble Faun is moving in." Restricted in her access to men, Edie tends to merge all of them into one composite and cannot always distinguish Jerry from the ones "who got away." Her attitude towards him remains ambivalent in the film. (The same could be said of the filmmakers who provide no context for Jerry other than what the women say about him. There is no indication as to what he thinks or feels about the women. He is one of the most unusual figures in any Maysles film because he appears frequently and yet never acknowledges in any remote way the camera's presence. Just as he is something of a ghost figure in the Beales' lives, so, too, does he remain something of a cipher to the audience.)

If Edie has difficulty differentiating the past and the present, the filmmakers prohibit the viewing audience from getting a clear view of either. Through the fragmentation of the narrative structure, the filmmakers jar the audience's sense of time and place, never letting them get a clean look at the women's lives. While the film maintains a certain voyeuristic quality, which evoked consternation from a few reviewers and theorists, it frequently allows little more than a quick peep behind the curtains. The reminiscence segment, for example, that follows soon after Edie's time pronouncement provides some insight into the women's past but also relentlessly generates more questions than answers. What exactly happened to Mr. Beale? What about Edie's two brothers? Why did Edith give up her singing career? When did Edie move back to Grey Gardens, and what prompted her return? Most of these questions *are* answered (although often ambiguously) in due course, but they emerge only in pieces. The burden of making sense of the fragments falls to the audience in whom, as with earlier films, the Maysles brothers invested a great deal of trust. And yet, as the film takes pains to show, the fragments may or may not piece together coherently. Like most lives, the Beales' are not reducible to a few simple truisms and could never be explained precisely in a ninety-minute film. Theirs is a complex and frequently ambiguous story; it is, therefore, true to life.

In establishing the time motif and the fragmented narrative, the filmmakers did not concern themselves with presenting events in the same chronological order in which they were filmed. In their work, the brothers and their collaborators had usually maintained a pure approach to time order; the audience is supposed to see events on-screen in the same order in which they occurred in real life. In the case of *Grey Gardens*, however, the material gathered "was very free-flowing, very repetitive—it didn't have an obvious structure."[7] The interest of the final product dictated that scenes could be interchanged, especially insofar as the subjects would not be placed in a different light. They discovered that the nature of the women's lives was repetitive, even obsessive; one day was much like the next. Therefore, the loose, repetitive structure of the film is totally appropriate to the material, as once again form and content coalesce in a Maysles film.

The ad hoc nature of the Maysles brothers' cinema has been extensively argued in earlier chapters, but certainly none of their films manipulate and play with the conventions to the extent that *Grey Gardens* does. The disregard for strict chronology is a prime example. In the reminiscence segment, the women look at old photographs, play scratchy recordings of Edith singing, and recall some of the men in their lives. Although the entire segment appears seamless, it actually comprises two different filmed sequences. The women have slightly different outfits ("costumes," as Edie calls them), but the film offers no clues that the segment was not filmed continuously in one day. For the sake of *narrative* continuity, however, Hovde, Meyer, and Froemke have attached these two sequences so that exposition about the past may be disseminated early enough in the film to provide some context for the women's perceived triumphs in life as well as their more powerful regrets. This also allows the filmmakers to establish the circularity of the women's memories; there are similar patterns and themes, articulated and repeated numerous times, within what they remember. The repetitive nature of their memories suggests that the conversations the audience witnesses on screen are typical of the kinds of conversations they have all the time.

This sequence concludes with a close-up of a portrait of Edith in her thirties, elaborately costumed and strikingly beautiful. The portrait no longer hangs on a wall (if it ever did) but rather rests against one, with piles of refuse and a cat's make-shift litter box in front of it. Albert pans to this portrait as the final strains of "Tea For Two," which Edith recorded many years before with her accompanist, Gould, are heard on the soundtrack. The camera zooms in on the portrait face as the music strikes a strong final chord and renders the point unmistakable: This elderly woman, now living in squalor, once possessed great beauty and a radiant voice. Here again, the filmmakers opt to violate direct cinema convention. The camera operator is not supposed to manufacture meaning or generate pathos; those effects, if they do occur, are usually allowed simply to happen via the spontaneous juxtapositions of life itself. Here, however, the point about Edith's lost youth is made more pronounced only because the camera has wandered over to the opposite wall, showing the viewer the portrait. The editors' choices here again reflect their desire to build a psychological structure and to let the narrative accrete in the viewer's mind. Because the film is almost "purely character development," notes Froemke, "we get deeper and deeper under the skin."[8]

Another segment makes a similar point. Edie gives a brief tour of her bedroom (the only scene filmed there), showing the brothers some of the memorabilia from her childhood. She laments that she has "not had time" to put up certain decorations, namely two theater masks, a birdcage, and an advertisement for an around-the-world tour. Such objects, of course, bear significant symbolic weight: One symbolizes her entrapment, another her chance for freedom. A fiction writer could not have scripted a more appropriate collection for Edie. She even holds the birdcage in one hand and the tour poster in the other as she demonstrates how she would place them side by side in her bedroom. The duality of the image is heightened by Albert's next shot. From the poster, he pans to a long shot of the ocean, with a ship in the distant horizon. The film then cuts to a scene of Edie on the beach.

Another example occurring near the end of the film is an even more conspicuous use of manipulated juxtaposition. The so-called pink-room scene featuring Edie's most intense diatribe about her fate was actually filmed quite early in the process. The editors' choice places the scene in a climactic position, strengthening its impact. In the scene, Edie expresses precisely and emotionally, more than she has in any other sequence, the wrongs she feels her mother has committed against her: "She never let me have anyone in the house I wanted to. . . . She chased Eugene away!" While similar sentiments have been conveyed several times before, there is a kind of raw emotion here that makes this scene all the more compelling. Edie's outburst gives the film a dramatic denouement and ushers in *Grey Gardens*'s closing images.[9]

Given a choice, however, Albert has always preferred discovering the juxtapositions of the moment, and again this film contains many of these. The scene in which mother and daughter listen to the inspirational words of Norman Vincent Peale on the radio features an ironic counterpoint that springs naturally out of the captured moment's absurdity. Sitting atop side-by-side twin beds, the women hear Peale proclaim that a person must "Try, really try," if he or she wants to "get on top of things." The juxtaposition of the Beales' squalor and Peale's unflappable optimism initially creates a comic effect. Later, the camera fixes on Edith's blank expression as she listens to the sermon's conclusion: "I am a child of God. I was intended to get on top of things, and I was intended to stay there." Here, the juxtaposition borders on the poignant; but Edith's enthusiastic response to Peale cuts through whatever pity the audience may have felt. She seems to support whole-heartedly his positive thinking despite her own circumstances.

That these women do not ask for nor desire pity is both ennobling and pathetic. Again, the push-and-pull of the modernist text asserts itself and leaves an unsettled feeling.

Both the manipulated and spontaneous juxtapositions underscore the idea that the film is designed to be an artistic re-presentation of reality rather than a purely documentary account of the Beales' lives. As in the Christo films, these manipulations work to support the film's thematic concerns and create a heightened dramatic impact. Indeed, all the ad hoc violations serve to preserve a finely tuned balance between disorder and order, both of which befit the complexity of the subjects. The resulting film, according to the Maysles brothers' film aesthetic, is "a true presentation of the Beales." Those who might look away in embarrassment or disgust are "denying the authenticity of these people."[10]

The key to the authenticity of *Grey Gardens* is the dynamic between mother and daughter. The filmmakers allow the women to reveal their relationship in their own terms, through their own peculiar amalgam of song, petty quarreling, and reminiscing. Granted, the women are encouraged verbally along the way, and the very presence of the camera invites their reactions, but even given those contrivances, the filmmakers show restraint as the story unfolds. There is respect for the subjects (and again for the audience, who, it is assumed, will accept that the narrative must accrete in their imaginations). Because the filmmakers are patient, the audience sees, gradually, the complexities and contradictions of the Beales' relationship.

In many ways, the film shows a contentious mother-daughter connection: Edith and Edie squabble over which pictures to show the filmmakers or which cats should be fed or even whether or not girdles ought to be worn. Yet, their isolation has bred a more complicated form of mutual dependence. Edie's inability to leave Grey Gardens (despite her proclaimed longing to do so) speaks to her reliance on her mother. "I've got to get out of here" is Edie's mantra, but, as the film makes evident, she is not really capable of leaving. She fears being on her own and has convinced herself that her mother needs her; these constraints are enough to hold her there. As for Edith, her incessant calling out for Edie whenever her daughter leaves the room indicates the extent to which she does rely on her daughter's companionship. Whenever Edie attempts to show other parts of the house to the filmmakers, she is persistently summoned back to the bedroom by her needy mother. Any doubt about Edith's reliance on her daughter is laid to rest when she confesses at a pivotal moment, "I didn't want my child to be taken away. I'd be entirely alone."

The interdependence of the relationship has engendered a singular communication system that simultaneously promotes greater intimacy and creates more division between them. Unlike *Salesman*, which shows the negative effects of depersonalized language, *Grey Gardens* depicts speech as almost exclusively personal. The Beales are constantly revealing their true characters or opening themselves up through what they say. They are equally adept at using words as weapons or as peacemakers. Although they repeat themselves often, they are highly articulate, frequently witty. They also *listen* very well. In *Salesman*, no one listens effectively, which helps pave the way for a communication crisis; in *Grey Gardens*, however, mother and daughter's constant and near-exclusive companionship has had the effect of finely tuning the way they hear each other. A conversation early in the film typifies the kind of banter that permeates *Grey Gardens*:

> EDIE: I suppose I won't get out of here until she dies or I die.
> EDITH: *(feigning innocence)* Who's she? The cat?
> EDIE: I don't know when I'm going to get out of here.
> EDITH: Why do you want to get out? Any place would be much worse. Any place on earth.
> EDIE: Yeah, but I like freedom.
> EDITH: Well, you can't get it, darling, you're being supported. You can't get any freedom when you're being supported.
> EDIE: You can't?
> EDITH: No, you can't.
> EDIE: I think you're *not* free when you're *not* being supported. *(Sighs)* It's awful both ways. . . .
> EDITH: When are you going to learn, Edie? You're in this world, you know, you're not out of the world.

Each woman follows the other's cue so precisely and listens so carefully to both the context and subtext of the other that the dialogue of the film often sounds like that of a play. Their exchanges have the feel of well-rehearsed scenes, each line freighted with meaning.

The dialogue also illustrates the way each woman manipulates the other. Edie's repeated threats of departure keep her mother wary, which in turn encourages Edie to exhibit passive-aggressive behavior (stealing her mother's pillow, withholding food, ignoring her calls for assistance). Still, there is little doubt that the mother knows how to ensure that the daughter will *not* leave her. Often, she condescends, as when she tells her she's "in the world" or when she calls her an "immature child." Playing on Edie's fears, insecurities, or, when necessary, vanity, Edith keeps her daughter under control. Twice, Edith quotes the advice a priest once gave her: "She needs a strong hand." While Edith holds little regard for the Catholic church, she obviously took the priest's advice to heart; she knows how to manage her daughter firmly. Edith gives Edie a long leash, but it is a leash nonetheless.

Other than passive-aggressive actions, Edie's primary defense against her mother's controlling behavior revolves around performance. Virtually every time she greets the camera, Edie immediately discusses her "costume for the day." Edie's continual references to her outlandish outfits underscore her desire to present herself visually to the brothers and for the camera. She is perpetually concerned with her appearance—whether her "costume," her hair (always hidden under an elaborate headdress), her weight, or her figure. She plays to the camera frequently, acknowledging its presence with a knowing grin, a raised eyebrow, or by directly approaching it. Edie also performs for her mother, alternately seeking Edith's approval or goading her mother into negative reactions. Indeed, performance serves as one of the principal ways Edie controls her mother.

Whereas *Gimme Shelter* questions the wisdom of Mick Jagger's relentless presentation of a manufactured version of himself, the perspective in *Grey Gardens* is that a certain amount of performing in everyday life represents a healthy form of "self-expression."[11] The filmmakers do not begrudge Edie's propensity to mug for the camera nor do they make fun of her inability to behave calmly when being filmed. Instead, they work with her personality, making her propensity to perform a part of the narrative, incorporating it as a vital part of the story of the women's lives. Just as Paul Brennan presents a sort of heightened self in *Salesman*, so, too, does Edie act as herself in this film. In both cases, the characters in the films are true and accurate presentations of the real people who (fortunately for the filmmakers and the viewing audience) are natural performers.

In *Grey Gardens*, Albert and David play their parts in the performance as well: They introduce themselves as "gentlemen callers" (in a nod to Tennessee Williams), sing along with Edith as she recalls several of her favorite recordings, and, more importantly, reveal their own images in mirrors in the midst of the two mother-daughter quarrels. Like the photograph in the montage sequence, the mirror shots show the brothers with their equipment and in the act of filmmaking. These reflections indicate that Albert and David (and the Hovde-Meyer-Froemke editing team) understand that they are an integral part of capturing and recording these events in the Beales' lives, and they are not ashamed to acknowledge it.

This is a far cry from the unobtrusive cameraman of early direct cinema; Albert and David are active participants. Their openness about their own involvement emphasizes their faith in themselves as sensitive film-makers; looking in the mirror, they do not see themselves as manipulators or intruders. Nor does this represent an effort to make *Grey Gardens* an autobiographical or confessional film. The brothers remain *supporting* characters in their own film and regularly permit Edie to become the director of her own show. After describing one of her outfits, she asserts, "I have to think these things up," as if she were the film's costume designer, and then suggests where the brothers should next shoot. She choreographs and stages a march to the Virginia Military Institute's fight song, a recording of which she plays on two different occasions. In another appearance, after describing her outfit as befitting a "staunch woman dressed for battle," she discusses a run-in with other family members who thought they could take advantage of her. "The relatives didn't know they were dealing with a staunch character [who won't] weaken no matter what." There, too, she played a role—convincingly, it seems—and dressed accordingly. In all of these moments, Edie asserts herself through performing. She clearly feels more liberated at these moments than at any other times.

In order to escape her mother's criticisms, Edie seeks opportunities to perform away from Edith's judgmental gaze. Her VMI marches, for instance, take place in the front hall or on the second-story patio. Although her mother calls to her from the bedroom, Edie ignores the pleas. She refuses to relinquish a rare unmonitored moment on center stage. Toward the end of the film, Edie finishes her dance and asks, "David, where have you been all my life?", referring not only to the notion that he would have been a prospective husband but also that he uncritically records her every word (and Albert films her every movement). A willing and eager audience who will hear and view the act she performs on a daily basis, the brothers are Edie's ultimate dream. The film audience by extension also bears witness to her performance (and she may have wondered where *they* had been all her life). Edie tells the brothers, "You don't see me as I see myself. But you're very good what you do see me as. I mean, it's okay." She recognizes the limitations of the camera/visitor but nevertheless values its perspective. At least it pays attention—and accepts her unconditionally.

Edith, too, frequently performs, but her attitude about performance differs from her daughter's. This difference marks an important distinction (and frequent point of conflict) between them. Having been a professional singer at one time in her life, Edith regards performance more seriously than her daughter. "I was a very successful singer," says Edith, as she listens to a 1934 recording of her singing "Tea For Two." "I like singing better than anything I've ever done since I was born." Recalling many fond memories, Edith boasts about her classical training and her musical successes. She sees herself as a consummate professional. Perhaps because she has had actual stage experience, she is frequently more cognizant of behaving well in front of the camera, as when she announces embarrassment at being filmed while eating or when she reprimands Edie for telling an untrue story in front of the brothers. "You're wasting that thing [film] on this," Edith states directly to Albert (and the camera). "That's nuts."

Edith cannot abide Edie's mocking performances. In one of the film's most comical moments, Edith coaches Edie through a rendition of "Don't Throw Bouquets at Me," scolding and correcting all the while. When Edie does not enunciate properly, her mother chastises her for "singing very incorrectly...very ugly" and for sounding like a "Czechoslovakian." When Edie forgets lyrics and fills in with nonsense words, Edith chides: "*La la le* doesn't make up for it." Later, in the pink-room scene, a frustrated Edith reprimands Edie for singing badly. "Stop that or I'm leaving the room," she warns. Then, cutting to the heart of the matter: "My voice was beautifully trained—*I* never used it to attract men." This rebuke in turn helps launch Edie's tirade. Thus, their different attitude towards performance also at times elicits their most hurtful jabs at each other.

As in the pink-room argument, Edith's criticisms tend to return, sometimes cruelly, to the fact that Edie has never married. She seems truly amazed that Edie never left Grey Gardens to live with a man. However, in a paradox reflective of human complexity, Edith's comments to her daughter also manifest her insecurities that her daughter *will* leave her. At this point in her life, she is too needy to be alone. She, unlike Edie, must emphasize the mundane needs of the present, whether signing a check for the gardener or worrying about the next meal. Thus, she continually either represses the past: "I can't go back to ancient history. How can you remember that? . . . I'm going to have to start drinking. I can't take it" or puts it in its most favorable light: "I was a very happy woman all my life," and "I had an extremely successful marriage". Meanwhile, she manipulates Edie through her vacillating expressions of love and contempt. One minute, she compliments her daughter's voice, looks, or poetry. The next, she is ridiculing the fact that she never found love—"France fell but Edie didn't fall"—or denigrating her daughter's appearance—"You could still look beautiful if you tried"— or treating her condescendingly—"I see her as a very immature child."

Despite its depiction of psychological warfare, the film is equally fascinated with what unites the two women. As their identical names seem to indicate, mother and daughter are in many ways mirror images of each other. Their shared past, their love of music and animals, and their common belief in the sanctity of family ultimately keep them together in loving company. Moreover, they are connected by their marginalized position in the community. As Froemke and Meyer have noted, *Grey Gardens* is in large measure about what happens to certain women of a certain social class whose options have been unduly constrained. In this way, the film makes a particular kind of feminist statement: As nonconformists against the traditional upper-class notions of womanhood, Big and Little Edie are united against the world even as the world has limited their options. Their mutual disdain for those who would drive them out of the house or, even more frightening, drive them apart gives them strength and a kind of staunch determination.[12]

For the Beale women, food is often the means by which they bond, and most of their quietest and closest moments in the film occur while sharing a meal. The concept of families bonding around the communal table is nothing unusual, but the Beales' meal-sharing scenes are quirky and fascinating because most of them occur in Edith's bedroom and involve odd variations on the usual qualities of meal-sharing. As each woman sits atop one of the room's two twin-sized beds, they nibble on everything from ice cream to paté to corn on the cob that Edith has prepared in a pot of water next to her bed. There is reference (although no film proof) to eating chicken in bed. Albert frequently zooms in on the preparing or eating of the food, as when he focuses on Edie using a plastic knife to get Hershey's ice cream out of a quart container. This rendition of family mealtime simultaneously normalizes the Beales and particularizes them. Although they are doing something to which most viewers can relate (sharing a meal) and doing it with a complete sense of their own normalcy, they vary from the norm in their own eccentric way. In describing her own life, Edith comments, "I had my cake, chewed it, masticated it, and thoroughly enjoyed it." All the references to food and eating may well betray the sad reality that the women sometimes went hungry; their resources by this time were wearing thin, and they relied in part on contributions from their extended family.

Again, the careful filming does not deride; there is respect afforded the women and a certain nobility given to their actions. In these scenes, the refuge of Grey Gardens reduces to an even smaller hide-out, as the women literally hole up in the bedroom, eating meals, sharing the space and food with the numerous cats that wander about the room, one of which defecates behind Edith's portrait. "At least somebody is doing what they want to do," the elder Beale comments. The camera registers the details of this bedroom/dining room, including close-ups of Edith's wrinkled skin, the scratching cats, and the liver paté on crackers. These are intimate family moments, recorded compassionately, with a sense of the universal.

Ultimately, both women want to do right by the other. Showing the camera an old photograph of herself with her three children, Edith entreats, "Was I a good mother?" She seems to be genuinely interested and uncertain as to the answer. One senses she did the best she could, but there are indications that she allowed too much freedom in her own life and in her children's. At this juncture, she provides Edie with necessary financial support as well as frequently helpful encouragement about how to cope with regret: "Everything's good that you didn't do. . . . [But] you didn't feel then as you feel now." Edie likewise wants to be a good daughter but doesn't always know how. She realizes she ought to help her mother lead a more ordered life, including feeding her balanced meals regularly, but "that takes timing." Facing the reality of being a woman who "never knows what time it is," she cannot hope to instill order to the chaos of Grey Gardens. That is one of the reasons she desires so much to leave. Nevertheless, she confesses in one of the film's final segments that her mother "is a lot of fun" and that she hopes her mother does not die. It is clear then that Edie will remain in the house as long as her mother remains alive.

Thus, the gray mansion in which Edie resides simultaneously shelters her from a hostile, outside world and imprisons her behind its dense greenery. The film's final scene illustrates her paradox. As Edie dances alone, free for a time from her napping mother's needs, the camera shows her entrapment as well. Filmed through the railing of the stair banister, Edie is dancing behind bars. And yet, she dances. This final image, which keenly illustrates the liberating power of artful expression as well as the confining responsibilities of family, echoes the duality contained in the opening shot of the screen door.

The Beale women, like all people, both succeed and fail as members of the complex human network known as the family. The filmmaking team's respect for this unusual yet oddly typical family of two is indicative of their own life experiences. Just as the Maysles brothers identified with Paul Brennan, seeing in him much of what they admired in their father, so, too, did the brothers forge a personal connection with Edith and Edie. Albert even admitted that Edith reminded him of his recently deceased mother.[13] The connection with Brennan actually enhanced *Salesman*'s effectiveness, much as the close relationship with Christo also infused the films about him with energy and sensitivity. In *Grey Gardens*, the personal fondness for the Beales likewise served well the understated yet profound statements about family. These connections do not make the films overly personal—they help universalize them. Albert has asserted, "The more personal [a film] is, the more it tells everybody's story."[14] *Grey Gardens* proposes to be the story of two women living in seclusion and then finds a way to implicate us all.

Perhaps it was too personal for some viewers. The ethical questions that had always shadowed direct cinema films emerged full-blown after *Grey Gardens* was released in 1976. Few films of the genre have so forcefully challenged its audience's sensibilities, and even fewer have generated as much controversy. While the controversy has usually centered on one essential question—Did Albert and David unethically exploit the Beales by making and releasing this film?—the negative criticism of this film was actually part of an ongoing backlash against the Maysles brothers and other direct cinema filmmakers. A new wave of documentarists and film theorists contended that direct cinema was inherently unethical and that all claims of objectivity were misguided and naive. *Grey Gardens* was for them a blatant and cruel example of a cinematic invasion. Simultaneous to this development, the quest for authenticity and the idealism of the late 1960s had lost momentum. In the early 1970s, the age of Aquarius had given way to the era of Richard M. Nixon and the Silent Majority. The shift in theoretical approaches to film, combined with the insurgence of less existential views of humanity, did not bode well for direct cinema. *Grey Gardens*, despite its attempt to stretch further the boundaries of the genre, arrived at an inopportune time.

TRUTHFUL WITNESS OR MERCILESS CAMERA?

The direct cinema documentary films of the early 1960s heralded a change in the way nonfiction films would be made. With brash talk and plenty of energy, the filmmakers who came to embody the movement—Robert L. Drew, Richard Leacock, D. A. Pennebaker, Albert and David Maysles—"committed themselves to furthering a new type of filmic expression" and to "find out some important aspect of our society by watching our society, by *watching how things really happen* as opposed to the social image that people hold about the way things are *supposed* to happen." The quest for the authentic, the "really real" as some called it, led them to believe that what they were doing was entirely new, something that had "nothing whatsoever to do with theater or drama as we've known it." Hyperbole aside, these filmmakers were breaking new ground, greatly aided by new technology, including lightweight, more portable cameras, and more sensitive sound-recording equipment. Furthermore, they were working in collaboration—and purposefully so—with film editors, sound recorders, additional camera operators, and producers. They adamantly believed in a group effort and a more democratic art form. Their ambitions paralleled other political and cultural movements that embraced authenticity and sought to create more cooperative, active, socially aware communities.[15]

Within a matter of years, however, direct cinema had lost momentum and was struggling for identity. Several factors contributed to its swift downturn. Perhaps most devastating to its long-term financial and critical success, many of direct cinema's conventions became commonplace, assimilated into fiction films, television news shows, and commercials, thereby reducing some of the once-new and realistic elements to cliché. A general familiarity with new cinematic techniques severely compromised the degree of spontaneity that was crucial to direct cinema. As early as 1967, a television documentarian was asking "Where's the wonder?" and noting that American "cinéma vérité, so fresh a few years ago, seems already overused." Calling for more experimentation, the filmmaker noted that direct cinema "has relied upon the magic of pure technique" and has been led "into the same blind alley—where the subject is all and interpretation is nothing." *Time* Magazine echoed this sentiment in 1969: "Now that methods and audiences are more sophisticated, pure documentary footage is not enough. . . . [I]t is necessary to do more than merely capture reality to achieve art." Direct cinema also suffered from the overexposure of its crisis structure, which after the initial novelty wore off increasingly seemed formulaic or contrived.[16] What once had been hailed as revolutionary was soon regarded as pedestrian, and its subject matter was now thought to be disconnected from society.

Meanwhile, direct cinema's tightly bound community of filmmakers splintered in the late 1960s and early 1970s. Drew, once the leader of this innovative cinema, found his influence waning as early as 1964 when his contract with ABC television expired. Nevertheless, he steadfastly continued to produce documentaries in the vérité manner. He believed direct cinema's problems stemmed not from a lack of wonder but from the changing nature of television. As the medium became increasingly reliant on sponsorship and advertising aimed at a middle-class American consumer, it moved away from highbrow cultural programming. Networks regarded hour-long documentaries as too expensive and potentially controversial; they shifted toward safe nonfiction like Jacques Cousteau's underwater adventures or films produced by National Geographic. The observational journalism Drew had wanted to produce for television never found a consistent audience.[17]

Whereas Drew continued to believe in the potential of television, his associate Leacock came to dislike the medium. Leacock grew tired of dealing with network executives and the creative constraints television required; he and fellow pioneer Pennebaker survived a legal battle with Drew and set out on their own separate paths. Within a few years, Leacock became almost exclusively interested in experimental cinema and video technology. In 1974, MIT hired him to develop a film program; he remained at the university for more than twenty-five years. Pennebaker followed a different course. After parting company with Drew and then Leacock, Pennebaker worked steadily in the late 1960s and early 1970s primarily on films that had a rock-music theme, as he directed *Dont Look Back* (1966), *Monterey Pop* (1968), *Keep on Rockin'* (1971), and *Ziggy Stardust* (1973).[18]

Other filmmakers of American direct cinema followed divergent paths. Willard Van Dyke retired from directing. After achieving some critical success with her controversial *Portrait of Jason* (1967), Shirley Clarke met with bitter disappointment over her foray into commercial film, leading her to shift her interest to experimental video. Frederick Wiseman, although prolific, created films that were increasingly subjective and personal. All of these filmmakers in their own ways continued to seek authentic means of expression but did so independently, often following new technology or more personal subject matter.

A concomitant trend exacerbated the turn away from direct cinema's methods. As Doug Rossinow's history of this time period suggests, the "politics of authenticity," which had energized so many for a few frenetic years in the 1960s, had given way to a "politics of identity," and the "era of 1960s radicalism ended with anything but a bang."[19] Many of the groups who had faith in a revitalized democracy that could change society and who had come together in the name of tackling social ills now reorganized into balkanized coalitions. Many Americans' utopian ideals of the 1960s had been dashed; the seemingly endless Viet Nam conflict and the so-called Silent Majority's growing support for Nixon's middle-of-the-road politics sent them into retreat.[20] And as the quest for authenticity was redirected, so, too, did the faith in authentic means of artistic expression diminish. An era had ended, and suddenly, the vitality and immediacy of direct cinema seemed less relevant. The Maysles brothers took the authenticity/modernism nexus to the extreme in *Grey Gardens,* but at the time of its release, fewer people were interested in this kind of artistic quest for an elusive truth.

Developments within academia hastened direct cinema's fall from favor. By the early 1970s, as direct cinema struggled for direction and as quests for authenticity abated, new theoretical approaches (structuralism, deconstruction, feminism, psychoanalysis, and Marxism to name a few) came to dominate academic film criticism. These postmodern approaches, which had initially infiltrated the fields of anthropology and linguistics, viewed with suspicion the modernist ideal of a quest for authenticity via an earnest exploration of the complexities of human behavior. Theorists held that cultural and artistic bias of all kinds reduced the artist's search for truth to just another search, no more or less pure or authentic than any other. Indeed, authenticity was dismissed as a sociohistorical construct that was itself laden with subjectivity. These theorists argued that because every film and every filmmaker must have a distinct point of view, only films that openly acknowledge their own processes for negotiating these limitations and biases could be considered trustworthy documents.[21]

Not surprisingly, this camp launched an increasingly vigorous attack against direct cinema. In 1975, just before *Grey Gardens* was released, Thomas Waugh delivered direct cinema's "eulogy," dismissing it as the "idiom of a decade ago":

> [American direct cinema's] aesthetic of the image, spontaneous, random, and true, was in effect a gospel of subjectivity, and too often, as it turned out, of inarticulacy as well. The movement's most serious liability was not this subjectivity per se, but its persistent pretense of impartiality. Most of the films of the era bore highly charged emotional statements beneath their posture of objectivity.

Waugh contended that the prevailing (and disingenuously hidden) subjective point-of-view of the direct cinema film had been one of "contempt." To him, the films offered no alternatives to the situations observed, no solutions to the societal problems recorded; in short, these films "had nothing to contribute to the real job that faced the counterculture," which was, according to Waugh, the elevation of "alternative politics." Waugh subsequently hailed a new era of documentary, led by Emile de Antonio, that was "moving purposefully forward through the seventies in its own unique direction."[22]

While Waugh was more strident than most, his views were borne out in many of the new academic journals that began to appear in the 1970s. In one of these, the *Quarterly Review of Film Studies*, founded in 1976, numerous scholars speculated as to what directions film studies ought to take within American universities. In holding up new approaches such as semiotics, they implicitly distanced themselves from what they regarded as the comparatively unsophisticated rhetoric and practice of direct cinema. "Without a semiotic awareness," announced Umberto Eco in the journal, "films are viewed as magic spells. . . . The semiotic approach is not only a criticism of the illusions of reality, it is also a continuous criticism of the ideological shaping of the reality on the part of the processes of semiosis." Ed Pincus, a filmmaker and professor of architecture who worked with Leacock at M.I.T., also published in *QTFS*. Offering a kinder rejection of direct cinema than Waugh's, Pincus highlighted several limitations of what he called cinéma vérité, including a lack of depth and breadth (due in part to financial restrictions on the amount of film that could be shot), varying degrees of insightfulness, "naively" used technology ("that is, without asking the self-referential question of the meaning of the act of filming"), and too great an emphasis on the filmmaker keeping his or her own personality out of the filming process.[23] In his own work, Pincus's solution at first was to reveal the artificial and intrusive nature of direct cinema (as in his *Panola*) and then to make films that relied on either very inexpensive technology (such as Super 8 film) or on highly autobiographical subject matter.

Other nonfiction filmmakers also offered their criticism. Waugh's favored director, de Antonio, excoriated direct cinema as

> two halves of an apple, half rotten and half rather decent eating. The decent part is the technical improvement of light sync-sound camera equipment that came from Leacock, the Maysles, Pennebaker. The rotten half is most of the work, the pretentiousness behind it. There lies behind cinéma vérité the implication of a truth arrived at by a scientific instrument, called the camera, which faithfully records the world. Nothing could be more false. The assumption of objectivity is false. Filmmakers edit what they see, edit as they film what they see, weight people, moments, and scenes by giving them different looks and values. As soon as one points a camera, objectivity is romantic hype.

In his own films, including *Point of Order!* (1963), *Rush To Judgement* (1967), *In the Year of the Pig* (1969) and *Milhouse* (1971), de Antonio never disguises his radical politics or his prominent (sometimes paranoid) distrust of American politics and politicians. He has kept himself and his point of view central in his own films. Mitchell Block took this notion one step further in his 1973 film *No Lies*, which demonstrates through the sardonic use of direct cinema technique that goading a woman on camera to discuss her rape is tantamount to a second rape, committed by the intrusive vérité filmmaker and his camera. For Block, "Rape becomes interchangeable with an act of [direct] cinema."[24]

Perhaps the most persistent and vitriolic attacks on direct cinema have come from British film theorist Brian Winston. For years, Winston has savaged direct cinema's "philosophy of documentary purity" (1978), its proponents' unethical propensity "to lurk and pry" into their subjects' lives (1983), which represents an exploitation of those subjects (1988). Winston has dismissed direct cinema's sometimes contradictory explanations of its own methods as a "miasma of circumlocutions" (1993). He also regrets that too many viewers incorrectly accept visual documentary evidence (first the photograph, then film) as unvarnished truth. Direct cinema filmmakers have taken full advantage of this illusion when they have claimed that they and their cameras are merely "observers." More recently, he has argued that direct cinema's "triumph" over other modes in documentary filmmaking has provoked a series of ethical dilemmas, including the recent controversies over fake documentaries and the frequently inappropriate blurring of lines between fact and fiction.[25]

As Winston's comments suggest, the ethical practices of direct cinema have been consistently called into question. The criticism started in the late 1960s (and were thus leveled at *Salesman* and to a lesser extent *Gimme Shelter*) and reached full voice by the time *Grey Gardens* came to theaters. Influenced by the theoretical approaches of ethnographers and anthropologists, many of those working in film studies argued that *any* documentary that presented a subject or subjects who could be regarded as suffering under difficult or primitive circumstances and which did not make explicit the filmmaker's biases and motives ran the risk of exploiting the subject(s). "Is it acceptable to use someone's life to illustrate a thesis?" one asked.[26] They contended that a subject of any nonfiction film must be able to give consent and that the subject must have a clear and rational understanding of how the footage will be used. Calvin Pryluck, one of this period's ethicists, maintained that direct cinema was condescending and coercive. First, "the film gear serves to intimidate the wary," and any "authentic" footage reflects that intimidation. He believed, for example, that *Salesman* had violated the privacy of the men who were filmed: "When we break down the defenses of a Paul Brennan ... and force [him] to disclose feelings [he] might prefer to keep hidden, we are tampering with a fundamental human right." Pryluck further emphasized the subjects' "competency" as essential to the ethical considerations of the filmmaker and asserted that "the requirement that consent be truly voluntary is a recognition of the fact that there is typically an unequal power relationship between investi-gators and subjects."[27] The new and relevant documentaries that Waugh and others advocated in the 1970s were not only aware of these power re-lationships, they made them as much a part of the film as the subjects themselves. The road was thus cleared for new, more radical perspectives, which included the emergence of minority and feminist points of view. Before long, filmmakers who were not actively discrediting authenticity and/or who were working within the realm of realism were marginalized.[28]

Postmodern theorists, along with many other film critics, simply could not abide the idealism of direct cinema filmmakers. *Grey Gardens*, for in-stance, faced stern opposition, most of which centered on the brothers' "cruel intrusion" into the Beales' lives. *Were* the Beales mentally compe-tent enough to consent to the film about them? Or did the Maysles brothers take advantage of these women in order to produce a film? Pryluck feared that in *Grey Gardens*, Albert and David had not allowed the Beales their right to privacy and that the women might not be competent to under-stand their right in the first place.[29] Pryluck's concerns echo much of the negative response from the popular press at the time of the film's release. Some reviewers called the film an "invasion" and seemed eager to protect the Beales from the film about them. Richard Eder posited that "the mov-iegoer will . . . feel like an exploiter. To watch *Grey Gardens* is to take part in a kind of carnival of attention with two willing but vulnerable people who had established themselves, for better or worse, in the habit of not being looked at. And what happens when the carnival moves on?" *Time* magazine's Jay Cocks concluded that the film is "an aimless act of ruptured privacy and an exploitation." Walter Goodman, the *New York Times* critic, held that *Grey Gardens* was relentlessly exploitative; his review blasted the entire project: "The sagging flesh, the ludicrous poses, the prized and private recollections strewn about among the tins of cat food—every-thing is grist for that merciless camera. The sadness for mother and daugh-ter turns to disgust at the brothers."[30] In the *Saturday Review*, film critic John Simon accused the Maysles brothers of feeling "glee over the Beales' pain." He further claimed that the Beales "are not worth knowing." David Sargent voiced an opinion shared by many: that this "unwarranted and cynical usage of people's lives [was done] in the dubious service of two men's careers."[31]

Much of the negative criticism of *Grey Gardens* also implicated the Maysles brothers' entire body of work. Citing the "chronic elements of indiscretion and callowness" in the brothers' films, one newspaper critic chastised them for showing the Beales' situation when "there's nothing we can do about it." The writer asked, "Since the Maysles' lack the eloquence necessary to persuade us of the Beales' nobility of feeling, what can one do with this picture except become futilely anxious, embarrassed, or remorseful?"[32] His criticism connected to Waugh's indictment of direct cinema's apoliticism: The genre presents a problem but offers nothing in the way of remedy or future direction. Similarly, Cocks castigated the brothers for being "inveterate seekers after the phantom of documentary 'truth.' This quest has been hampered by the peculiar insularity of their vision and by its glib spontaneity." And Goodman believed the "sideshow" quality of *Grey Gardens* was "distasteful enough to call the [Maysles brothers'] whole enterprise into question."[33]

The questions about ethics were generally intertwined with the issue of self-reflexivity. Those eager to denounce direct cinema's "posture of objectivity" also rejected the idea that direct cinema was at all self-reflexive. Filmmaker and anthropologist Jay Ruby considered the kind of reflexivity evident in *Grey Gardens* as "accidents of the moment." In an influential essay, Ruby suggested that the Maysles brothers merely tolerated, for the sake of the film, the Beales' acknowledgments of the camera and the interactions with them. "In one sense, [they] were allowing the circumstances of the shooting to dictate the form of the film, which consequently revealed the process and the producer." Ruby, like many others at this time, advocated the more overt reflexivity of Jean Rouch and de Antonio.[34] Again, the preference for filmmaking that embodied the new theoretical and academic approaches colored the way these critics read the obvious moments of self-reflexivity in films like *Grey Gardens* even though, ironically, the Maysles brothers had moved towards a more open presentation of themselves and their process—at least in *Grey Gardens*. But these critics defined self-reflexivity very narrowly; for them, filmmakers needed to appear on-camera either in body or voice, own up to their cultural and sociopolitical biases, and explicitly delineate the limitations of their own point of view. Ruby's essay insists, "To be reflexive is to reveal that films—all films, whether they are labeled fiction, documentary, or art—are created, structured articulations of the film-maker and not authentic, truthful, objective records." The filmmaker has an obligation to make the audience aware of the interdependent relationship among producer, process, and product, something which he believed direct cinema rarely if ever did.[35]

That opinion has continued to hold sway in film studies. Bill Nichols, for example, has written that direct cinema's "claims of 'objective knowledge'" are no more authentic than the authoritative stance taken by mid-century documentaries with their "voice-of-God commentary." In neither case, Nichols has argued, does the filmmaker do a sufficient job of revealing himself or herself, of understanding that "those who confer meaning . . . exist within history rather than at the periphery, looking in like gods." A truly self-reflexive film "avoids invoking the power of disembodied knowledge and abstract conceptualization in favor of the enabling power stemming from situated knowledge and the subjectivities of corporeal experience."[36] Nichols's position squares him with numerous contemporary ethnographers and anthropologists who, like documentary filmmakers, have grappled with the issues of objectivity and ethical treatment of study subjects. Clifford Geertz, James Clifford, David MacDougall, and Judith MacDougall, among others, have reasoned that a truly enlightened anthropologist must acknowledge his or her point of view that, like everyone else's, is a product of a unique, historically and culturally situated subjectivity, not of some godlike omniscience—infused with scientific knowledge—that can responsibly and ethically impose judgement on other cultures or peoples.

As a result, authenticity itself became a target for these critics—dismissed as a kind of "jargon" used in certain nonfiction films.[37] This argument simultaneously discredited the idealism of the 1960s and withdrew support for artistic expression unabashedly striving for authentic expression. Anyone who had tried to pursue authenticity—whether in politics, religion, or the arts—became fodder for those who decried their efforts in the early 1970s. In politics, the reenergized right, led by Nixon and then championed by Ronald Reagan, helped to "rout the liberals" and sent activists scrambling for new coalitions and new outlets for their passions. Political scientists like Samuel Huntington led a backlash against the radical developments of the 1960s, noting that certain aspects of government—including "hierarchy, coercion, discipline, secrecy, and deception"—were legitimate and ought to be supported.[38] In the case of nonfiction film, the onslaught came from the far left, with Marxist-based approaches leading the charge. The pendulum had swung back the other way quickly; authenticity never had a chance.

It is not surprising that direct cinema met with fierce rebukes. Part of what plagued direct cinema then and continues to do so today is the result of its own practitioners saying the *wrong* things for too long. Defending themselves against the challenges of the 1970s, filmmakers still working in direct cinema responded weakly or not at all. Furthermore, direct cinema's leaders were moving in separate directions, which meant they were unable to form a unified front of defense. As a result, the established, often dated rhetoric of the direct cinema movement rather than its films dominated the rebuttals to these charges and even when responding to unfair criticism, that rhetoric had historically been either too idealistic or stubbornly evasive. There are no published interviews with David, for example, after 1971. As a result, his initial definitions of what his brother and he were trying to do had to stand, even though his films developed and matured. Rather than admit that the style had any inherent flaws or discuss how filmmakers and editors were working to negotiate these issues (as they seemed to be in the films themselves) or to refocus the conversation toward what their films had always done well and were continuing to do effectively, the Maysles brothers and others usually ignored or sidestepped the criticism, especially on the objectivity issue. Or they simply rehashed what had happened in the heyday of the early 1960s. Or, like Wiseman and Leacock, they became increasingly obscure or flippant in their defenses.[39] For his part, Albert has sometimes lacked eloquence. In defending the goals of Maysles Films, Albert once remarked, "But we will be damned, and yet we won't let ourselves be damned, by critics who say that our truths are not truths. We won't let ourselves be forced into the position of saying that what we do is entirely objective and so deny ourselves the opportunity to express ourselves subjectively. . . . We express ourselves in an indirect fashion by expressing ourselves through what we find to be interesting around ourselves."[40] In light of such a convoluted explanation, Winston's miasma charge seems justified.

Thus, it is essential to go directly to the films themselves. Although it would seem an obvious course of action, it has not been particularly well traveled, especially in the case of the Maysles brothers' films, which too often have been ignored or treated monolithically. The films themselves are more accomplished and multilayered than many of their detractors recognize. One cannot help but notice how little Winston's work, for one, examines what is actually in the films he condemns. He has lamented that direct cinema often proves that "filming the surface of things reveals [only] the surface of things," yet too much of direct cinema criticism has done no better.[41] A careful look at the films reveals a surprising inconsistency between rhetoric and practice. Albert has maintained a purist's stance in theory, but in practice, his films—after the intervention of editors—are not pure "spontaneous eruptions." Every finished film to which he has contributed at times violates direct cinema convention, including prohibitions on the use of voice-overs, music, crosscut editing, montage, and on-camera appearances by the filmmakers. Condemning direct cinema for its blind allegiance to the tenets of a naive objectivity does not allow for the countless examples in films like *Grey Gardens* that, at least in part, contradict those tenets.

One such violation in *Grey Gardens* is the frequent appearance of the brothers, whose on-camera acknowledgment of themselves and the filmmaking process goes well beyond what Drew envisioned when he launched his film group. Although self-reflexivity takes on a less conspicuous form in direct cinema, it nonetheless helps carry much of the thematic weight of the film, just as it does in *Grey Gardens*. According to Richard Barsam, "Direct cinema self-reflexive cinema, cinema about the nature and process of cinema itself, calling the attention of the serious viewer to its form and language, as well as to the process of its making."[42] William Rothman also offers a helpful rebuttal to direct cinema detractors on this issue. Informed by the writing of Stanley Cavell, Rothman states,

> Documentaries are not inherently more direct or truthful than other kinds of films. But from this fact it does not follow that documentaries are too naive to take seriously unless they repudiate the aspiration of revealing reality. What particular documentary films reveal about reality, how they achieve their revelations, are questions to be addressed by acts of criticism, not settled a priori by theoretical fiat.

Accordingly, Rothman reads both *Dont Look Back* and Leacock's *A Happy Mother's Day* (1963) as self-reflexive films. While Rothman appreciates and applauds the more blatantly self-reflexive films of, say, Pincus or Ross McElwee, he has also been amazed at "the centrality and depth of the acknowledgment of the filmmaker's role" in American cinéma vérité.[43]

Rothman and Barsam both allow for a broadened view of self-reflexivity, much different than what Ruby had in mind. Whereas Ruby demanded that the work "contain sufficient indications that the producer intends his product to be regarded as reflexive" lest the viewer "be uncertain as to whether they are reading into the product more or other than what was meant,"[44] those who made direct cinema films trusted and encouraged their audiences to read into the films. Barsam maintains that "in direct cinema, meaning develops through a process of accretion, in which the images grow and coalesce in the viewer's perception. . . . Direct cinema does not elude interpretation, but rather encourages it, making the viewer aware of both its form and value." Film editor Patricia Jaffe, who worked on the early Maysles brothers films, confirmed this view: "The answer lies in allowing the viewer to experience what the film maker felt in the screening room."[45]

A 1971 interview with the brothers identified a "definite contradiction between the Maysles' notion of spontaneity and the very formal structure of their work."[46] But this contradiction actually represented the sophisticated negotiation between Albert's freely expressive and highly flexible camera work and the editors' goal of shaping the work into a coherent package. Again, the editor's role was vital to the process: She shaped the film so that the viewer might undergo the same emotional response (Jaffe's use of the word "felt" is important here) that she did when viewing the raw footage. This kind of film would ideally be a "total experience, and the job of the film maker is to preserve the spark that is kindled by the ordinary interchange of people and events."[47] Is this subjective? Absolutely, but there is an interesting degree of trust undergirding the process. The editor believed the viewer would come to a similar emotional place without having to be unduly manipulated or told directly within the film itself.

The issue of self-reflexivity is therefore a highly complex one in direct cinema. Neither Ruby's definition (which implies direct cinema is never or only accidentally self-reflexive) nor Barsam's (which asserts that it always is) provide or even allow a middle-ground position, where most of the Maysles brothers' films reside. Rothman makes a case for a kind of measured self-reflexivity, handling it on a case-by-case basis. So, too, should the issue be considered within a Maysles Films production; the work should not be treated monolithically on this issue either. Just as violations of direct cinema conventions occur when it is in the best interest of the finished product to do so, self-reflexivity in the Maysles brothers' films appears to a greater or lesser extent, depending on what they and their editors believed was appropriate. In general, their decision-making in this regard provided one more example of their ad hoc direct cinema; after all, life-as-it-happens dictated different responses and strategies from the filmmakers. Yet, the filmmakers were not given enough credit for their openness about the filmmaking process in *Grey Gardens*—partly because of their undeserved reputation as being resistant to such openness but also because the self-reflexivity of *Grey Gardens* is not that film's central concern, as some detractors would have it. In making the film the way they did, the filmmakers were not responding to critics; they were creating a film they felt was most suited to the story of the Beales.

Their public defenses against the charges of unethical behavior proves this point. Albert and David, of course, vigorously rebuffed the criticism they and *Grey Gardens* received, but they did so by promoting the Beales' competence rather than by identifying the strengths of their art. For them, the humanistic side of the enterprise superseded the artistic or philosophical issues. Mother and daughter, the brothers argued, were willing and supportive subjects during the filming and after the film was released. In a 1976 interview, Albert articulated their position:

> The Beales aren't squeamish and neither are we. The Beales are very vulnerable, anyone who exposes himself is, especially such raw feeling, such true honesty. But who's going to hurt them, how can they be hurt? When you lay yourself wide open, to filmmakers you trust, is that an injury or a strength? They trust the vulnerability of just being, letting our private lives be known.[48]

For the Maysles brothers, the established trust between subjects and filmmakers creates an openness in the film that they thought should be hailed as remarkable, not condemned as coercive. After all, such trust was at the core of their process. However, defending themselves along these lines steered them toward a potentially arrogant or condescending position, a we-know-better defense that often fell on deaf ears, especially in light of the widespread dismissals of direct cinema. Albert and David often attempted to turn the tables on their critics, suggesting that those who had trouble with *Grey Gardens* were manifesting their own psychological issues. Many who would object to the footage of the mother's "sagging flesh," Albert argued, "are people who are very much afraid of growing old. That's all there is to it. They are afraid to face it." And, "We feel that people who worry about exploitation wouldn't like the Beales anyway. . . . They would be put off by the dirt and the cats and the odd clothes and that they're old."[49] This was an aggressive approach, similar to the one taken in defense of *Salesman* that while containing a measure of truth probably only fueled the opinions against them.

On several occasions, the brothers defended *Grey Gardens* by pointing to the Beales' own positive reactions to the film, much as they had defended *Salesman* by saying that Paul Brennan liked it: "You talk to the Beales about the film . . . and they don't really have any serious complaints about [it], although there are many scenes where they are very open in their pain and their anger; and all of that was shown. But they had no objection to that, because it was so much a truthful witness to them."[50] Codirector and principal editor Hovde concurred: "Now the criticism in this film is that they did not have any knowledge of what was going on, but *I* think that they *did*. At the time of cutting it, I was not sure that they did, but since it was made, it is clear to me that they knew and accepted a great deal about themselves, that other people had no idea of."[51] The Beales, especially Edie, did applaud *Grey Gardens*. At the film's October, 1975, premiere in New York, Edie Beale handed out roses to the audience and repeatedly said, "I love you, and I love the Maysles." The brothers were "factual," Edie told *Newsweek* in 1976, and they "get the pith of every situation. There is no difference in the way we lead our lives and what you see." When the film was re-released in 1998, Edie's position had not changed. (Her mother had died in 1977, allegedly saying on her deathbed that no "final words" were necessary: "It's all in the film.")[52]

Albert's awkward defenses notwithstanding, the question of ethics should have been dismissed, and the ethical concerns should not have dominated the discussion of the film. Like Brennan and his cohorts, the Beales consented to the film and never attempted to block its release. Although they were eccentric, they showed every indication of being competent enough to make their own decisions. Even Alan Rosenthal, a proponent of high ethical standards in documentary films, accepted that the "duty of care" shown by the Maysles brothers towards the Beales was sufficient. The result for Rosenthal, not generally an admirer of direct cinema, "is a beautifully wrought film revealing more about human relationships than almost any film I can remember."[53]

In the end, the trusting relationship between the Beales and the Maysles brothers allowed the Beales a chance to assert themselves in the film. The so-called cruel intrusion proved actually to be a liberating experience for the two women. The filmmaking team all recognized that they were bringing to light the story of two women who would otherwise have been discarded by society, again highlighting the feminist perspective. As Hilton Als commented at the time, "The Beales confer style upon the Maysleses. In *Grey Gardens*, the Maysleses find their true voice in the vindication of the dispossessed who live unaware that they are so." David Sargent of the *Village Voice* emphasized that the "story works like any tragedy in which the plight of everyone is raised in magnitude by the nobility of the protagonists." He concluded his review with an assessment that Albert and David must have loved: "*Grey Gardens* is a film that exalts people, and you will like it if you like yourself."[54]

Exalting people is what the Maysles brothers always claimed to do and what bolstered their modernist expressions in film. For them authenticity was linked to the desire to expand human connectedness. The power of an individual text should be transcendent, they believed; a reader, viewer, or listener, being moved by the experience of art, is changed in ways that are often inexpressible and difficult to measure. The brothers also took for granted that the person would become more socially aware and more positively interested in other human beings as a result. A key ingredient of any Maysles film and of other well-made direct cinema has always been an abiding faith in the audience's ability to be moved by the seemingly shapeless material, such as that found in *Grey Gardens*. Albert and David reasoned not only that the audience would be as sensitive to the subjects as they had been while filming but could also handle the slow pace, gradual revelations, and lack of voice-over explanation. Any self-conscious calling attention to director biases was regarded as talking down to the audience.[55]

Despite what Waugh and others have argued, this attitude about art made direct cinema a political genre. It clearly connected it to the early-twentieth-century avant-garde movements, which hailed art as the answer to many of society's ills, but the stronger affinity was to a later era: Effecting change one individual at a time was one of the hallmarks of the New Left and other 1960s-rooted social and political movements. One of the famous maxims of the era noted that the personal and political were interconnected. Potentially, direct cinema films could be personal accounts (i.e., one individual's story) *and* highly articulate documents on social issues as well. The Maysles brothers' earlier films, for instance, caution against an overzealous media, the hype surrounding celebrities, artistic censorship, prejudice against others based on race or ethnicity, and, generally, those who lead an unexamined life. And *Grey Gardens* is eloquent indeed about family dynamics and the effects of the past on a person's present life. The film's efficacy in articulating these points remains to a large degree up to the individual viewer, reflecting again the filmmakers' trust in the audience. They offered no course of action, no plan of attack to address any of the above issues. Rather, they asked their audiences to observe, to think, and then to act according to their own consciences. The Maysles brothers thereby promoted their own liberal humanist perspective in all their films.

Grey Gardens marked a substantial achievement for the Maysles brothers and the editing team of Hovde, Meyer, and Froemke. Ultimately, however, they were unable to defend the film against a new wave of critical hostility. With the idealism of the 1960s behind them, many scholars working in the relatively new field of film studies were eager to move away from the authenticity claims of direct cinema toward more integrated and challenging approaches.[56] This incursion of new attitudes and theories about film did not bode well for those working within direct cinema. They were in many ways unprepared for the tide to turn so rapidly against them; the Maysles brothers, for instance, continued to work steadily and could not devote all their energy toward rebuffing often-unfair charges. As a result, they and other direct cinema practitioners and proponents failed to convince their critics of one essential point: that their preferred mode of filmmaking had never been a one-dimensional genre despite its tendencies toward certain structures or conventions. Not every Drew film follows the same pattern—despite some general similarities—nor every Pennebaker nor every Maysles.

In their recent work, film scholars Jeanne Hall, William Rothman, and Stella Bruzzi have provided much-needed correctives to the misperceptions about direct cinema. While none of them are unabashed defenders of the genre, they have focused discussion back on to the films themselves rather than on the rhetoric surrounding the films. Hall, in her important essay "Realism as a Style in Cinéma Vérité: A Critical Analysis of *Primary*," summarizes the discussion that had existed up to that point: "Documentary scholars . . . simply dismissed cinéma vérité films for not being 'windows on the world' and denounced cinéma vérité filmmakers for believing or pretending that they were. And many relied upon the rhetoric of the movement for information about the films rather than on the sounds and images of the films themselves." Hall points out that the pioneer *Primary* features voice-over narration and nonsynchronous sound, both supposedly anathemas to direct cinema's nonintervening style. She concludes that *Primary*, like many early Drew films, is actually a "hybrid" that "bear[s] traces of a struggle between convention and innovation in this transitional period."[57] This struggle is also played out quite often in the Maysles brothers' films.

In her reading of *Dont Look Back*, Hall argues that Pennebaker's "liberal concern for the proper role of the press in democratic societies" informs his film, as he allows Bob Dylan to challenge "traditional newsgathering and reporting practices" through his acerbic interactions with members of the media. (The Maysles brothers had already presented a nearly identical critique in *Meet Marlon Brando*.) Significantly, Hall also points out that Pennebaker himself disavowed such a reading of the film; he chose instead to downplay his motives (with typical direct-cinema-objectivity rhetoric) and to emphasize that the film should speak for itself.[58] Here again, one must trust the film more than the filmmaker.

Similarly, William Rothman's richly detailed analysis of *Dont Look Back* in his *Documentary Film Classics* allows him to see the film as in many ways a *rejection* of some of its direct cinema predecessors. According to Rothman, in this ultimately optimistic and liberating film, "the tyranny of the 'crisis structure' is overcome by an idea of selfhood, exemplified by filmmaker and subject alike, that embraces the principle that human character is not fixed, that human beings are capable of changing, are incapable of not changing, are changing at every moment." He also contextualizes the film, noting that it came out at a time when several important developments were occurring simultaneously: (1) "Cinema-verite's break with, or expulsion from, network television"; (2) Dylan's impending shift from folk music to rock and roll; and (3) the emergence of the new French thought (spearheaded by Jacques Lacan, Jacques Derrida, et al.) as the dominant influence in film theory.[59] These three factors combined to charge the film with a dramatic tension that is visible not only in the performance of Dylan himself but also in the way the film is edited and structured. Understanding this film in its very particular American context imbues it (and Rothman's interpretation of it) with a great deal more meaning than is possible when considering it as simply another link in the chain of similar direct cinema films.

Bruzzi, in her work *New Documentary: A Critical Introduction*, notes the need for an "alternative way of discussing documentary," which will recognize "documentary as a perpetual negotiation between the real event and its representation." In other words, discounting the zealous claims to the real of certain filmmakers does not simultaneously exclude the films themselves from careful consideration. Bruzzi understands that "if one strips the [direct cinema] films of the theoretical baggage they come burdened down by, they offer less stifling, more exciting possibilities." She also argues against what she calls a "family tree" approach to documentary studies whereby one style of nonfiction filmmaking *replaces* another without building on or referencing previous films. Such treatment has unfairly boxed in direct cinema and has made it too convenient for critics to judge newer documentary films in opposition to direct cinema practices. Her readings of such direct cinema classics as *Salesman, Meet Marlon Brando,* and *Primary* open up those films to broader critical analysis, much as I have attempted to do in the preceding chapters.[60]

But these responses had not emerged in the 1970s when the Maysles brothers' work came under fire. With the idealism of the 1960s behind them, many scholars working in the relatively new field of film studies were eager to move away from the authenticity claims of direct cinema toward more integrated and challenging approaches. The incursion of new attitudes and theories about film sent direct cinema into a kind of forced dormancy. Ironically, the Maysles brothers' fate was left, to a great degree, in the hands of academics, whose world Albert and David themselves eluded when they left Boston University in order to pursue film careers. Without greater support and interest from these men and women, the Maysles brothers' artistic ambitions and their desire to test the boundaries of direct cinema faced an uncertain future.

7

Taking Direct Cinema into the 1980s

Grey Gardens was not the intentional endpoint in the Maysles brothers' long journey. Without the form-content tension that infuses their best work, however, none of their subsequent attempts matched the quality or daring of *Grey Gardens*, a film that may now be considered their final attempt at redefining what "cinema could really do." Their particular brand of authentic filmmaking, steeped in a modernist aesthetic and enhanced by the integral collaboration of codirectors and coeditors, reached a climax in the Beale film. It proved to be the last great film on which they would work before David's sudden death from a stroke in 1987.

To a significant extent, the financial realities of filmmaking impinged on the brothers' joint career and shaped its conclusion. Direct cinema had never proven to be a lucrative art form, and a lack of commercial success plagued the Maysles brothers throughout their careers. Despite critical acclaim—especially from such champions as Jonas Mekas, James Blue, Vincent Canby, and Louis Marcorelles—none of their films, including the feature-length *Salesman*, *Grey Gardens*, and *Gimme Shelter*, received widespread distribution or attracted enough viewers upon initial release to earn profits for the brothers. Feature-length direct cinema documentaries remained unseen by the majority of the viewing public. This lack of viewership disappointed the brothers, even if at least initially it did not discourage them from taking on other projects. Yet, the limited box office success and lack of consistent television or theatrical exposure hampered the growth and acceptance of direct cinema generally and specifically hindered the brothers' ability to pursue projects in which they could exercise their full creative powers. And when critical support languished in the early 1970s, the Maysles brothers lost much of the momentum they had built just a decade before.[1]

As a result, Albert and David turned more frequently to commercial ventures in the 1970s, creating direct cinema–style advertisements and promotional films for companies like IBM, Ragu, American Express, Clinique, and Citicorp. Although their motivation was financial, they nevertheless took on such projects enthusiastically and maintained faith in themselves as filmmakers turned advertisers. They insisted on creative control over the work and held true to many of the same principles they always had: They used real people instead of actors, they shot a great deal of footage as they awaited spontaneous events to occur, and they avoided overt manipulation of the audience's emotions. Much as they had laid claim to breaking new ground in nonfiction features, they felt their commercials and promotional films journeyed into unchartered territory and were more authentic than those of other production companies. They touted a particular kind of work as a "bouquet commercial," which, they boasted, "put people directly in touch with one another."[2] Harboring no ill will toward the realities of the film business, they, along with several of their collaborators, turned Maysles Films into a more financially stable enterprise. Although the brothers maintained that these commercial projects were undertaken in order to fund later efforts in nonfiction experimentation, they did so without apparent regret even as the time commitment involved in commercial work diminished their opportunity to make features. Personal developments also played a significant role in the brothers' career shift: Both men married and started families during this time, further limiting their available hours to make longer films.[3]

One might conclude that the turn toward more commercially oriented ventures was a classic case of artistic compromise. After all, Albert, the same man who had consistently denigrated television product, willingly made commercials as well as nonfiction films that appeared primarily in that medium. The subtle but persistent critiques of American materialism that had permeated their work gave way to a seemingly unbegrudging acceptance. Their modernist impulses were all but abandoned in favor of more conventional modes of representation and expression. The Maysles brothers never again seized the opportunity to make a film "as one would write a novel or do a painting or even compose a song." Yet, it is too easy to fault artists who face the commercial realities of their situations. Calling such compromises selling out ignores the harsh market of filmmaking. Moreover, the humanistic side of the Maysles brothers' later work should not be over-looked: They consistently strove to bring people together and, as much as possible, emphasized the positive aspects of human potential, whether in their commercial work or in their feature-length profile films. The com-mercials of this period therefore sought to personalize what they saw as the cold world of advertising while their films documented and advocated for artists they truly admired.[4]

During the two particularly hectic years of 1975 and 1976, the Maysles brothers and their crews simultaneously worked on three different projects. While their codirectors completed the editing of *Grey Gardens* and *Running Fence*, the brothers filmed and recorded one segment of a six-part PBS se-ries entitled *Six American Families*. For their episode, the brothers hoped to find a rural family who had undergone hard times. Albert consulted with a friend in Dalton, Georgia, who helped them find the Burk family. The subsequent one-hour film, *The Burks of Georgia*, depicts a large and im-poverished clan who has survived numerous travails by virtue of being "very, very devoted to one another."[5] Much like the Beales of East Hamp-ton, the Burks of Dalton, Georgia, have been marginalized within their community. Yet, their plight as outcasts helps keep them together, hover-ing around the crowded home base. "Too many families get separated," observes Grace Burk, the mother of ten living children; hers stays together. And like Edie and Edith Beale, many of the Burks are willing to reveal their character strengths and flaws on camera.

The Burks contains numerous poignant moments, including one Burk son's tearful recounting of his brother's sudden death in a suspicious train accident. Other scenes are memorable for the humor they invoke, as when Arlon Burk, the near-toothless patriarch, watches professional wrestling on television, twisting and wrenching in his armchair. Like *Grey Gardens*, *The Burks* achieves its impact through the accretion of detail. Only slowly, gradually, do we learn of the family's troubles, of the interpersonal rela-tionships that have persisted as well as those that have been strained, and of Grace Burk's power as the matriarch of this clan. To underscore the importance of detail, Albert brings his camera close-up on the Burks' lives: We see images of haircombing, men working on cars, doors and mailboxes being opened and closed, hands washing dishes. The brothers' sensitivity for the subjects proves to be the film's greatest asset; what could have been a condescending or clichéd portrait of a Southern family instead displays at times great compassion.

Overall, however, the film suffers from the numerous restrictions of the assignment. The producers of the film (Westinghouse Broadcasting Company) and the series' writer (Paul Wilkes) interjected their own editorial demands, including subtitles for some of the family's dialogue (a concession Albert Maysles regarded as a "put-down" of the family) and an awkward scene at the end of the film in which the family is asked to comment on the finished film.[6] Whereas the Rolling Stones's responses to themselves on film provided an important distancing effect, with the reaction scenes seamlessly integrated into *Gimme Shelter*, the Burks' responses provide no great insight, and the whole staged conclusion comes off as a patronizing attempt on the producers' part to understand Southern poverty. Even worse, the incessant din of several roosters crowing in the background all but drowns out the family members' comments. Combined with the unwarranted sixty-minute time constraint, *The Burks* has the feel of a partially finished scrapbook or a family photograph that has been inexplicably cropped. Certainly, more time and creative freedom would have led to a stronger final product; potentially, a *Grey Gardens*–like portrait could have been constructed from the raw footage.

Similar constraints encumbered another production, *Muhammad and Larry* (1980), a twenty-six minute, made-for-British-television special that aired the night before a major heavyweight boxing match between Muhammad Ali and Larry Holmes. Held in Las Vegas, the title fight took place on 2 October 1980. (Holmes won the bout, retaining his heavyweight title.) The producers of the film, the Deerlake Company, desired a well-focused lead-in to the title fight, and the resulting film primarily shows both Ali and Holmes at their respective training camps, preparing to battle each other. The ever-loquacious Ali is in rare form, and although the on-screen time is divided evenly between the two men, he dominates the proceedings. The film opens with a close-up of Ali as he is addressing an unseen audience. "People desire to understand what they cannot understand," he says. "People like to be puzzled." Here the film is self-referential, as we struggle to make meaning of what we are seeing, much like the opening of *Christo's Valley Curtain*. In a moment, there is partial clarity: A wider shot reveals Ali doing sit-ups, pummeling himself in the stomach as he moves upward and back. Then the film cuts to one of Ali's trainers massaging the boxer, as Ali describes how he is going to "shock the world." The title frame, MUHAMMAD AND LARRY, follows (no other credits are provided at this juncture).

The next cut shows Holmes driving his car. He says "I know him like a book," obviously referring to Ali, then silently listens to an inspirational disco song about himself and occasionally mouthing the words. Quickly, we see the sharp contrast between the two men: One boxer's speech is as fluid as his fighting style; the other quietly but confidently goes about his business both inside and outside of the ring. In this way, Kate Hirson and Janet Swanson, the editors of this film, create drama through the juxtaposition of the Ali camp in Louisiana and the Holmes camp in Las Vegas, visually marking the contrast between the rather rustic setting of Ali's training quarters and Holmes' more lavish one. Still, the editing cannot overcome what is a highly conventional film. There are moments of captured spontaneity (the last scene in which Ali admits to liking Holmes is the strongest case in point), but there is little underlying tension as in, for instance, *Meet Marlon Brando*, that would help this effort transcend the commission. Nor did a Maysles hunch lead them toward an additional story underneath the surface. The viewer therefore meets Ali and Holmes in an entertaining but uncomplicated way.

After a long hiatus from feature-length filmmaking (with commercial work and family taking center stage), a call from Peter Gelb of Columbia Records brought the brothers back to two larger projects in the early 1980s. Gelb happened to become acquainted with Albert at a party on Fisher's Island, just outside of Manhattan, where Albert lives and Gelb was vacationing. After several conversations, Gelb convinced the brothers that they would be ideal for the kinds of film projects he was intending to produce.[7] Two personality-profile films followed in 1985: *Ozawa*, a study of the Boston Symphony's conductor Seiji Ozawa, and *Vladimir Horowitz: The Last Romantic*, an intimate concert film featuring the legendary pianist performing at his home in New York City.

In both works, Albert focuses his camera on the hands and faces of the artists. *Ozawa* opens with a head-and-shoulder shot of the conductor; his face, dripping with sweat, is a study in concentration as he gently guides the orchestra through a quiet moment of the piece. The music is audible, but the filmmakers never show us the orchestra nor anything but Ozawa for more than a minute. Similarly, in *The Last Romantic*, the camera consistently zeroes in on the maestro's aging hands, nimble as ever, deftly playing a series of compositions by composers of the last hundred years.[8] These close-ups help these films achieve an intimacy and authenticity rarely achieved in works of this nature.

Both films feature moments of spontaneous candor and humor as well. Ozawa's filmed interactions, first with a young conducting student at the Tanglewood Music Center and then a young (and already immensely talented) Yo-Yo Ma, reveal his effective and engaging teaching methods. At ease with these protégés, he imparts technical expertise as well as advice about the difficulties of his profession. A central theme emerges from these scenes: An Asian interested in Western classical music once faced unique challenges and pressures because his or her individual successes might run counter to cultural norms that stipulate conformity and selflessness. Indeed, this conflict eventually drove Ozawa out of Japan to the United States. As he shows in the film, the personal turmoil still troubles him. He admits to being "sensitive" about this matter, and he even asks the brothers at one point to stop filming.

We also see vulnerability in Horowitz, especially when he acknowledges that he is the last survivor of the cadre of musicians and composers he has known over the years. Although he is confident at the piano, at one point he demurs from playing Robert Schumann's "Novelette." "I cannot do it!" he proclaims, shortly before a flawless performance. The film exposes a playful Horowitz, too: He chats amiably with the assembled group and spars lovingly with his wife, Wanda Toscanini Horowitz. In these brief scenes from a marriage, we get a clear picture of this relationship: the patient, earnest wife has sublimated herself to the delightful but self-absorbed pianist. (Wanda sums it up herself: "He married an angel, and I married a devil.")[9]

The strength of both films lies in the editing, for which Deborah Dickson was primarily responsible. (Patricia Jaffe coedited the Horowitz film.) The structure of *Ozawa* is deceptively simple. The film moves back and forth from performance or rehearsal to off-stage activities (teaching, swimming with his family, talking directly to the camera about his career), which permits the viewer to see him in action but also allows the conductor to tell his own story. As in most direct cinema, narration is thus rendered unnecessary. Intercut black-and-white archival footage of a young Ozawa provides visual verification of some of the biographical information he shares. Often, Dickson brings in these biography pieces in the middle of a performance or teaching lesson, creating a kind of parenthetical phrase for the contemporary footage.

In *The Last Romantic*, the similar decision to move back and forth between musical performance and casual conversation serves both the artist and the film about him. He has the opportunity to tell stories about his past or about the composer whose piece he is about to play. In the end, we have learned much less about Horowitz than we have about Ozawa, but the personal stories provide depth and context for the performances. Thus, while *The Last Romantic* is essentially a concert film (albeit on a small scale), it builds an appreciation for Horowitz's character as well as for his musical talent.

The artists in these two films espouse a Maysles perspective on art and its place in the world. At one point in *Ozawa*, the conductor affirms that in order to get the performance he wants from his orchestra, "a good conductor must go through the Himalaya Mountain." The statement—which recalls Christo's similar comment about himself and his work in *Running Fence*—suggests that good art is akin to a kind of exploration; there is a physical dimension to it, as evidenced repeatedly in Ozawa's energetic conducting. But such exploration is meaningless without a reconnection with other human beings. As Horowitz notes in his film, a true artist "must have acquaintance with the world." This duality of being both an independent and single-minded explorer as well as a person who knows his world captures the humanistic philosophy the Maysles brothers espoused.

The Horowitz film premiered at Carnegie Hall in November, 1985, and went on to earn numerous accolades, including an Emmy Award for Outstanding Individual Achievement in Classical Music/Dance Programming-Directing in 1987. Ozawa played to enthusiastic audiences at the U.S.A. Film Festival (the precursor to the Sundance Festival). Both efforts received distribution via television and videotape, thanks to the backing of Gelb and Sony Classical. Other than a short industrial film commissioned by the Foundation Center, the Horowitz project would be the last the brothers completed together.

Around the same time, editing of the third Christo collaboration was completed, and the film called *Islands* was released in 1986. Despite its title, the film chronicles three works in simultaneous progress of Christo and Jeanne-Claude *Surrounded Islands* in Miami, the wrapping of the Pont Neuf in Paris (eventually completed in 1985), and the wrapping of the Reichstag in Germany (completed in 1995). The intercutting among the three projects provides glimpses into the negotiation processes behind each large-scale undertaking. The opening ninety-second sequence of the film, which takes the viewer from the studio to the three project sites, vividly illustrates how Christo and Jeanne-Claude maintain a dizzying schedule, simultaneously juggling the planning and execution of the projects.

The use of crosscutting within the film also highlights the couples' increasing salesmanship. Their reliance on commercial means to their artistic ends has heretofore seemed secondary to the grand artistic vision; in *Islands*, this salesmanship emerges as a necessary evil. The kind of compromising for the sake of the project, to which Alfred Frankenstein objected after the *Running Fence* project, occurs much more blatantly in this film. In order to obtain permission to proceed with both the *Surrounded Islands* and Pont Neuf projects, Christo and Jeanne-Claude must sacrifice some of their idealism for the sake of "getting the job done," as they are shown winding their way through a more overtly political maze than we have seen in the earlier films.

Incorporating this maze into a dramatic storyline, the filmmakers try to build tension through the familiar overcoming-the-obstacles format. As in the first two Christo films, the brothers and Charlotte Zwerin relied on variations on direct cinema's conventional crisis scenes. The question of whether Christo can complete the projects despite a range of challenges provides dramatic tension in both *Valley Curtain* and *Running Fence*. In *Islands*, however, this tension develops less successfully. Two issues hinder the effect: No usual people contribute to the eventual resolution of the crises, and Christo's compromised integrity severely reduces the audience's sympathy for him.

The first crisis moment involves a long-awaited meeting with Paris mayor Jacques Chirac. In the first half of the film, Christo and Jeanne-Claude negotiate with a series of French politicians and influential figures, including Gen. Jacques de Guillebon (a French elder statesman who also happens to be Jeanne-Claude's father), and former prime minister Michel Debre, who holds sway with the ruling Gallist party. These two men pave the way toward the ultimate encounter with Chirac. In all these meetings, the artistic process becomes a decidedly political one; Christo and Jeanne-Claude must convince French officials not on the aesthetic merits of the project but on the premise that it will not damage anyone's political career. (Chirac, for instance, had initially refused to meet with them because of the public's unsubstantiated concerns over the project's costs.) Having finally been granted an audience with Chirac, Christo and Jeanne-Claude fear the worst. The film builds tension through a series of quick cuts and close-ups, showing a diffident Christo dismissing his wife's advice to think of the pending meeting as a "friendly chat" between two men. Despite the anticipation, the meeting itself is anticlimactic. Christo pitches the project breathlessly; he even distributes postcards of the concurrent *Surrounded*

Islands site. A seated Chirac betrays little emotion. Finally, he offers, "Personally I am in favor of the project. But no one must know that yet. It would make things difficult. This affair must not be turned into a political battleground." He agrees to meet with the couple again in one year, after the next election, which he assumes he will win. A smiling Christo departs, victorious for now, thanks to political expediency. It is a decidedly anticlimactic resolution of the kind that most direct cinema films had been fortunate enough to avoid.

The second crisis moment reaches a similarly unexceptional conclusion. In two different scenes of the Dade County Commission's proceedings, Miami councilman Harvey Ruvin objects to the *Surrounded Islands* project's "exploitive" nature. He further challenges the "legitimacy of the artform itself." (He thereby covers two of the usual three positions against Christo and Jeanne-Claude's work.) The couple must therefore persuade Ruvin to reverse his initial rejection of the *Surrounded Islands* project. The film builds toward another showdown meeting scene, but it, too, disappoints. Whatever genuine convictions Ruvin may hold on the environment or on art become moot after a private lunch meeting with Christo and Jeanne-Claude in which Ruvin shamelessly admits that he is looking for a way to "enhance the community." Having listened carefully to the artist's lengthy explanation of his philosophy, Ruvin ignores the rhetoric and looks simply for "a significant flowback to the resource." By this, of course, he means a financial contribution; he suggests a figure of $250,000. Christo eventually relents, agreeing to "donate" one thousand signed "photographic images" (Christo eschews the term "poster"—it sounds "cheap," he says) to the Miami council, which the Chamber of Commerce will sell. Ruvin has gotten his "flowback." Here, the film makes a striking point. Ruvin and Chirac may be thousands of miles apart, but their political motivation is much the same. For them, the "shocking" nature of Christo's art is secondary to keeping diverse constituencies at bay. Still, their requests are only as regrettable as Christo's acquiescence to them. Like Paul Brennan and the other Bible salesmen, Christo seems willing to compromise for the sake of closing a deal. The idealism of the *Valley Curtain* project has been replaced here by a less inspiring pragmatism.

The reliance on two less-than-stellar crisis moments is not the film's only weakness. The music, composed by Scott Cottu, is New Age orchestration at its worst: "Eerie" synthesizer accompanies the underwater photography, and tinkling piano underscores Christo at work in the studio. The music strains to direct our emotions in scene after scene, much like the "Take It to the Limit" sequence in *Running Fence*. The artist's struggle and vision receive the "appropriate" accompaniment, as if the audience cannot be trusted to decide how to feel. This represents a reversal of the usual Maysles confidence in the audience to respond personally to the scenes transpiring on the screen.

Similarly, Christo's voice-overs hinder rather than help the final product. In three segments, Christo explains his artistic philosophy as he travels or works in his studio. The speeches are quite similar to those heard not only in the first two films but within *Islands* itself—especially in the Chirac and Ruvin meetings segments. The voice-overs do not clarify the picture or broaden the perspective; they merely support the film's positive treatment of the artist. The enhanced photography—both from the air and in the water—performs much the same function. The opening and closing segments of the film especially, providing lengthy shots of the pink-wrapped islands, strain to sell the beauty of the project, again steering the audience toward a particular point of view. The problem is exacerbated by the lack of ordinary people reacting to the process and the finished product. Albert actually filmed some reaction scenes from "people who don't ordinarily come into contact with art," but, inexplicably, these were cut from the finished product.[10] Such scenes might have helped energize the film.

At the end of the film, as husband and wife gaze out upon one of the surrounded islands from the coast, Jeanne-Claude asks, "Is it like you wanted? Did we do a good job for you?" Christo, hugging her, replies, "Much beautiful job." Like much of the film, this moment fails to deliver much of an impact; the end product is shown through a filtered lens. While *Islands* may be the most technically precise of the Christo films, it is also the least interesting. In the end, the beauty of the project is emphasized too ardently; as a result, *Islands* becomes merely a "much beautiful job."

Whereas the film could make an interesting statement about the intersection of politics and art or the extent to which the bold ideas of both subject and filmmakers have entered the mainstream, it leaves these issues unconsidered. Direct cinema's objective position typically shuns that kind of perspective, yet the film calls out for some sort of perspective other than that of Christo and Jeanne-Claude (or by extension the Maysles brothers). The underlying problem is two-fold. First, by this time, the filmmakers had become too close to this particular subject. Whatever objectivity may have existed in the first two films had now gone, and the filmmakers seemed primarily to want to "do a good job" for Christo. In one instance, David, off-camera, is heard advising Christo to "take it easy" for the sake of his health. Christo smiles and assures David that vitamin C will help him endure. In other scenes, Christo looks knowingly at the camera (i.e., at Albert); on one occasion, he even winks. This kind of casual relationship benefits neither the filmmakers nor the subjects of this film. Second, too many people had become involved in making *Islands*. Albert had done nearly all the photography for the first two films, but for *Islands*, he was aided by two other photography teams as well as a special underwater cameraman. Their collective work is patched together admirably by codirector Zwerin (returning to this Maysles Brothers project nearly ten years after her last collaboration with them) and coeditor Hirson, but the total package is not coherent.

To be fair to the Maysles brothers and their collaborators, part of the reason for the decline in effectiveness in *Islands* has to do with the subjects, Christo and Jeanne-Claude, themselves and the era in which the film was made. In 1973, when footage for *Valley Curtain* was shot, Christo was young and energetic, and his projects seemed outrageously unique. There is an innocence about him in the first film especially—as when he marvels that the curtain "looks just like the model"—which is endearing and sincere. By the third film, however, Christo has become such a salesman for his projects, and the projects themselves have become almost prosaic despite their size and scope, that he no longer elicits the same sympathy. His artist-against-the-world process has become routine, his projects less surprising in the postmodern 1980s when the challenging nature of modern art had become commonplace—so much so that many viewers regard it cynically or with a yawn. The optimistic spontaneous projects espoused by Christo, Jeanne-Claude, and the Maysles brothers had lost their edge. The controversies that environmental art or direct cinema had once engendered belong to an earlier era.

Project historian Jonathan Fineberg has acknowledged that wrapping the islands "passed from physical presence into pure idea more smoothly than any Christo project to date," which is in turn reflected in the film—to its detriment.[11] David Edelstein, in the *Village Voice*, recognized this smoothness and mocked the film for believing that the "Is it art or isn't it?" question is still a relevant and interesting one to ask. Dismissing the film as "hagiography," Edelstein also poked fun at Christo, "determined—visionary that he is—to fight, fight, fight to wrap those islands in pink."[12] This critic's perspective suggests that 1960s idealism failed to make much of an impact in the mid-1980s. Moreover, as Edelstein implied, the persona of Christo, so integral to his success, has seemingly overwhelmed the man. With his Woody Allen glasses and relentless salesmanship, he frequently cuts a comic figure in *Islands*: the Broadway Danny Rose of environmental art.

Islands is not the final Maysles Films–Christo collaboration, however. A fourth Christo film, *Christo in Paris*, was released in 1990. The work features much of the footage Albert and David shot and recorded in the mid- to late 1980s, and David received a posthumous credit as one of four directors, along with Albert, Dickson, and Susan Froemke. A stronger and more cohesive work overall than *Islands*, the film went on to win several honors, including a Grand Prize at the 1990 Amsterdam Film Festival. Since then Maysles Films has also produced *Umbrellas* (1995), the film record of the ambitious, 1991 project in which thirty-one hundred umbrellas were positioned on rolling hillsides throughout southern California and central Japan.

David's death in 1987 more than anything else determined the post–*Grey Gardens* trajectory of Maysles Films. Without David's gentle prodding and enthusiasm, the creative energy of the Maysles Brothers team did not continue in the same way; plans for future "outrageous acts of faith" lost much of their impetus. Albert has ventured on since the late 1980s, teaming up most frequently with Froemke, Dickson, and Henry Corra, but he has not completed any project that matches the audacity of the brothers' best joint efforts. Two works-in-progress have the potential to be in much the same vein as *Salesman* and *Grey Gardens*. One of these, first titled *Fellow Passengers* and now called *In Transit*, is a series of real-life vignettes about people traveling on trains, which for Albert has been a lifelong obsession. The other is a Maysles family portrait entitled *Blue Yonder*, a piece that would certainly take the Maysles-style modernism further into an autobiographical mode than ever before. Both projects, started while David was still alive, may yet be completed. (*In Transit* was shown as a work-in-progress in New York City in September, 2004.) If so, they will add dimension to the already complex and varied career of the Maysles Brothers.[13]

In the twenty-first century, Maysles Films continues to be a vital player in the world of nonfiction film. Led principally by Froemke until her departure in 2004, the company has produced several first-rate nonfiction films since the early 1990s, including *Abortion: Desperate Choices* (1992), *Letting Go: A Hospice Journey* (1996), *Concert of Wills: Making the Getty Center* (1997), and *Lalee's Kin: The Legacy of Cotton* (2001), an Academy Award nominee for best feature-length documentary. Albert continues to shoot footage for these films, but as always, he plays no part in the editing process. He is now officially credited as a cinematographer, rather than as codirector. Thanks in large measure to the increasingly popular film festival circuit and to the support of HBO Films, the Maysles filmmakers have more opportunity to reach a wider audience than they have had in many years. In 2002, Froemke asserted that the company was still devoted to carrying on its initial "verité mission" and was still seeking "the most interesting ways filmically to tell a story."[14] Meanwhile, Maysles Shorts, the commercial-producing arm of Maysles Films, has continued to flourish, making direct cinema-style commercials and short industrial films. In 2004, filmmaker and cinematographer Robert Leacock, son of Richard, joined Maysles Shorts and will be a principal force of that branch of the company.

At the same time, films in the Maysles catalog continue to generate interest, in some cases even more than they did at the time of their original release. *Salesman*, which finally reached a national audience in 1990 when PBS aired it as part of its "P.O.V." series, has screened in numerous retrospectives and was named to the Library of Congress's list of one hundred films "saluted for their historical, cultural, and aesthetic significance."[15] National re-releases of *Grey Gardens* and *Gimme Shelter* have brought new attention and new critical acclaim to those films. Indeed, both films enjoy something of a cult status: *Gimme Shelter* plays regularly on cable movie channels and is still featured as a midnight movie at college campuses across the country; *Grey Gardens* attracts a devoted following, many of whom know all the dialogue in the film and is especially popular among urban gay populations.[16] In 2000 and 2001, *Salesman, Grey Gardens,* and *Gimme Shelter* were all selected to be part of the Criterion Collection DVD series, which at this date includes nearly three hundred of the finest international films ever produced. With the full cooperation of Maysles Films, Criterion has restored these three films to superior quality and has added an exhaustive list of DVD extras, including directors' commentaries and rare recordings of the Maysles brothers and their subjects.

Albert's individual legacy has been publicly recognized via several film retrospectives and lifetime-achievement awards, most notably the American Society of Cinematographers' 1997 President's Award. Calling him the "father of direct cinema," the organization also wrote that Albert has "made a unique contribution to the art of filmmaking. . . . [H]is films include some of the most unique, interesting, and innovative works" ever made.[17] He is the only nonfiction filmmaker to have earned this award.

What is the broader legacy of the Maysles brothers' direct cinema films? Although there have been a few nonfiction films in the direct cinema mode since 1990 (notably, *Truth or Dare*, *The War Room*, *Unzipped*), some of which have fared well critically and financially, today few filmmakers hold rigidly to the original precepts of the genre. Rather, its techniques and conventions have been absorbed into the collective aesthetic consciousness of nonfiction filmmaking. Today's filmmaker often avoids voice-over narration, for instance, underscoring a greater trust in the audience. And filmmakers today make liberal use of the close-up, recognizing what the Maysles brothers consistently advocated: that the most-effective nonfiction films are about people instead of generalized issues; and an individual story in turn can be a powerful means of revealing larger truths. In addition, the controversy and debate surrounding direct cinema's claims to authenticity opened up more discussion about nonfiction film and ultimately helped lead to an expansion of the definition of what a documentary could be. Albert and David thereby paved the way for future nonfiction filmmakers like Michael Moore and Erroll Morris, whose commercial successes would not have been possible without forerunners priming an audience of nonfiction viewers.

With the advent of videotape and then digital photography, hand-held cameras have become commonplace, and so has the kind of on-the-scene filmmaking that was so revolutionary in the late 1950s and early 1960s. Audiences today frequently see live or videotaped footage of unrehearsed, spontaneously unfolding scenes—whether the Rodney King beating, the panic-stricken students and faculty of Columbine High School, or O. J. Simpson's Bronco ride—so that aspect of direct cinema's novelty has certainly dissipated. Moreover, because television news shows and documentary programs have adopted many of direct cinema's aesthetic and philosophical principles, real events are continually played out in front of the television viewer. In the 1990s, shows like *Cops*, CBS News's *48 Hours*, and MTV's *Real World* have tapped into people's fascination with reality, banking on the fact that audiences will find actual events more exciting than anything concocted by Hollywood.[18] Even more recently, reality-based shows like *Survivor*, *The Amazing Race*, *Newlyweds*, and even the *Osbournes* abound in the prime-time line-up. (One could argue that many of these programs are as indebted to the classic game show or situation comedy as they are to documentary film, but viewers' desire for "authentic" programming fuels their fascination with such product.) This of course has taken the contemporary version of direct cinema in a more commercialized and less humanistic direction than the Maysles brothers would have hoped.

Still, the Maysles brothers' most important legacy is that subsequent generations of filmmakers will strive to depict, as Albert described, "a direct relationship with reality. . . . We're interested in what you can't escape from and presenting it."[19] That is a more problematic goal than Albert himself has realized, yet the striving for ever-greater authenticity in film has its roots in direct cinema—and in the modernist impulse that dominated arts of all media in the twentieth century. The brothers adhered to an unshakable faith that what they were doing was worthwhile and had integrity and that the people they filmed were worth knowing. Despite sometimes being dismissed as condescending, the brothers never expressed anything but positive feelings toward the people they filmed, even if they did not admire every activity in which those people were engaged. They faced the truth and tried to present that truth as authentically as they could. A self-proclaimed "religiously committed documentarian," Albert has asserted that the "essential thing about our work is not making believe, but finding out."[20] In 1969, David told *Newsweek* magazine, "We think of each film as a sort of trip. And if we knew what was going to happen, we would be terribly bored and we would never make a film about it."[21] That idealism, that spirit of adventure, of traveling down an unknown road, infused all of the Maysles brothers' films and continues to be at the heart of the Maysles Films projects.

Filmography
Notes
Bibliography
Index

Filmography

This list of the Maysles brothers' major works is divided into two time periods. The first includes films made by Albert and David Maysles, with collaborators when that was the case, before David's death in 1987; the second period includes all major Maysles Films productions completed after David died. The filmmaker credits are given as they are officially listed by Maysles Films.

1962–1986

Showman. Albert and David Maysles. 1962.
What's Happening! The Beatles in the U.S.A. Albert and David Maysles. 1964.
Meet Marlon Brando. Albert and David Maysles. 1965.
With Love from Truman: A Visit with Truman Capote. Albert and David Maysles. 1966.
Salesman. Maysles Brothers and Charlotte Zwerin. 1968.
Gimme Shelter. David and Albert Maysles, Charlotte Zwerin. 1970.
Christo's Valley Curtain. Maysles Brothers and Ellen Hovde. 1974.
Grey Gardens. David and Albert Maysles, Ellen Hovde, Muffie Meyer, Susan Froemke. 1976.
Running Fence. David and Albert Maysles and Charlotte Zwerin. 1978.
Muhammad and Larry. David and Albert Maysles. 1980.
Vladimir Horowitz: The Last Romantic. David and Albert Maysles, Susan Froemke, Deborah Dickson, Pat Jaffe. 1985.
Ozawa. David and Albert Maysles, Susan Froemke, Deborah Dickson. 1985.
Islands. Albert and David Maysles and Charlotte Zwerin. 1986.

1987–2001

Horowitz Plays Mozart. Albert Maysles, Susan Froemke, Charlotte Zwerin. 1987.
Jessye Norman Sings Carmen. Susan Froemke and Albert Maysles. 1989.
Christo in Paris. Albert Maysles, David Maysles, Deborah Dickson, Susan Froemke. 1990.

Soldiers of Music: Rostropovich Returns to Russia. Susan Froemke, Peter Gelb, Albert Maysles, Bob Eisenhardt. 1991.

Abortion: Desperate Choices. Susan Froemke, Deborah Dickson, Albert Maysles. 1992.

Conversations with the Rolling Stones. Susan Froemke, Kathy Dougherty, Albert Maysles. 1994.

Umbrellas. Henry Corra, Grahame Weinbren, Albert Maysles. 1995.

Letting Go: A Hospice Journey. Susan Froemke, Deborah Dickson, Albert Maysles. 1996.

Concert of Wills: Making the Getty Center. Susan Froemke, Bob Eisenhardt, Albert Maysles. 1997.

Recording The Producers. Susan Froemke, Kathy Dougherty. 2001.

Lalee's Kin: The Legacy of Cotton. Susan Froemke, Deborah Dickson, Albert Maysles. 2001.

Notes

1: DIRECT CINEMA AND THE MAYSLES BROTHERS

1. Richard Leacock, "Richard Leacock Remembers the Origins of 'Direct Cinema,'" 253–54.

2. James Blue, "Thoughts on Cinéma Vérité and a Discussion with the Maysles Brothers," 23.

3. Stephen Mamber, *Cinéma Vérité in America: Studies in Uncontrolled Documentary*, 71.

4. Louis Marcorelles and Andre S. Labarthe, "An Interview with Robert Drew and Richard Leacock," 19. On the early history of direct cinema, see P. J. O'Connell, *Robert Drew and the Development of Cinéma Vérité in America*.

5. Robert L. Drew, "An Independent with the Networks," 393.

6. Erik Barnouw, *Documentary: A History of Non-fiction Film*, 254–55. For early comparisons of the French and American styles, see Peter Graham, "Cinéma Vérité in France," and Louis Marcorelles, "Nothing But the Truth."

7. On issues of authenticity, see especially Doug Rossinow, *The Politics of Authenticity: Liberalism, Christianity, and the New Left in America*; Kenneth Cmiel, "The Politics of Civility," in David Farber, ed., *The Sixties: From Memory to History*, 263–90; and Marshall Berman, *The Politics of Authenticity: Radical Individualism and the Emergence of Modern Society*. On social critics, see Daniel Joseph Singal, "Towards a Definition of American Modernism," in Singal, ed., *Modernist Culture in America*, 20; Allen J. Matusow, *The Unraveling of America: A History of Liberalism in the 1960s*, 386–88; Rossinow, 280, 297. On social science, see Clifford Geertz, *The Interpretation of Cultures: Selected Essays*, and James Clifford, *The Predicament of Culture*. On the New Left specifically, see James Miller, *"Democracy Is in the Streets": From Port Huron to the Siege of Chicago*, which includes the "Port Huron Statement," and Kevin Mattson, *Intellectuals in Action: The Origins of the New Left and Radical Liberalism, 1945–1970*.

8. Miller, 16; 144 (quoting SDS leader Tom Hayden). However, "authenticity was never explicitly defined in the *Port Huron Statement*" even though "Tom Hayden had linked authenticity with 'genuine independence' and 'an intuitive

alertness to that which is capable of occurring'" (205). Authenticity was a slippery concept but "it was an ideal that captured some deep meaning," according to SDS activist Sharon Jeffrey (205).

9. Singal, 20.

10. Drew, 393. See also O'Connell, 22–25.

11. Paul Arthur, "Jargons of Authenticity (Three American Moments)," in Michael Renov, ed., *Theorizing Documentary*, 119.

12. Albert uses the term *truthful witness* in an interview with filmmaker Hamid Naficy (Naficy, "'Truthful Witness': An Interview with Albert Maysles," 156, 157).

13. Blue, "Thoughts," 23. Louis Marcorelles, a leading French film critic for the influential *Cahiers du Cinema*, concurred. See M. Ali Issari and Doris A. Paul, *What Is Cinéma Vérité?*, 127.

14. The origin of the term *direct cinema* has been the subject of some debate. In explaining the origin of the phrase, Albert also stated his working philosophy: "To classify these things is some kind of sin. Nevertheless, people force us into giving it a name. So the name 'direct' came into being—if only because people are set off on a rampage by the use of the word 'verite.' I think the word 'direct' is more dispassionate. We go directly to things as they take place, and almost in spite of ourselves we are bound to come up with something that's more truthful" (Robert Phillip Kolker, "Circumstantial Evidence: An Interview with David and Albert Maysles," 185). Albert may have first used the term publicly in an interview published in *Film Comment* in 1964: "If you have to use a label, I suppose direct cinema is the one that's the most meaningful. What we're doing is direct in every way" (Maxine Haleff, "The Maysles Brothers and 'Direct Cinema,'" 22). In his survey of film history, Robert Sklar confirms that Albert dubbed the term *direct cinema*; Barnouw concurs (Sklar, *Film: An International History of the Medium*; Barnouw, 240).

15. On the Maysles brothers' technical innovations, see Brooke Comer, "Man of the People," 86; Charles Reynolds, "Focus on Al Maysles," 400–5.

16. Haleff, 22, 19; Kolker, 186.

17. To cite one example of many: "The whole thing is based on faith . . . the most outlandish faith" (qtd. in Lawrence Van Gelder, "Maysles: Filming the Impossible," 1).

18. Blue, "Thoughts," 24; Reynolds, 401; Blue (interviewing Leacock), "One Man's Truth," 406.

19. Marcorelles, "Nothing but the Truth," 117.

20. Boston Film and Video Foundation Master Class, 11 June 1998, as quoted in the *Fourth Annual Boston Film/Video Foundation Vision Award Ceremony Honoring Albert Maysles*, 21.

21. Comer, 86.

22. Naficy, 159.

23. Kolker, 184. Sometimes Albert can take this point too far, as when he said in 1971: "Our motivations for making films aren't intellectual ones" (qtd. in Arthur, 119).

24. Rosenthal, *New Documentary*, 82.

25. Kolker, 185.

26. Blue, "Thoughts," 24.

27. Calvin Pryluck, "Seeking to Take the Longest Journey: A Conversation with Albert Maysles," 13.

28. Blue, "Thoughts," 22; Kolker, 184.

29. Albert and David Maysles, "Direct Cinema," 31.

30. Naficy, 168.

31. Richard M. Barsam, "American Direct Cinema: The *Re*-Presentation of Reality," 140, 146.

32. Tony Pinkney has perhaps best described the bedeviling nature of modernism: "Modernism is the most frustratingly unspecific, the most recalcitrantly unperiodizing, of all the major art-historical 'isms' or concepts" (Introduction, in Raymond Williams, *The Politics of Modernism: Against the New Conformists*, 3). My discussion of modernism is informed by a wide range of sources, especially David Davidson, "Direct Cinema and Modernism: The Long Journey to *Grey Gardens*"; Andreas Huyssen, "Mass Culture as Woman: Modernism's Other," in *After the Great Divide: Modernism, Mass Culture, Postmodernism*; Fredric Jameson, *Postmodernism, or, The Cultural Logic of Late Capitalism* and *Signatures of the Visible*; Gilberto Perez, *The Material Ghost: Films and Their Medium*; Daniel Joseph Singal, "Towards a Definition of American Modernism," in Singal, ed., *Modernist Culture in America*; Raymond Williams, *The Politics of Modernism: Against the New Conformists*; and Slavoj Zizek, *Looking Awry: An Introduction to Jacques Lacan Through Popular Culture*.

33. Singal, 4.

34. As quoted in Perez, 369.

35. Perez, 292–93; 371, et passim.

36. Malcolm Le Grice, *Abstract Film and Beyond*. In the United States, experimental filmmaking took on a slightly less radical tone in the 1920s and 1930s. Several factors help to explain this difference: The nation historically had a less-developed propensity towards radical expression of any kind; World War I had been less devastating to Americans; and, perhaps most importantly, commercial story films had swallowed up nearly everyone who had the resources or expertise to make films. In any event, there are very few American films from this period that fully embrace the art-for-art's-sake mentality of the European artistic circles. *Manhatta*, a film made by photographer Paul Strand and artist Charles Sheeler in 1920 and 1921, comes closest. Jan-Christopher Horak has compiled a group of essays that trace the development of avant-garde film in the United States from 1919 to 1945. Horak widens the definition of avant-garde to include all films that express "a formal opposition to classical Hollywood cinema" (6). He shows that American filmmakers "demonstrated a wild eclecticism" and "an extremely contradictory relationship to the modernist project" (30) (*Lovers of Cinema: The First American Film Avant-Garde 1919–1945*).

37. David Hollinger, "The Knower and the Artificer," in Singal, 43, 49.

38. Ray Carney, *The Films of John Cassavetes: Pragmatism, Modernism, and the Movies*, 163–64, 95.

39. Kolker, 185.

40. Kolker, 184. Robert Drew said "that there was something about sitting at an editing table hour after hour that immobilized" Albert Maysles (396).

41. Alan Rosenthal, "Ellen Hovde: An Interview," 9.

42. Blue, "Thoughts," 24. Even Stephen Mamber, generally friendly to direct cinema, acknowledges that "editing can be as much a form of 'fictionalization' as scripting or acting. It is often harder to spot, possibly insidious, and sometimes scarcely credible." Therefore, the "sanctimonious repetition of the claim to undiluted reality" purported both by the filmmakers and within the films themselves by the opening narration, potentially "undermin[es] the whole approach" (126).

43. Naficy, 166. Interviews with the Maysles brothers' collaborators confirm this opinion. Susan Jaffe, "Editing Cinéma Vérité"; Rosenthal, "Ellen Hovde" and "Charlotte Zwerin," in Rosenthal, *The New Documentary*, 86–91. The films achieve a greater complexity as a result, contends Gerald O'Grady in "Just Two Guys," 9.

44. Blue, 29.

45. Reynolds, 402.

2: CELEBRITY AND AUTHENTICITY: THE FILMS OF 1962–1966

1. Albert Maysles, "Letter to the Editor," 64.

2. Maxine Haleff, "The Maysles Brothers and Direct Cinema," 20. Albert Maysles noticed, "Movie camera manufacturers are very concerned with camera engineering, but they are not concerned enough with human engineering" (qtd. in Charles Reynolds, "Focus on Al Maysles," 404). He relates that "by positioning the viewing tube of the Angenieux zoom lens on my camera above the camera itself, the camera is always out of my field of view. In addition, all the controls are completely visible to the cameraman by simply glancing down" (404).

3. Haleff, 20; Reynolds, 401, 404. Occasionally David would place a second remote microphone on the subject being filmed. See also Jonas Mekas, "Movie Journal," 21.

4. Daniel J. Boorstin, *The Image: A Guide to Pseudo-Events in America*. David Riesman, "The Uncommitted Generation." Tom Hayden quoted in James Miller, *"Democracy Is in the Streets": From Port Huron to the Siege of Chicago*, 144.

The classic Marxist text on this point is Horkheimer and Adorno's "The Culture Industry: Enlightenment as Mass Deception." For a discussion of this and other important works on the same topic, see P. David Marshall, *Celebrity and Power: Fame in Contemporary Culture*, 9–12.

5. Boorstin, 19.

6. Quoted in Joshua Gamson, *Claims to Fame: Celebrity in Contemporary Amer-ica*, 57.

7. On the difficult process of getting Jane Fonda to stop acting, see P. J. O'Connell, *Robert Drew and the Development of Cinéma Vérité in America*, 138–41.

8. Quoted in James Blue, "Thoughts on Cinéma Vérité and a Discussion with the Maysles Brothers," 29.

9. "Maysles Brothers," 114. On the making of *Showman*, see Mark Shivas and Ian Cameron, "Cinéma Vérité," 19.

10. Quoted in Gerald O'Grady, "Just Two Guys," *Fourth Annual Boston Film/ Video Foundation Vision Award Ceremony Honoring Albert Maysles*, 7. O'Grady notes David's interesting use of the pronoun *we* as if the brothers somehow "shared a shoulder" (11).

11. Maysles Films mission statement, Maysles Films, New York, 2002.

12. "Maysles Brothers," 114. Susan Jaffe, a cinéma vérité editor, compliments the brothers for "allowing the film a leisurely pace—by refusing to hoke it up with fast cutting or excessive narration. . . . [T]he job of the film maker is to preserve the spark that is kindled by the ordinary interchange of people and events" ("Editing Cinéma Vérité," 47).

13. Peter Graham, "Cinéma Vérité in France," 34. Two other writers indicated that the Maysles brothers were "lucky" that this "childhood poverty" revelation occurred during their watch (see Shivas and Cameron, 19; and M. Ali Issari and Doris A. Paul, *What Is Cinéma Vérité?*, 125). To some extent, of course, direct cinema does rely on the fortuitous unfolding of interesting and revealing human moments, but pointing to the Maysles brothers' fortune seems to downplay their own ability to be ready for and to capture sensitively such moments.

14. On audience reactions, see Blue, 23–24; Graham, 40; Reynolds, 400; Shivas and Cameron, 19.

15. Among others, Italian director Roberto Rossellini criticized the "formless and shapeless" film (qtd. in Louis Marcorelles, "Nothing but the Truth," 117; see also O'Grady, 10–11).

16. Quoted in Issari and Paul, 130. Elsewhere, Marcorelles raved that *Showman* "seemed to me to be the most beautiful, the purest" of the films shown at a Lyon festival. "I would easily rank it among the ten or fifteen great films that it has been my fortune to see since the war" (qtd. in Haleff, 20).

17. Reynolds, 402.

18. Mekas, 21.

19. Blue, 27.

20. "Maysles Brothers," 114; Naficy, "'Truthful Witness': An Interview with Albert Maysles," 162–63.

21. Blue, 29.

22. Kenneth Cmiel, "The Politics of Civility," in David Farber, ed., *The Sixties: From Memory to History*, 275–76. Cmiel argues, for example, that when the Beatles burst on the scene, the discussion of long hair did not zero in on the "basic rottenness of a civilization" but had a much more innocent and fun-loving dimension. It was not until the late 1960s that long hair seemed to stand for something more profound. See also Hunter Davies, *The Beatles*, 189–94.

23. George Lipsitz, "Who'll Stop the Rain? Youth Culture and Social Crises," in Farber, 212.

24. See, for example, George Harrison, *I Me Mine*, 15–45; Mamber, 147–49.

25. Davies, 194–96.

26. Indeed, the film ultimately did its part too well. Once the group was recognized as a hugely successful business venture, the Beatles were quickly steered into entertainment films, beginning with *A Hard Day's Night* in 1964. When that project was slated, the Beatles' management refused to allow the Maysles brothers' documentary further distribution (Comer, "Man of the People," 86–87).

27. Robert Steele, "Meet Marlon Brando," 2.

28. Steele, 4.

29. Marshall, 90.

30. "Maysles Brothers," 114; Mekas, 21.

31. Mekas, 21.

32. Mekas, 21.

33. Gamson, 156. The postmodern celebrity and fan are much more skeptical than their predecessors. Thus Madonna's documentary/biography *Truth or Dare* (Alex Keshishian, 1991) is not a film that reveals the surprising fact that Madonna is a controlling guardian and manipulator of her own image but rather a film in which she and her audience can share a kind of inside joke about celebrity manipulation while they all agree to love and appreciate her as a hard-working artist. Madonna's then-boyfriend Warren Beatty's on-camera objections to her manipulations may be on target, but in the context of the film, they are brushed off as old-fashioned.

34. Howard Thompson, "Film Festival: Something for Youths," 78; Steele, 2; Comer, 87.

35. Boorstin, 57, 61.

3: *SALESMAN* AND THE LIMITS OF LANGUAGE

1. For general background on the making of *Salesman*, see Alan Rosenthal, "Salesman," in Rosenthal, ed., *The New Documentary in Action*, 77–80; Howard Junker, "Production Notes," in *Salesman: A Film by the Maysles Brothers and Charlotte Zwerin*, 106–21; Erik Barnouw, *Documentary: A History of Non-fiction Film*, 241–44; Bob Sitton, "An Interview with Albert and David Maysles," 13–15. The Criterion Collection's 2001 DVD release of *Salesman* also features audio commentary by Albert Maysles and Charlotte Zwerin.

2. Junker, 108, 110, 117; Rosenthal, 79; 81–82.

3. Sitton, 13.

4. Walker Gibson, "Introduction," in Gibson, *The Limits of Language*, ix.

5. Walker Gibson, "A Note on Style and the Limits of Language," in Gibson, 105.

6. Daniel Joseph Singal, "Towards a Definition of American Modernism," in Singal, *Modernist Culture in America*, 13.

7. Singal, 19.

8. Albert Maysles, audio commentary, Criterion Collection DVD of *Salesman* (2001). In an earlier interview, Albert spoke of "an idealism about life. *Salesman*

could have been merely about exploitation, about people hurting each other and doing unethical things. But our idealism consists in a childlike belief in life as it is" (Sitton, 18).

9. Junker, 113.

10. Junker, 120.

11. Blue, "Thoughts on Cinéma Vérité and a Discussion with the Maysles Brothers," 30; Jonas Mekas, "Movie Journal," 21.

12. Zwerin notes that she and David "saw things the same way," and she worked well with the younger Maysles on this project (Zwerin, audio commentary, *Salesman* DVD).

13. Timothy B. Spears, *One Hundred Years on the Road: The Traveling Salesman in American Culture*, 1–2.

14. Truman E. Moore, *The Traveling Man: The Story of the American Traveling Salesman*, 231.

15. Moore, 161.

16. Victor P. Buell, "Door-to-Door Selling," 38, 36.

17. Spears, 3–4; Moore, 224–25; literary models include Eugene O'Neill's *The Iceman Cometh* and Booth Tarkington's *Penrod*. On the converse, several Norman Rockwell covers for *Saturday Evening Post* took a more nostalgic and sympathetic look at the traveling salesman.

18. Moore, chapters 12–15, and especially 171; Buell, 39–41. The Bursk and Hutchison sales management book includes chapters entitled "What Makes a Good Salesman" and "Get the Most Out of Your Sales Force."

19. The entire creed may be found in Richard M. Baker Jr. and Gregg Phifer, *Salesmanship: Communication, Persuasion, Perception*, 20–21.

20. Of course, this kind of demanding work ethic predates the traveling salesman; Puritan settlers ascribed to it, and their descendants helped foster in the young nation a spirit of individualism through hard work and independent accomplishment. Benjamin Franklin took the idea of the self-made man in a more secular direction, but even in Franklin, the rhetoric has a certain spiritual quality. Not surprisingly, then, the inspirational messengers who encouraged salesmen in the 1950s and 1960s took a quasi-religious position, preaching a "gospel of salesmanship [that] was harsh in its demands on the individual" (Moore, 223). The grandfather of these "business evangelists" was Russell Conwell, Baptist minister and founder of Temple University, whose "Acres of Diamonds" public presentations "combined the American taste for emotional, inspiring lectures and sermons with the democratic belief that anything could be done by a free man of solid resolve" (Moore, 222). Bruce Barton took the religion-work nexus in an even more direct and bizarre direction. His best-selling *The Man Nobody Knows* (1925) called Jesus the most successful adman ever, praising the historical figure for his religious fervor and business acumen (Spears, 8; Moore, 229–30).

21. Unfortunately, many of those who have written or spoken about this film—including, usually, the Maysles brothers and Zwerin themselves—have treated *Salesman* as "Paul's film" (see, e.g., Zwerin's interview with Alan Rosenthal in

"Salesman," *The New Documentary*, 86–91). The film should not be categorized so neatly as the study of one man and his way of life, as many have been quick to do, because that reading of the film unfairly limits it. It also often leads critics to pan the film. Brennan's story "fails," they believe, to hold our interest strongly enough or to rise to the level of true tragedy (see, e.g., Ernest Callenbach, "Short Notices: *Salesman*," 54–55; and Joseph Morgenstern, "God and Country," 116, 120). Even Stephen Mamber, whose overview of direct cinema includes many close readings of the numerous films he mentions, falls victim to this trap, spending the majority of the pages devoted to *Salesman* discussing whether Brennan's situation merited the film's focus (*Cinéma Vérité in America: Studies in Uncontrolled Documentary*, 161–69).

22. Zwerin defends her editing choices, even though she notes that the "cinéma vérité police" have chastised her for this scene. She feels confident that because Paul has been to these sales meetings many times before and can clearly envision what they will be like, he is in fact pondering his own sales slump vis-à-vis the more positive testimonials he knows he will hear in Chicago (Zwerin, audio commentary, *Salesman* DVD). The scene represents one of the few times direct cinema convention is violated in this film. Albert did not particularly like this scene for that reason, calling the crosscutting an "artificial device" that was "so unlike us" (Robert Phillip Kolker, "Circumstantial Evidence: An Interview with David and Albert Maysles," 184). For a shrewd analysis of the "violations of direct cinema's code" in this film, see Stella Bruzzi, *New Documentary: A Critical Introduction*, 70–73.

23. Moore, chapter 14.

24. Baker and Phifer, 140.

25. Sitton, 15; Rosenthal, 77–78.

26. As quoted in *The Fourth Annual Boston Film/Video Foundation Vision Award Ceremony Honoring Albert Maysles*, 24.

27. Albert Maysles, audio commentary, *Salesman* DVD.

28. Mamber, 169.

29. John Craddock, "*Salesman*, a Review," 8.

30. Like Miller, some said, the Maysles brothers had exposed the dark underbelly of the American dream or the American success myth, with Paul Brennan standing in for Willy Loman as a tragic common man (see, e.g., Hollis Alpert, "That Great Territory in the Sky"; Sitton, 14; Judith Crist, review of *Salesman*).

In the end, both Miller's play and the Maysles/Zwerin film raise important questions about the life of a salesman; both are realistic in that they detail the pressures facing many individual salesmen, especially in light of a pervasive and abnegating individual work ethic. Both Willy Loman and Paul Brennan come to doubt themselves, and in a profession in which confidence is vital, their self-doubt undermines their performances as salesmen and simultaneously causes each man to think less of himself. Their plights call attention to the inherent flaws in a materialistic society that equates individual worth with sales production. Neither work offers a solution. Willy's suicide and Paul's impending return to Boston make it clear that they cannot tolerate their respective situations, but neither the play nor the film instructs the audience how to learn from these particular cases and make meaningful changes in society. In this regard, *Salesman*, a product of direct cinema, is traditionally nonsolution oriented.

The brothers themselves rejected comparison to Miller's play. Albert distinguished *Salesman* from the Miller play particularly in terms of process:

> One great difference is that when a playwright begins to set down his play, he necessarily has to start with the general and then specify the particular. He has in mind a certain character, and in the descriptive process he fits in all the facts of that imagined person's life. The process with us is entirely different. We select particular people about whom we know very little. We are prepared at any moment to change our notions about them. In the process of watching and setting down the particulars, maybe we reach generalizations; maybe we never do. (Sitton, 14)

Adds David, "We discover everything in the filming. We discover the theme and the point of view" (Sitton, 14). Obviously, Miller cannot discover his theme as he presents his play to an audience; he has written a script, not an outline for an improvisation. The Maysles brothers seemed more comfortable with a different comparison, as when David noted, "Ours are more O'Neill characters than Miller characters. Miller's characters are all more or less external. You don't get very close to them. . . . However, the tragic condition of O'Neill's characters is timeless. Their dilemmas are relevant to any age" (Sitton, 14). Interestingly, Miller, who saw and enjoyed *Salesman* "immensely" according to Vincent Canby of the New York *Times*, qualified his praise by noting that films such as *Salesman* could only scratch the surface of a person's life. There is no past available to the audience so "you are stopped at the wall of skin" (Canby, "*Salesman*, a Slice of America," 32).

31. P. J. O'Connell, *Robert Drew and the Development of Cinéma Vérité in America*, 202–3.

32. John Simon, "A Variety of Hells," 466–67.

33. Stanley Kauffmann, "Salesman," 24, 32; Callenbach, 54, 55.

34. "Byro," Review of *Salesman*, *Variety*, 26 February 1969; Simon, 468; New York critic quoted in "*Salesman*," *FilmFacts* 12 (May 1969), 179; Crist, 55.

35. Junker, 121.

36. Craddock, 12; Canby, 32. Other supportive comments: In the San Francisco *Chronicle*, critic Paine Knickerbocker remarked, "The Maysles' offer only the report . . . no mockery, no condescension marks the picture" (qtd. in "*Salesman*," *FilmFacts*, 179). Hollis Alpert also understood this: The Maysles brothers "are much more than reporters; they sense the drama in ordinary lives. Above all, they are human and compassionate" (75). In his history of direct cinema, Richard M. Barsam argues that the film avoids condescension because it manages "control of the tension between film form and content. . . . It is Zwerin's editing that maintains this tension between the Maysles' affection for Paul Brennan [expressed in interviews if not directly in the film itself] and their desire to remain objective

in filming" ("American Direct Cinema: The *Re*-Presentation of Reality," 146). Zwerin reported that she had to work to like Paul as she saw him only in the film rushes, whereas she knew David and Albert had a genuine affection for him (Rosenthal, 88).

37. Sitton, 13.

38. Rosenthal, 87.

39. Junker, 116. The *New Yorker's* Penelope Gilliatt exemplifies this kind of critic's discomfort. In her review ("The Current Cinema: About Thy Father's Door-To-Door Business"), she maintained that the people in the film often behave awkwardly, betraying an awareness of the camera's presence. At times, they seem like "children who have run out of words [and] have been told to go on talking and being natural while Daddy finishes the reel in a home-movie camera" (149).

40. Paul Johnson's *A Shopkeeper's Millennium: Society and Revivals in Rochester, New York, 1815–1837* illustrates how an emergent bourgeois in upstate New York turned to the religious revivals of the Second Great Awakening as a means of easing their anxiety about the sundry societal changes they were experiencing (and actively pursuing). Johnson, influenced strongly by the work of Emile Durkheim, argues, "Revivals were a means of building order and a sense of common purpose among sovereign, footloose, and money-hungry individualists" (9).

41. As quoted in Barsam, 139.

42. Alpert, 75. The glowing review concludes, "Obviously their work is infused with a point of view; it wouldn't be so effective otherwise. But nevertheless they see clearly; at the same time they feel for, even admire, their subjects as they attempt to fulfill the American dream by selling washable Bibles. Their film is strong without being harsh. It must be seen." Sitton, 13. Mamber, 161. Others agreed. Andrew Sarris referred to the film as the brothers' "masterwork . . . a miraculously merciful contemplation of lives of drab desperation such as never been seen on any movie screen" (56). John Craddock says *Salesman* "is a classic, perhaps the definitive, direct cinema film" (10). Joseph Gelmis of *Newsday* wrote it was "the most important film you will see this year" (qtd. in "*Salesman*," *FilmFacts*, 180). In an otherwise mixed review, *Time* magazine called it "surely one of the most moving and accomplished examples of cinéma vérité so far" ("The Drawbacks of Reality," 83). Barnouw quote, 241. The same space was afforded the film in the 1983 and 1993 editions of Barnouw's history, thereby testifying to *Salesman's* lasting historical significance.

43. Simon, 468.

4: CAN WE SEE HOW THEY LOOK?: OBSERVING THE ROLLING STONES IN *GIMME SHELTER*

1. As of early 1971, the brothers had lost "about $80,000 on a $200,000 investment" in *Salesman* (Winster, "Rages & Outrages," 47). However, in 1981, Albert reported they had lost as much as $150,000 on the film (Naficy, "'Truthful Witness': An Interview with Albert Maysles," 169). On the making of the film, see

Lester Bangs, et al., "Let It Bleed," *Rolling Stone*, 26. On the Criterion Collection DVD of *Gimme Shelter* (2000), Albert, Charlotte Zwerin, and sound editor Stanley Goldstein provide audio commentary that also elucidates much of the background to making the film.

2. Albert and David Maysles, "*Gimme Shelter*: Production Notes," 29. Albert reports in the audio commentary in the DVD version of *Gimme Shelter* that the Stones paid the brothers $14,000 to film at Madison Square Garden, then an additional $120,000 for the California trip. The film eventually would cost $500,000 to produce.

3. Norman Schreiber, "Desire and Discovery: A Film-maker's Journey," 33. Audio commentary, *Gimme Shelter*.

4. Held 16–18 August 1969, the festival in the rural town of Bethel, New York, epitomized the counterculture's self-proclaimed spirit of cooperation, with three hundred thousand people together for "three days of peace and music," mixed with an ample amount of sex, drugs, and alcohol. The subsequent film of that experience, Michael Wadleigh's *Woodstock* (1970), was an enormous box-office and public relations success, grossing millions of dollars and presenting a barrage of images, not only of the leading musical acts of the time but also of the counterculture turning peaceful ideals into reality. Within the film, Max Yasgur, on whose land the concert occurred, summarizes the positive impressions generated by Woodstock: "You've proven something to the world. . . . A half a million young people can get together and have three days of fun and music. And have nothing but fun and music. And I God-bless you for it."

5. *Rolling Stone* magazine, in a lengthy and thorough report, January, 1970, sardonically itemized ten decisions that had "worked out a blueprint for disaster" at Altamont:

1. Promise a free concert by a popular rock group which rarely appears in this country. Announce the site only four days in advance.
2. Change the location 20 hours before the concert.
3. The new concert site should be as close as possible to a giant freeway.
4. Make sure the grounds are barren, treeless, desolate.
5. Don't warn neighboring landowners that hundreds of people are expected. Be unaware of their out-front hostility toward long hair and rock music.
6. Provide one-sixtieth the required toilet facilities to insure that people will use nearby fields, the sides of cars, etc.
7. The stage should be located in an area likely to be completely surrounded by people and their vehicles.
8. Build the stage low enough to be easily hurdled. Don't secure a clear area between stage and audience.
9. Provide an unreliable barely audible low fidelity sound system.
10. Ask the Hell's Angels to act as "security" guards. (Bangs, 20)

Distributing blame to a wide range of factors and people, including the Rolling Stones and their well-tuned image as the bad boys of rock and roll, the magazine concluded, "Altamont was the product of diabolical egotism, hype, ineptitude, money manipulation, and, at base, a fundamental lack of concern for humanity."

There is still debate over the nature of the Hell's Angels' presence at the concert. Stanley Goldstein contends that Hell's Angels were not hired per se; rather there was an "unspoken agreement" that they would play their "traditional role" at a California outdoor concert, namely to surround the stage, establishing what was called "Angel Land," a buffer zone between the audience and the performers. The Grateful Dead and other San Francisco–based acts had been using Hell's Angels as security for years, generally paying them in beer or small amounts of cash. It was on their advice that the promoters and producers of Altamont hired—or at least tacitly accepted the inevitable presence of—the Angels for their event (Goldstein, audio commentary, *Gimme Shelter* DVD). David Crosby, for one, defended Hell's Angels after Altamont by referring to the "dozens" of events where they had behaved peacefully (Bangs, 30), so the extent of their violence at Altamont was unprecedented. They also enjoyed a certain cult status that had been reified through their depiction in Hollywood B-movies such as *The Wild Angels* (1967) and *The Savage Seven* (1968). Clearly, however, the faith in the motorcycle group was misplaced and naive. The Angels as a group tended to "subscribe to a highly ritualized code of behavior . . . that aspires, unlike Jagger and his minions, to undiluted authenticity," which included violence if necessary (Richard Porton, "*Gimme Shelter*: Dionysus at Altamont," 85). As for the Stones, apparently they had never been exposed to the "really real" Angels before. When they had employed Angels as security for a Hyde Park concert in London, they had actually gotten a mellower European version of Hell's Angels (Goldstein, audio commentary; Bangs, 34; Geoffrey Stokes, "Woodstock . . . and Altamont", in Ed Ward, Stokes, and Ken Tucker, *Rock of Ages: The Rolling Stone History of Rock and Roll*, 447–48).

6. Todd Gitlin, *The Sixties: Years of Hope, Days of Rage*, 406–8; Berkeley *Tribe* quoted in David Cauté, *The Year of the Barricades: A Journey Through 1968*, 448.

7. In *The Unraveling of America*, Allen J. Matusow notes that the Woodstock crowd "created a living community" amidst "disastrous" conditions, whereas at Altamont, "rock revealed an equal affinity for death" (304). The film *Gimme Shelter*, Matusow contends, reveals "as much as any counterculture document of the time . . . Thanatos unleashed" (305). The counterculture "faded" after 1970, he further argues, just after the Altamont concert, as its Dionysian impulses were "absorbed into the dominant culture and domesticated" (307). The contrast between the two events often invited overwrought metaphor: "The loving community of *Hair* was disintegrating into Hobbes's state of nature" (Cauté, 448). Even Geoffrey Stokes in an otherwise measured treatment of the event declares that it was at Altamont where "a generation's faith in itself was mortally wounded" (446) and later: "The era had been one of communalism, a coming together that reached its spiritual apex at Woodstock, its nadir at Altamont" (452). Admittedly, the "symbolism *was* too easy, but it was a way of making sense out of chaos" (446).

In actuality, Woodstock's publicized peacefulness proved to be an exception. The majority of festivals in 1969 were, like Altamont, marred by unruly behavior. In June, a rock music festival in Northridge, California, turned violent, leading to numerous injuries; police had to use tear gas at an Atlanta folk music festival in September to bring a crowd under control; a festival in West Palm Beach in November included confrontations with police and numerous arrests. Of course, even Woodstock had its downside: Three people died in accidents, numerous others endured bad trips, and scuffles broke out over food and water (Stokes, 428–29; see also "Breaking Boundaries, Testing Limits," episode 3, PBS film series *Making Sense of the Sixties*, David Hoffman, 1991).

8. Robert Phillip Kolker, "Circumstantial Evidence: An Interview with David and Albert Maysles," 186. In the same interview, David acknowledged that he and codirector Zwerin "were developing different themes" as they sought some sort of organizing principle for the film. "We had a hundred different formulas for the structure of the film at different stages. It just finally evolved into what it is. We could give you all the reasons why it is that way now, but we couldn't possibly give you those reasons before" (185–86).

9. John Berger, *Ways of Seeing*, 7. Gilberto Perez, *The Material Ghost: Films and Their Medium*, 287.

10. David and Albert Maysles, "*Gimme Shelter*: Production Notes." 29.

11. Kolker, 186.

12. Albert and David Maysles and Charlotte Zwerin, "A Response to Pauline Kael," in Kevin Macdonald and Mark Cousins, *Imagining Reality: The Faber Book of Documentary*, 394.

13. Although most reviewers and historians have insisted on describing *Gimme Shelter* as being *about* Altamont and the Hunter murder, at least one has recognized that the film is more accurately "a meditation on the excesses of celebratory zeal." Richard Porton's treatment of *Gimme Shelter* is one of only two published essays that deal with the film primarily as an artistic statement rather than as a documentary of an event or a rock group. In the film journal *Persistence of Vision*, Porton notes, correctly I believe, that *Gimme Shelter* marks a turning point in direct cinema, when the assumption that "unscripted documentaries suffused with an aura of spontaneity could unveil a reality that was relatively conclusive" or that could at least bring the audience closer to something more true than other documentaries or fiction (83). Porton goes on to illustrate the extent to which nearly everyone in the film is "engaged in a meticulous 'presentation of self,'" which renders virtually impossible any hope of reaching an objective assessment of their behavior (83). The "Apollonian detachment" that the filmmakers take in the film, via their "circumambient" structure, emphasizes their belief that the violence in Altamont is not easily explained nor easily accounted for (88). In 1971, English professor David Sadkin published "*Gimme Shelter*: A Corkscrew or a Cathedral?", an article meant to be a corrective to other contemporaneous criticism of the film. In the essay, Sadkin contends that the film must not be considered "in relation to what extent it was or was not accurate reporting. The film is not

journalism" (27). Instead, the end product "was created in the editing room and was true to the artists' view of the situation derived largely after the fact" (20). He argues that the filmmakers have *constructed* tension and an "atmosphere of self-delusion" through editing, with the film building toward the grim conclusion. The structure heightens the inevitability like a Greek tragedy, as if to suggest that everyone involved moved blindly toward a devastating finish they should have been wise enough to foresee. In this way, Sadkin read the film as an artistic rather than a journalistic success.

Occasionally in their treatments of individual segments within the film, both Sadkin and Porton miss the mark. Sadkin, for instance, calls the film's final image of concert-goers walking into bright sunlight "a terrible artistic misjudgment" that threatens to undermine what the Maysles brothers and Zwerin have established up to that point. Porton's essay, thick with theory, does not consider enough of the evidence within the film and emphasizes too strongly the negative role of attorney Melvin Belli. Still, in general their arguments do a valuable service to the film. Both men free *Gimme Shelter* from being something the filmmakers resisted and try to understand it on its artistic terms.

14. Bangs, 30, 31.

15. Stokes, 284–85. Paul Friedlander has also described the Stones's desire to imitate rhythm-and-blues singers (Paul Friedlander, *Rock and Roll: A Social History*, 109). Michael Hicks argues that the group "embodied the antagonism to which garage bands aspired" so they "adapted a rural black assertion of personal dissatisfaction into an urban white assertion of cultural repression" (Michael Hicks, *Sixties Rock: Garage, Psychedelic, and Other Satisfactions*, 26–27).

16. Maysles and Zwerin, 394.

17. On the issue of celebrity, see P. David Marshall, *Celebrity and Power: Fame in Contemporary Culture*, 46–56. The more recent concert/rock group profile film *Depeche Mode: 101* (Chris Hegedus and D. A. Pennebaker, 1988) effectively delineates, by following the parallel stories of a rock band on tour and a contingent of fans on a road trip of their own, how different are the experiences of celebrities and those who watch them.

18. Patrick MacFadden, "*Gimme Shelter*," 41.

19. In an essay on performance in personality-profile documentaries, William F. Van Wert argues that any time a performer is aware of being filmed, "We can be reasonably sure that we are witnessing a lie and not a reality, an artifice as opposed to a truth, a performance as opposed to a true personality." Everyone in *Gimme Shelter* performs constantly, according to Van Wert's reading (Van Wert, "The 'Hamlet Complex' or, Performance in the Personality-Profile Documentary," 258).

20. Leo Braudy, *The Frenzy of Renown: Fame and Its History*, 570.

21. Belli's performance in the film earned him harsh criticism. Richard Porton identifies Belli's "oleaginous presence" as a "farcical prelude to the mass hysteria at Altamont. . . . He appears to believe that his own self-infatuation will defeat any human or natural disaster" (Porton, 86–87). David Sadkin contends, "If the Stones did not realize what was going on in California, Belli surely did, and greed

must have been his major motive" (Sadkin, 22). On this matter, I tend to concur more with Joel Haycock's opinion that Belli "is reduced to a harmless comic figure" (Haycock, Review of *Gimme Shelter*, 60). See also Van Wert, 261–62.

22. Stanley Booth, who traveled with and wrote about the band, recalls, "A kid ran up to Mick, said 'I hate you,' and hit him in the face" (Stanley Booth, "The True Adventures of Altamont," *Gimme Shelter*, Criterion Collection DVD booklet).

23. David allegedly attempted to perform some on-site censoring at the concert, reportedly telling one of the several cameramen hired for the event not to film something that was "ugly." Producer Porter Bibb agreed this could have occurred because no one was "emotionally set" for what had happened at Altamont (Bangs, 31).

24. Craig McGregor, "Rock's 'We Are One' Myth," 5, 25. See also Doug Rossinow, *The Politics of Authenticity: Liberalism, Christianity, and the New Left in America.* For a more cynical account of the same issues, see Matusow, chapter 10.

25. Bangs, 22. Another observer reported that the stabbing occurred so close to Jagger that he could and should have seen it: "*If the Stones were looking*, they saw [the knife] too" (Bangs, 23; emphasis added).

26. Booth, 19.

27. While the freeze-frame of Jagger may be inconclusive, rock-music historian Geoffrey Stokes has surmised that Altamont did in fact have a sobering effect on the band. The Stones laid low in 1970, charting no new singles; their only musical release that year was, ironically, a live album compiled from the 1969 tour (Stokes, 450; see also Friedlander, 116). Jagger avoided the media spotlight. From late 1968 to early 1970, he had appeared in three other films besides *Gimme Shelter:* another more experimental documentary about the group, Jean-Luc Godard's *One Plus One (Sympathy for the Devil)*, which failed to attract audiences at the few art houses in which it played, and two fiction films, Tony Richardson's futuristic drama *Ned Kelly* and the debut film of British cinematographer-turned-director, Nicolas Roeg, the appropriately titled *Performance*, in which Jagger plays a mysterious hedonist. In all four films, Jagger's acting is much the same; the art of performance for him blurs the lines between fiction and documentary. His participation in the films not only garnered him more financial satisfaction but also highlighted his desire to create a particular kind of image. In the wake of the Altamont concert, however, Jagger backed away from this strategy of relentless media exposure. The band waited three years before allowing another concert film, and Jagger's next feature film appearance was not until 1991.

28. Zwerin appreciates the multiple interpretations of the more ambiguous ending. She also believes that part of Jagger's muted response on film has to do with his stunned understanding of his own vulnerability at Altamont. Hunter was brandishing his weapon only twenty feet from the stage and could have targeted any of the band members (Zwerin, audio commentary, *Gimme Shelter*). See also Sadkin, 26–27, for a less kind treatment of the decision-making process.

29. Sadkin, 27.

30. Initially, no one was interested in distributing the film. CBS rejected it for television broadcast, and other potential backers found it to "too depressing." Finally, a financier affiliated with Andy Warhol's Factory came through with enough money to get the film off the shelf and into movie theaters (Albert Maysles, audio commentary, *Gimme Shelter*).

31. MacFadden, 42. In the British film journal *Sight and Sound*, David Pirie offers a similar assessment, declaring that *Gimme Shelter* "communicates better than any other pop festival film the poignant desperate hopefulness of the occasion, as well as the helplessness of those caught up in it. . . . The faces we are shown span many emotions from gentleness to sheer hatred and, together with the apocalyptic tone of birth and death, they are less reminiscent of a pop jamboree than some kind of overwrought religious vision." Pirie describes the film as a "definitive record of the hippie experience," not because it painstakingly documents every detail leading up to Altamont but because it remains equivocal in its approach, "exploring both [the] vulnerable hedonistic idealism" of the counterculture as well as "its terrifying capacity for self-destruction" (Pirie, "*Gimme Shelter*," 227).

32. Haycock, 58.

33. Michael Goodwin, "Films" (review of *Gimme Shelter*), 58. These kinds of readings persisted. Years later, film historian Richard M. Barsam, generally a supporter of the Maysles brothers, wrote that *Gimme Shelter* "is unsatisfying precisely because it is so detached and thus overlooks the festival's significance as a major turning point of the decade." He sees the film as skillfully made but also as a missed opportunity (Barsam, "American Direct Cinema: The *Re*-presentation of Reality," 146). Elsewhere, his assessment of Altamont underscored why he wanted more from the film: "Clearly Altamont ended what Woodstock began" (Barsam, *Nonfiction Film: A Critical History*, 290).

34. Albert Goldman, "Delicately Handled Dynamite or a Whitewash of Jagger?", 9. John Simon, quoted in Sragow, "Critics," 18. (In a 1984 essay, Doug Tomlinson echoes Simon: "[T]he film attempts to relieve [Jagger] of any responsibility. . . . The directors do not contort the facts so much as present them in a biased way. The blame is shoved squarely onto the broad shoulders of the Hell's Angels, the hired peacekeepers for the concert" [Tomlinson, "Gimme Shelter," 172]). Haycock, 60.

35. Review, "*Gimme Shelter*," *Variety*, 25 November 1970, 13. Haycock, 60. Pauline Kael, "Beyond Pirandello," 112–15.

36. Maysles and Zwerin, 394.

37. Cauté, 448; Bangs, 22.

38. Sadkin, 24.

39. In an interview with the *New York Post*, Albert admitted that he and his brother "love life and tend to see good in everything." The article relayed, "When a picture like *Gimme Shelter* doesn't turn out like that, he begins to fear he may be some kind of Cassandra. . . . He would like to make a picture that glorifies life" (Winster, 47).

40. Stephen Mamber, "Cinéma Vérité and Social Concerns," 15. The brothers did forge a personal relationship with the Stones as the years went on; the film-makers and the band were united through the permanence of the popular film. Indeed, when the Stones wanted to make a short film about their 1994 reunion tour, they called Albert. The resulting twenty-four-minute film, *Conversations with the Rolling Stones*, was codirected by Susan Froemke, Kathy Dougherty, and Albert and was aired on the VH-1 network.

5: WORKING WITHIN THE LIMITATION OF REALITY:
THE CHRISTO FILMS

1. Hamid Naficy, "'Truthful Witness': An Interview with Albert Maysles," 164.

2. Ellin Stein, "It's a Wrap!", 10.

3. *Fourth Annual Boston Film/Video Foundation Vision Award Ceremony Honoring Albert Maysles*, 21. Since 1994, after the completion of the Maysles-Christo films, Christo and Jeanne-Claude have insisted on joint credit for all of their projects (see Charles Green, "Disappearing and Photography in Post-Object Art: Christo and Jeanne-Claude," 13–15).

4. Stein, 10; *Fourth Annual*, 21.

5. Michele Cone, "A Sublime Folly: Christo's *Running Fence*," 91.

6. Nancy Scott, "The Christo Films: *Christo's Valley Curtain* and *Running Fence*," 61.

7. Jonathan Fineberg, "Essay," 27.

8. Naficy, 158.

9. Scott, 62.

10. Robert Phillip Kolker, "Circumstantial Evidence: An Interview with David and Albert Maysles," 184.

11. Kolker, 185.

12. Victor Canby, "*Christo's Valley Curtain* Is a Real Tall Story," 20; Calvin Tomkins's comment appears on the VHS edition of *Christo's Valley Curtain*.

13. Dominique G. Laporté, *Christo*, 48; original emphasis.

14. Denise Hare, "Film" (review of *Running Fence*), 76.

15. Naficy, 158.

16. Hare, 76.

17. Ian Christie, Review of *Running Fence*, 28.

18. Additionally, the poor quality of the song's performance is not, unfortunately, "deliberate parody" as Christie suggested, but simply a less costly alternative to the Eagles's high-priced rendition. Judy Maysles, David's wife, acknowledged that the song "Take It to the Limit" was one of their favorites (*Fourth Annual*, 25).

19. Of course, this kind of criticism is not unique to the Christo projects. At least as long as artists have challenged tradition, as most of the important artists of the twentieth century had, there have been those who have ridiculed the artist and the art. If the New York Armory Show of 1913 serves as modern art's first great public statement in this country, then the criticism of that show also serves as the first great backlash against such art. A *New York Times* headline advised, "Nobody

who has been drinking is let in to see this show." The same newspaper featured illustrated parodies including "The Rude Descending a Staircase" (see *New York Times* 11 May 1913, et passim). Theodore Roosevelt weighed in, noting that the "extremists whose paintings and pictures were represented [in the show] are [not] entitled to any praise, save, perhaps that they have helped to break fetters" (The-odore Roosevelt, "A Layman's View of an Art Exhibition," *Outlook* 103, 29 March 1913, 719; for a summary of the range of responses to the Armory Show, see J. M. Mancini, "'One Term Is as Fatuous as Another': Responses to the Armory Show Reconsidered"). Although he did not care for the show, Roosevelt had identified the key ingredient of the artists whose works were in that exhibit. Many twentieth-century artists, Christo included, were and still are seeking to redefine art. In a modern world in which the photographer and the filmmaker can create highly realistic art, artists in other media often turned away from representational painting, drawing, or sculpture. They believed that they could comment more trenchantly on the world around them by broadening the notion of what art could be. "It is not what the artist makes," one art critic has noted, "but what he points out, identifies, labels, categorizes, that is art" (Marina Vaizey, *Christo*, 10). Such an artist looks first to challenge rather than to entertain or to please. Christo and Jeanne-Claude endeavor to create works that have some aesthetic or even theatrical value but, more importantly to them, that awakens the audiences to the world around them.

20. Richard Chon, "Once in a Lifetime," C1.

21. Calvin Tomkins, "Onward and Upward with the Arts: *Running Fence*," 54.

22. Laporté, 69–70.

23. Fineberg, 27.

24. A key difference was that the French tended to manipulate and transform the objects whereas Americans presented them as they were, for ironic effect (Tomkins, 46, 49).

25. Cone, 96.

26. Tomkins, 61.

27. Janet Maslin, "*Running Fence* Films Story of an Art Event," 11; Penelope Gilliatt, "The Current Cinema," 120; Alec Dann, "Don't Fence Me In," 15; Scott, 65.

28. Alfred Frankenstein, "Report from California: Christo's *Fence*, Beauty or Betrayal?" 58–61.

29. Cone, 92.

30. Tomkins, 45.

31. Tomkins, 80.

32. J. Hoberman, "Nylon Sheets and Vinyl Freaks," 51.

33. Christie, 28.

34. Cone, 91.

35. Chon, C1; Stephanie Morimoto, "Filmmaker Albert Maysles Addresses Salomon Crowd," 2.

6: LOOKING INTO *GREY GARDENS*

1. Michael Tolkin, "What Makes the Maysles Run?", 141. Alan Rosenthal, "Ellen Hovde: An Interview," 10–11. The audio commentary of the Criterion Collection's

DVD of *Grey Gardens* also features further comments from Albert, Susan Froemke, and Muffie Meyer on the background to making the film.

2. David Davidson's "Direct Cinema and Modernism: The Long Journey to *Grey Gardens*" does a thorough job of placing the film in a modernist context, utilizing the literary criticism of Irving Howe and Roger Shattuck. Kenneth Robson (in "Grey Gardens") focuses primarily on the unconventional narrative structure of the film, pointing out that "the aesthetic effect [is] very similar to that of many modernist novels" such as Virginia Woolf's *Mrs. Dalloway* (43).

3. In this way, the film is distinct from a postmodern text, even though postmodern art forms were coming to the fore at the time the Maysles brothers made *Grey Gardens*. One can only imagine the level of irony (an essential ingredient of postmodernism) that would have accompanied this film if virtually any other contemporary filmmaker had looked to the Beales as subjects. Moreover, the degree of autobiography and self-revelation would have been much greater in such a film; a few glimpses of Albert and David would be regarded (as it was by many critics) as not nearly revelatory enough. Or the film would have revolved around some dilemma, conflict, or dramatic question—for example, Will the Beales be evicted from their house due to health code violations? An interesting comparison is *Brother's Keeper* (Joe Berlinger and Bruce Sinofsky, 1992), the story of eccentric brothers living in seclusion in rural New York, whose lives are brought to the public's attention when one of the them is accused of killing another. (Berlinger started in the film business as a production assistant at Maysles Films.)

4. Jay Ruby, "The Image Mirrored: Reflexivity and the Documentary Film," 73.

5. The audience, of course, can easily read the newspaper clippings as well; the articles therefore become substitutes for voice-over narration. While the Maysles brothers maintained their opposition to narration (the one precept over which they would not be moved), the editors found a way around the requirement via the articles. The film is better off with this minimum amount of context as it establishes a certain degree of curiosity and empathy for the Beale women from the outset. It also links them to the Bouvier and Kennedy families, about which curiosity never seems to wane. While Ellen Hovde reported that she was not "fond of" the newspaper scene, she did want somehow to establish a context for the women. In true modernist fashion, Albert has argued that context was not important. The newspaper clippings represented a compromise (Rosenthal, "Ellen Hovde," 13). Susan Froemke and Muffie Meyer concur that there was a necessity for some background information and that they were "very against using a narrator" (audio commentary, *Grey Gardens* DVD).

6. Gilberto Perez, *The Material Ghost: Films and Their Medium*, 371. Reality itself, according to Albert, can frequently be unsettling. "[O]ur films make it damn near impossible to escape. We're interested in what you can't escape from and presenting it. One of the things that happens is that some people get a little edgy when they see something that is of most value to them because it is so personal. They don't know where to turn to look for the kind of buffer that most movies give them" (qtd. in Lawrence Van Gelder, "Maysles: Filming the Impossible," 19).

7. Rosenthal, "Ellen Hovde," 11.

8. Personal interview with Susan Froemke, New York, New York, 22 July 2002.

9. Hovde related that the pink room scene "happened very near the beginning of the shooting. . . . And when we saw that, it moved us, we thought we had something. . . . [W]e thought it gave us some kind of insight into the relationship between these two women, and what kind of pain they could cause each other" (Rosenthal, "Ellen Hovde," 10). Froemke agrees, adding that once they had that scene, they felt they had an ending to the film, something "that they were cutting *to*" (Froemke interview).

10. As quoted in Leendert Drukker, "Cinéma Vérité: End of the Trail?", 70.

11. Drukker, 70.

12. A feminist reading makes even more sense when one considers that three women worked on this film for nearly two years. *Grey Gardens* reflects their deep interests and concerns (audio commentary, *Grey Gardens* DVD; Froemke interview).

13. Rosenthal, "Ellen Hovde," 11; Norman Schreiber, "Desire and Discovery: A Film-maker's Journey," 33. The connection between the Beales' and the Maysles brothers' own family relationships is also discussed in Tolkin, 141, and in Judith Trojan, "Who's Who in Filmmaking: Albert Maysles," 26–30.

14. *The Fourth Annual Boston Film/Video Foundation Vision Award Honoring Albert Maysles*, 22.

15. James Blue, "One Man's Truth: An Interview with Richard Leacock," 406, 411, 418. Richard M. Barsam, "Defining Nonfiction Film," 374.

16. Daniel Klugherz, "Documentary—Where's the Wonder?", 451, 456. "The Drawbacks of Reality," 83. Stephen Mamber, *Cinéma Vérité in America: Studies in Uncontrolled Documentary*), 138–40.

17. P. J. O'Connell, *Robert Drew and the Development of Cinéma Vérité in America*, 203, and Robert L. Drew, "An Independent with the Networks," 399–401. Eventually, hard-hitting and more concise news magazines like CBS's "Sixty Minutes" supplanted direct cinema's leisurely spontaneity. Drew Associates, minus many of the creative forces that helped launch it, remains a vital filmmaking company. Its output has consisted primarily of culturally based films on topics such as space exploration, jazz, and visual-arts biographies (O'Connell, 239–49). Since the mid-1970s, the Public Broadcasting Service (PBS) has in many ways picked up where Drew left off, offering challenging documentaries on many controversial and complex issues. More recently, Home Box Office (HBO) has become a major supporter of independent documentary filmmakers. Free of many of the constraints facing the for-profit networks, PBS's "Frontline" and "P.O.V." programs and the documentary films supported by HBO Films currently fulfill much of the promise Drew foresaw for television as a whole.

18. Blue, "One Man's Truth," 413. O'Connell, 166–67; 196–97. Louis Marcorelles, "Leacock at M.I.T.," 104–7. For Leacock's current views on filmmaking, see his statement in Macdonald and Cousins, *Imagining Reality: The Faber Book of Documentary*, 377–79. Since the direct cinema heyday, D. A. Pennebaker has contin-

ued to direct and produce films, many in collaboration with his wife, the film-maker Chris Hegedus. Titles include *Depeche Mode: 101* (1989), a film about the new-wave band and its dedicated fans; *The War Room* (1994), an Academy-Award–nominated film about Bill Clinton's 1992 campaign for the presidency; and *Moon over Broadway* (1998), a behind-the-scenes look at the making of the stage comedy *Moon over Buffalo*.

19. Doug Rossinow, *The Politics of Authenticity: Liberalism, Christianity, and the New Left in America*, 335. See also David Farber, "The Silent Majority and Talk about Revolution," in Farber, ed., *The Sixties: From Memory to History*, 291–316.

20. James Miller, *"Democracy Is in the Streets": From Port Huron to the Siege of Chicago*, 215, 317; Allen J. Matusow, *The Unraveling of America: A History of Liberalism in the 1960s*, 335–43.

21. One need only peruse the first few volumes of what was at the time a new academic film journal, the *Quarterly Review of Film Studies*. Founded in 1976, the first eight issues include numerous articles that posit semiotic, psychoanalytic, or Marxist readings of films or that focus generally on the question, "What is the theoretical basis of the discipline of film studies?" (see, e.g., J. Douglas Gomery, "Film Industry Studies: The Search for a Theory," in *QRFS* 1 [February 1976], 95). See also Jeanne Hall, "Realism as a Style in Cinéma Vérité: A Critical Analysis of *Primary*," 44.

22. Thomas Waugh, "Beyond *Verite*: Emile de Antonio and the New Documentary of the Seventies," in Bill Nichols, ed., *Movies and Methods*, Vol. 2, 234–36.

23. Umberto Eco, "Semiotics and the Cinema," 14. Ed Pincus, "New Possibilities in Film and the University," 169–71.

24. De Antonio quoted in Barbara Zheutlin, "The Politics of Documentary: A Symposium," 235. In Block's film, the victim and the filmmaker are fictional for the purposes of the experiment; Vivian C. Sobchack, "*No Lies*: Direct Cinema as Rape," 335. Other documentarians apparently felt a similar disdain for direct cinema: "There are filmmakers who will tell you that the Maysles are blatant liars and exploiters, that their adherence to 'true honesty' is only an excuse for bear baiting" (Tolkin, 140).

25. Brian Winston, "Documentary: I Think We Are in Trouble" (1978); "Direct Cinema: The Third Decade" (1983); "The Tradition of the Victim in Griersonian Documentary" (1988); and "The Documentary Film as Scientific Inscription" (1993). In the latter, Winston is strongly influenced by Walter Benjamin, "The Work of Art in the Age of Mechanical Reproduction," in Gerald Mast and Marshall Cohen, eds., 612–34. For his most recent views, see especially chapter 1 of *Lies, Damn Lies and Documentaries*.

26. Jay Ruby, "The Ethics of Imagemaking," 316.

27. Calvin Pryluck, "Ultimately We Are All Outsiders: The Ethics of Documentary Filmmaking," 257, 259, 262. Winston made much the same objection about *Salesman* in one of his several anti–direct cinema essays: "Other problems [in ethics] arise from the fact that these texts have extended, perhaps nearly indefinite, lives. Paul, the failed salesman in the Maysles film of that name, is constantly

exposed as such wherever documentary film classes are taught or Maysles retrospectives are held" ("Tradition of the Victim," 278).

28. Postmodern theorists like Winston would continue to develop these ideas in the 1970s, 1980s, and 1990s. They recognized that there are inherent fictive qualities in any text, whether the text identifies itself as fiction or nonfiction. They understood truth and authenticity to be historically situated constructs, influenced by whomever or whatever holds power at a given historical moment. (See Michael Renov's introduction to his *Theorizing Documentary* book and Trinh T. Minh-ha, "The Totalizing Quest of Meaning," in the same book.) French cinéma vérité filmmakers like Jean Rouch, Edgar Morin, and Jean-Luc Godard gained favor with postmodern theorists because they seemed better able and more willing to incorporate their own "subjectivity and involvement" into their films. (See Ellen Freyer, "*Chronicle of a Summer*: Ten Years After" for a concise report on why that film by Rouch and Morin is considered exemplary.)

Alexandra Juhasz has written insightfully about her marginalized status as a feminist (but) realist filmmaker in "They Said We Were Trying to Show Reality— All I Want to Show Is My Video: The Politics of the Realist Feminist Documentary."

29. Pryluck, "Seeking to Take the Longest Journey," 11–12.

30. Richard Eder, "Grey Gardens" (review), 21. Jay Cocks, "Slumming Expedition," 67. Walter Goodman, "'Grey Gardens': Cinéma Vérité or Sideshow," 15.

31. John Simon quoted in Tolkin, 144. David Sargent, "When Does Invasion of Privacy Become Art?", 134. Other negative reviews: Vincent Canby worried that the "film's expression is impassive. Also a little cruel" (*Grey Gardens* review, 15). *Film Heritage's* J. E. Siegel "suspect[ed] that we are all a bit poorer in spirit for having seen" *Grey Gardens* (34). Chad Curtis of *Vogue* called the film "one of the most exploitative, tasteless, and frankly reprehensible films of them all" (192). Molly Haskell of the *Village Voice* concurred: "[T]here are some people we should close our eyes to" (qtd. in Naficy, 171).

32. Gary Arnold, "A Disquieting *Grey Gardens*," 13.

33. Cocks, 67; Goodman, 15.

34. Jay Ruby, "The Image Mirrored: Reflexivity and the Documentary Film." Ruby, "The Ethics of Imagemaking," 314.

35. Ruby, "The Image Mirrored," 74–75; 65.

36. Bill Nichols, "The Voice of Documentary," 52; Nichols, "'Getting To Know You . . .': Knowledge, Power, and the Body," 188.

37. See especially Paul Arthur's essay "Jargons of Authenticity (Three American Moments)," 119.

38. Farber, 309; Matusow, 439; Miller, 321. See Samuel Huntington, *Political Order in Changing Societies*.

39. Naficy, 161, 162; Mamber, 113. See also Drew, "An Independent with the Networks" and Winston, "Documentary as Scientific Inscription," 49–50. As another example, Jeanne Hall argues that Pennebaker was purposefully evasive when discussing and "explaining" his film *Dont Look Back* (1966) in order to support his central thesis. Whatever his intent, Pennebaker contributed to the misper-

ceptions of direct cinema filmmaking (Jeanne Hall, "'Don't You Ever Just Watch?' American Cinéma Vérité and *Dont Look Back*"). Ironically, Wiseman's films—so relentless and so formulaic—became less and less ambiguous and more clearly subjective. See also Leacock's defense of *Chiefs* (1969) in Mamber, 212–13.

40. Robert Phillip Kolker, "Circumstantial Evidence: An Interview with David and Albert Maysles," 185.

41. Winston, "Direct Cinema," 520.

42. Richard M. Barsam, "American Direct Cinema: The *Re*-Presentation of Reality," *Persistence of Vision*, 133 (emphasis added). While he acknowledges that direct cinema is frequently self-contradicting or even obfuscatory in its approach, Barsam does not wish to confuse direct cinema's ambiguity with a lack of self-reflexivity. Direct cinema "refuses to impose direct control over meaning and thus asks the viewer to confront the ambiguities in any subject" (139). Furthermore, Barsam argues, the essential nature of direct cinema emerges only in the editing process, during which the editor must be "both organizational and creative; the successful direct cinema editor is guided by a sense of integrity to *re*-presenting actuality as it was filmed" (142). The editor therefore "produces a model of reality" (136) that must be "true" to the reality of the filmed events without necessarily taking pains to illustrate how that is done or by whom. In the end, direct cinema "is disguised self-revelation, in which the filmmaker (either visible or invisible in the film) both expresses and conceals himself" (137). In the Maysles brothers' films, he believes "form and content are seamlessly joined" (145).

43. William Rothman, *Documentary Film Classics*, xiii, xii. It should be noted, however, that he does not use the term "self-reflexive." He prefers, at times, "truth-in-cinema" and emphasizes the way "camera" and "subject" operate together to create a world on film in which there is clear mutual understanding of the film-making process, even if that understanding is not explicitly stated within the film. He sees, for instance, "the developing relationship between Mrs. Fischer and Leacock's camera" in *Happy Mother's Day* (1963) as "internal to the drama" of the film (125). It is also vital to the affirmation of American cinéma vérité as an important mode of observational cinema. "The capacity to transfigure America, to celebrate the mythical in the typical, is the secret bond between Mrs. Fischer and Leacock's camera" (143). See his chapters V and VI.

Similarly, Jeffrey K. Ruoff maintains that direct cinema's detractors overlook the "ubiquitous references to the filmmaking process" that occur in films such as *An American Family* (Craig Gilbert, 1973) and *Grey Gardens*. He suggests there is a middle ground between "the pronounced reflexivity" of Rouch and the "mostly transparent approach" of Wiseman. One need not explicitly explain or acknowledge the filmmaker to have a film that is self-reflexive (Jeffrey K. Ruoff, "'A Bastard Union of Several Forms': Style and Narrative in *An American Family*," 298).

44. Ruby, "The Image Mirrored," 66.

45. Barsam, 139. Susan Jaffe, "Editing Cinéma Vérité," 45.

46. Kolker, 183.

47. Jaffe, 47.

48. Tolkin, 140. Defending the film specifically against Goodman's harsh rebuke, the brothers asked in a letter to the *New York Times* editor: "Who is anyone to judge another person unfit for filming? The implications here are chilling, even medieval. Why suggest that Edith Beale at 78 is senile, or that her daughter Edie is not quite all there? The Beales may be eccentric, obsessively individualistic, tormented if you will; and they choose to live in seedy, unorthodox surroundings. But they are not mad" (Albert and David Maysles, "The Maysles Defend Their Film," 15).

49. Naficy, 159–60; Sargent, 134. When the film was shown to a Brown University audience in 1995, Albert continued to defend the film and the Beales on these grounds, noting that no one ever wanted to "think about what [the Beales] have going for them . . . their signs of health" (qtd. in Stephanie Morimoto, "Filmmaker Albert Maysles Addresses Salomon Crowd," 2). Reviewer Denise Hare took a similar approach when she observed that *Grey Gardens* will "stir up a storm of very personal responses and raise questions to which there are no answers, thus forcing the spectators to think, reflect, and *react* according to their individual temperaments and sensibilities. And this means *critics*, too" (Denise Hare, Review of *Grey Gardens*, 77; emphasis in original). Ellen Hovde supported the film in much the same way. She admitted (more readily than Albert ever would) that she struggled with the ethical questions as she was cutting the film, but

> As for exploitation, [codirector and coeditor] Muffie [Meyer] and I worried a great deal during the cutting about exploiting the [Beales], and exposing them to ridicule from people who wouldn't understand them, and so on. David and Al never did. They felt that everything that had gone on was all right, and that if the Beales revealed themselves completely, fine. . . . I think that what really happens in that film is that an audience is amazed and identifies with them, and is frightened, maybe repelled. But when people say that those women were exploited, I think that what they are really thinking about is themselves. . . . I think that people are aware in our society of what a camera is, and very aware of what they ought to be doing in front of it, so unless a person is really *non compos mentis*, it is pretty hard to put someone in a film with their own knowledge and consent, without them having a good idea of what is going on." (Rosenthal, "Ellen Hovde," 14–15)

50. Naficy, 161.

51. As quoted in Rosenthal, "Ellen Hovde," 14. Hovde reported that the two women "saw the film at their house and loved it."

52. On the Beales' reaction to the film: Marjorie Rosen, "*Grey Gardens*: A Documentary about Dependency," 30. Charles Michener and Katrine Ames, "The Eavesdroppers," 87. Hilton Als, "Dept. of Legacies: A Rare Chat with the Bouviers' Miss Havisham," 32. Schreiber, 33. At the time of the film's release, Michael Tolkin worried that the Maysles brothers, in support of their film and in the name of creating publicity for it, were "dragging 'Little' Edie Beale around like a trained seal with a half a lobotomy" (Tolkin, 140).

53. Alan Rosenthal, Introduction, in Rosenthal, *New Challenges*, 250, and Rosenthal, *The Documentary Conscience: A Casebook in Film Making*, 373.

54. Als, Review of *Grey Gardens*, 68. Sargent, 134. Martyn Auty of the *Monthly Film Bulletin* noticed much the same phenomenon as Als: "The Beales direct *Grey Gardens* as much as do the Maysles—indeed they fictionalise the documentarists' ostensible subject at every opportunity" (Auty, Review of *Grey Gardens*, 49). Other positive reviews: John Coleman observed that the film "is an astounding, completely gripping filmed intrusion on the wildly eccentric life-styles" of the two women (Coleman, "Mixed Doubles," 643). Charles Michener, reviewing the film for *Film Comment*, opined that the film is "an extraordinarily craft invasion" into the Beales' lives. *Grey Gardens* "achieves what cinéma vérité aims for but seldom conveys: a sense that the material is telling itself" (Michener, "Grey Gardens," 38; see also his *Newsweek* article, note 52 above).

55. Filmmaker Susan Woll has noted, for instance, that the Maysles brothers were "surprised when some viewers didn't share their affection for their subjects" (qtd. in the *Fourth Annual Boston Film/Video Foundation Vision Award Ceremony Honoring Albert Maysles*, 19). See also Hall, "Realism as a Style," 45, for Pennebaker's views on audience.

56. See Michel Benamou, Forward, vii–ix; Marshall Cohen and Gerald Mast, Introduction, v–ix, and the subsequent papers from the Conference on Film and the University (1976).

57. Hall, "Realism," 27, 45.

58. Hall, "Don't You Ever," 226–27, 236. Paul Arthur also discusses this subject-as-intermediary aspect of many direct cinema films (Arthur, 122–23).

59. Rothman, 148, 144–45.

60. Stella Bruzzi, *New Documentary: A Critical Introduction*, 1, 9, 72.

7: TAKING DIRECT CINEMA INTO THE 1980S

1. On the commercial results of the early films, see chapter 2. *Salesman* and *Grey Gardens* both played nationwide in selected theaters, but neither made back their original costs. It has only been through later exposure—*Salesman* aired nationally on PBS's "P.O.V." series in 1990, and *Grey Gardens* was re-released to theaters in 1998—and video sales that these two films have been modest successes. *Gimme Shelter* broke even when it played nationally in 1970 and has continued to bring in some revenue for the brothers, although they have only a limited part of the revenue stream. See also Hamid Naficy, "'Truthful Witness': An Interview with Albert Maysles," 168–69, and Brooke Comer, "Man of the People," 87. After the limited successes of *Salesman* and *Gimme Shelter*, David told an interviewer: "Evidently, from what we can gather, people don't go to the movies to experience anything but a very light kind of amusement. I don't think it's going to change us any" (Robert Phillip Kolker, "Circumstantial Evidence: An Interview with David and Albert Maysles," 186).

2. Albert Maysles, "Persistence of Vision" (September, 1992), 24. See also Albert Maysles, "Persistence of Vision" (January, 1993), 22, 24; David and Albert Maysles,

"Direct Cinema," 31–33; and Norman Schreiber, "Desire and Discovery: A Film-maker's Journey," 33–34.

3. Personal interview with Susan Froemke, New York, New York, 22 July 2002; Lawrence Van Gelder, "Maysles: Filming the Impossible," 19. See also Naficy, 170; Schreiber, 34.

4. See Kolker, 186.

5. Albert Maysles, as quoted in Judith Trojan, "Who's Who in Filmmaking: Albert Maysles," 26–30. On the making of this film, see also William J. McClure, "Finding the Six Families," 16.

6. Trojan, 29. Catherine Egan, "Six American Families and How They Reacted to Their Portrayals," 13.

7. Froemke interview.

8. In *The Last Romantic*, the brothers had a special platform constructed so that Albert could film Horowitz from above. See Lawrence Loewinger, "Digital Recording in the Field."

9. Walter Goodman observed that Mrs. Horowitz "treats him rather as an adult might treat a precocious but sometimes prankish child" ("Screen: Documentary on Vladimir Horowitz," 12).

10. Ellin Stein, "It's a Wrap!", 10.

11. Christo and Jeanne-Claude had also become much more media savvy; see Jonathan Fineberg, "Essay," 28.

12. David Edelstein, "It's Been Reel," 72.

13. Schreiber, 30, 34; Gerald O'Grady, "Just Two Guys," the *Fourth Annual Boston Film/Video Foundation Vision Award Ceremony Honoring Albert Maysles*, 7, 11. Albert is also at work on *The Jew on Trial*, a film about Mendel Beilis, a Jew from Kiev who was falsely accused of murdering an eleven-year-old boy in 1913.

14. Froemke interview.

15. See "25 Films for 1993," *American Cinematographer*, March 1993, 100.

16. On this phenomenon, see, for example, the video interviews with fashion designers Todd Oldham and John Bartlett in the *Grey Gardens* DVD.

17. Comer, 83–84. Robert Koehler, "Zero Attitude, Just Humanity," A1.

18. On the way videotaped and audiotaped reality seem to be more highly regarded as the "really real," see Bruce J. Schulman, "Taping History."

19. Van Gelder, 19.

20. Albert Maysles, as quoted in O'Grady, 9.

21. Paul D. Zimmerman, "Shooting It like It Is," 134.

Bibliography

Alexander, William. *Film on the Left: American Documentary Film from 1931 to 1942*. Princeton, NJ: Princeton University Press, 1981.

Alpert, Hollis. "That Great Territory in the Sky." *Saturday Review* (22 March 1969): 75.

Als, Hilton. "Dept. of Legacies: A Rare Chat with the Bouviers' Miss Havisham." *New Yorker* (8 June 1998): 31–32.

———. Review of *Grey Gardens*. *Village Voice* (7 April 1992): 68–69.

Arnold, Gary. "A Disquieting *Grey Gardens*." *Washington Post* (8 October 1976): B1, 13.

Arthur, Paul. "Jargons of Authenticity (Three American Moments)." Renov 108–34.

Auty, Martin. Review of *Grey Gardens*. *Monthly Film Bulletin* 47 (March 1980): 48–49.

Bahr, David. "View to a Kill." *Time Out New York* (10–17 August 2000): 176.

Baker, Richard M., Jr., and Gregg Phifer. *Salesmanship: Communication, Persuasion, Perception*. Boston: Allyn and Bacon, 1966.

Bangs, Lester, et al. "Let It Bleed." *Rolling Stone* (11 January 1970): 18–36.

Barnouw, Erik. *Documentary: A History of Non-fiction Film*. 2d rev. ed. New York: Oxford University Press, 1993.

Barsam, Richard M. "American Direct Cinema: The *Re*-presentation of Reality." *Persistence of Vision* 3/4 (summer 1986): 131–56.

———. "Defining Nonfiction Film." Mast and Cohen 366–78.

———. *Nonfiction Film: A Critical History*. New York: E. P. Dutton, 1973.

Benamou, Michel. "Forward." *Quarterly Review of Film Studies* 1 (August 1976): vii–ix.

Benson, Thomas W., and Carolyn Anderson. *Reality Fictions: The Films of Frederick Wiseman*. Carbondale: Southern Illinois University Press, 1990.

Berger, John. *Ways of Seeing*. London: BBC/Penguin, 1972.

Berman, Marshall. *The Politics of Authenticity: Radical Individualism and the Emergence of Modern Society*. New York: Atheneum, 1970.

Blue, James. "Direct Cinema." *Film Comment* 4 (summer/fall 1967): 80–81.

———. "One Man's Truth: An Interview with Richard Leacock." Jacobs 406–19.

———. "Thoughts on Cinéma Vérité and a Discussion with the Maysles Brothers." *Film Comment* 2 (winter 1964): 22–30.

Boorstin, Daniel J. *The Image: A Guide to Pseudo-Events in America.* New York: Vintage Books, 1987. Originally published 1961.

Braudy, Leo. *The Frenzy of Renown: Fame and Its History.* New York: Oxford University Press, 1986.

Breitrose, Henry. "On the Search for the Real Nitty-Gritty: Problems and Possibilities in Cinéma Vérité." *Film Quarterly* 17 (summer 1964): 36–40.

Bruzzi, Stella. *New Documentary: A Critical Introduction.* London: Routledge Press, 2000.

Buell, Victor P. "Door-to-Door Selling." Bursk and Hutchison 35–41.

Bursk, Edward C., and G. Scott Hutchison, eds. *Salesmanship and Sales Force Management.* Cambridge: Harvard University Press, 1971.

"Byro." Review of *Salesman. Variety* (26 February 1969): 6.

Callenbach, Ernest. "Short Notices: *Salesman.*" *Film Quarterly* 23 (fall 1969): 54–55.

Canby, Vincent. "*Christo's Valley Curtain* Is a Real Tall Story." *New York Times* (15 March 1974); 20.

———. "Making Murder Pay?" *New York Times* (13 December 1970): sec. 2, pp. 3, 45.

———. "Of Sticks and Stones and Blood at Altamont." *New York Times* (7 December 1970): 60.

———. Review of *Grey Gardens. New York Times* (5 October 1975): sec. 2, p. 15.

———. "*Salesman*, a Slice of America." *New York Times* (18 April 1969): 32.

———. "Why, Even You and I Can Be Stars." *New York Times* (27 April 1969): sec. 2, pp. 1, 11.

Capote, Truman. *In Cold Blood.* New York: Random House, 1965.

Carney, Ray. *The Films of John Cassavetes: Pragmatism, Modernism, and the Movies.* Cambridge: Cambridge University Press, 1994.

Carroll, Noël. *Theorising the Moving Image.* Cambridge: Cambridge University Press, 1996.

Cauté, David. *The Year of the Barricades: A Journey Through 1968.* New York: Harper and Row, 1988.

Cavell, Stanley. *The World Viewed.* Enlarged Edition. Cambridge: Harvard University Press, 1979.

Chon, Richard. "Once in a Lifetime." *Bakersfield Californian* (20 January 1991): C1.

Christie, Ian. Review of *Running Fence. Monthly Film Bulletin* 45 (February 1978): 27–28.

Christo. John Kalder Art Project. Sydney: Art Gallery of New South Wales, 1990.

Christo: The Running Fence Project. Text by Werner Spies. New York: Harry N. Abrams, 1980.

Christo: Surrounded Islands: Complete project. New York: Harry N. Abrams, 1986.

Christo: Surrounded Islands. Introduction by Werner Spies. New York: Harry N. Abrams, 1985.

Christo: Valley Curtain. Complete project. New York: Harry N. Abrams, 1973.

Clifford, James. *The Predicament of Culture.* Cambridge: Harvard University Press, 1988.

Clurman, Harold. Review of *Salesman. Nation* (10 March 1969): 318.

Cmiel, Kenneth. "The Politics of Civility." In *The Sixties: From Memory to History,* edited by David Farber. Chapel Hill: University of North Carolina Press, 1994. 263–90.

Cocks, Jay. "Slumming Expedition." *Time* (1 March 1976): 66–67.

Cohen, Marshall, and Gerald Mast. Introduction. *Quarterly Review of Film Studies* 2 (May 1977): v–ix.

Coleman, John. "Mixed Doubles." *New Statesman* (25 April 1980): 643.

Comer, Brooke. "Man of the People." *American Cinematographer* 79 (January 1998): 83–88.

Cone, Michele. "A Sublime Folly: Christo's *Running Fence.*" *Atlantic* 238 (September 1976): 90–96.

Craddock, John. "*Salesman,* a Review." *Film Library Quarterly* 2 (summer 1969): 8–12.

Crist, Judith. Review of *Salesman. New York* (28 April 1969): 55.

Curtis, Chad. Review of *Grey Gardens. Vogue* 165 (November 1975): 192.

Dann, Alec. "Don't Fence Me In." *Afterimage* 6 (December 1978): 15.

Davidson, David. "Direct Cinema and Modernism: The Long Journey to *Grey Gardens.*" *Journal of the University Film Association* 33 (winter 1981): 3–13.

Davies, Hunter. *The Beatles.* 2d rev. ed. New York: Norton, 1996.

Dembitzer, Beth. "Hand Held and from the Heart: The Stories of Albert Maysles." *Dox* (June 2000): 8–11.

"The Drawbacks of Reality." *Time* (7 March 1969): 83, 85.

Drew, Robert L. "An Independent with the Networks." Rosenthal, *New Challenges* 389–401.

Drukker, Leendert. "Cinéma Vérité: End of the Trail?" *Popular Photography* (19 August 1976): 66, 70.

Eco, Umberto. "Semiotics and the Cinema." *Quarterly Review of Film Studies* 2 (February 1977): 14–24.

Edelstein, David. "It's Been Reel." *Village Voice* (20 October 1987): 72.

Eder, Richard. Review of *Grey Gardens. New York Times* (27 September 1975): 21.

Egan, Catherine. "Six American Families and How They Reacted to Their Portrayals." *Film Library Quarterly* 11 (spring 1978): 5–18.

Farber, David, ed. *The Sixties: From Memory to History.* Chapel Hill: University of North Carolina Press, 1994.

Fineberg, Jonathan. Essay. *Christo: Surrounded Islands.* New York: Harry N. Abrams, 1986.

Fourth Annual Boston Film/Video Foundation Vision Award Ceremony Honoring Albert Maysles. Boston: BF/VF, 1998.

Frankenstein, Alfred. "Report from California: Christo's *Fence*, Beauty or Betrayal?" *Art in America* 64 (November 1976): 58–61.

Freyer, Ellen. "*Chronicle of a Summer*: Ten Years After." Jacobs 437–43.

Friedlander, Paul. *Rock and Roll: A Social History*. Boulder, CO: Westview Press, 1996.

Froemke, Susan. Interview by the author. Tape recording. Maysles Films, New York, New York, 22 July 2002.

"The Frontiers of Realist Cinema: The Work of Ricky Leacock." *Film Culture* 22/23 (summer 1961): 12–23.

Gaines, Jane, and Michael Renov. *Collecting Visible Evidence*. Minneapolis: University of Minnesota Press, 1999.

Gamson, Joshua. *Claims To Fame: Celebrity in Contemporary America*. Berkeley: University of California Press, 1994.

Geertz, Clifford. *The Interpretation of Cultures: Selected Essays*. New York: Basic Books, 1973.

Gibson, Walker, ed. *The Limits of Language*. New York: Hill and Wang, 1962.

Gilliatt, Penelope. "The Current Cinema." *New Yorker* (17 April 1978): 119, 120.

———. "The Current Cinema: About Thy Father's Door-to-Door Business." *New Yorker* (19 April 1969): 149–52.

Gimme Shelter. 1968. Dir. David and Albert Maysles and Charlotte Zwerin. Criterion Collection, 2001. DVD.

"*Gimme Shelter*." Review. *Variety* (25 November 1970): 13.

Gitlin, Todd. *The Sixties: Years of Hope, Days of Rage*. Toronto: Bantam Books, 1987.

Godmilow, Jill, and Ann-Louise Shapiro. "How Real Is the Reality in Documentary Film?" *History and Theory* 36 (December 1997): 80–101.

Goldman, Albert. "Delicately Handled Dynamite or a Whitewash of Jagger?" *New York Times* (3 January 1971): sec. 2, p. 9.

Goodman, Walter. "Christo, in 'Islands.'" *New York Times* (16 October 1987): sec. C, p. 4.

———. "'Grey Gardens': Cinéma Vérité or Sideshow?" *New York Times* (22 February 1976): sec. 2, p. 15.

———. "Screen: Documentary on Vladimir Horowitz." *New York Times* (15 November 1985): sec. C, p. 12.

Goodwin, Michael. "Films." Review of *Gimme Shelter*. *Rolling Stone* (24 December 1970): 58.

Graham, Peter. "Cinéma Vérité in France." *Film Quarterly* 17 (summer 1964): 30–36.

Grant, Barry Keith, and Jeannette Sloniowski, eds. *Documenting the Documentary: Close Readings of Documentary Film and Video*. Detroit: Wayne State University Press, 1998.

Green, Charles. "Disappearing and Photography in Post-Object Art: Christo and Jeanne-Claude." *Afterimage* 27 (November/December 1999): 13–15.

Guzzetti, Alfred. "Notes on Representation and the Nonfiction Film." *New Literary History* 27 (spring 1996): 263–70.

Haleff, Maxine. "The Maysles Brothers and 'Direct Cinema.'" *Film Comment* 2 (spring 1964): 19–23.

Hall, Jeanne. "'Don't You Ever Just Watch?': American Cinema Verite and *Dont Look Back*." Grant and Sloniowski 223–37.

———. "Realism as a Style in Cinéma Vérité: A Critical Analysis of *Primary*." *Cinema Journal* 30 (summer 1991): 24–50.

Hare, Denise. "Film." Review of *Grey Gardens*. *Craft Horizons* 36 (June 1976): 12; 76–79.

———. "Film." Review of *Running Fence*. *Craft Horizons* 38 (April 1978): 6, 76–77.

Harrison, George. *I Me Mine*. New York: Simon and Schuster, 1980.

Hartung, Philip T. "The Screen" Review of *Salesman*. *Commonweal* (2 May 1969): 207–8.

Haskell, Molly. "Film: Gimme Shelter." *Village Voice* (10 December 1976): 71, 77.

Hatch, Robert. "Films." Review of *Gimme Shelter*. *Nation* (4 January 1971): 30.

———. "Films." Review of *Grey Gardens*. *Nation* (13 March 1976): 317.

Haycock, Joel. Review of *Gimme Shelter*. *Film Quarterly* 24 (summer 1971): 56–60.

Hicks, Michael. *Sixties Rock: Garage, Psychedelic, and Other Satisfactions*. Urbana: University of Illinois Press, 1999.

"Hitch." Review of *Islands*. *Variety* (5 November 1986): 14.

Hoberman, J. "Nylon Sheets and Vinyl Freaks." *Village Voice* (17 April 197): 51.

Hollinger, David. "The Knower and the Artificer." Singal 42–69.

Hollowell, John. *Fact and Fiction*. Chapel Hill: University of North Carolina Press, 1977.

Horak, Jan-Christopher, ed. *Lovers of Cinema: The First American Film Avant-Garde, 1919–1945*. Madison: University of Wisconsin Press, 1995.

Huntington, Samuel. *Political Order in Changing Societies*. New Haven: Yale University Press, 1968.

Huyssen, Andreas. *After the Great Divide: Modernism, Mass Culture, Postmodernism*. Bloomington: Indiana University Press, 1986.

Issari, M. Ali, and Doris A. Paul. *What Is Cinéma Vérité?* Metuchen, NJ: Scarecrow Press, 1979.

Jacobs, Lewis. *The Documentary Tradition*. 2d ed. New York: Norton, 1979.

Jaffe, Susan. "Editing Cinéma Vérité." *Film Comment* 3 (fall 1965): 43–47.

Jameson, Fredric. *Postmodernism, or, The Cultural Logic of Late Capitalism*. Durham, NC: Duke University Press, 1991.

———. *Signatures of the Visible*. New York: Routledge, 1992.

Johnson, Paul. *A Shopkeeper's Millennium: Society and Revivals in Rochester, New York, 1815–1837*. New York: Hill and Wang, 1978.

Jolson, Marvin A. "The Salesman's Career Cycle." In *Contemporary Readings in Sales Management*, edited by Jolson. New York: Petrocelli, 1977.

Juhasz, Alexandra. "They Said We Were Trying to Show Reality—All I Want to Show Is My Video: The Politics of the Realist Feminist Documentary." Gaines and Renov 190–215.

Junker, Howard. "Production Notes." In *Salesman: A Film by the Maysles Brothers and Charlotte Zwerin*. New York: Signet, 1969. 106–21.

Kael, Pauline. "Beyond Pirandello." *New Yorker* (19 December 1970): 112–15.

Kauffmann, Stanley. "*Salesman*." *New Republic* (5 April 1969): 24, 32–33.

Keith, Jean Hennelly. "Reality Revealed: Documentary Proof of the Maysles Film Achievements." *Bostonia* (spring 2002): 18–21.

Klugherz, Daniel. "Documentary—Where's the Wonder?" Jacobs 451–58.

Knight, Arthur. "Cinéma Vérité and Film Truth." *Saturday Review* (9 September 1967): 44.

Koehler, Robert. "Zero Attitude, Just Humanity." *Variety* (6 March 1998): A1.

Kolker, Robert Phillip. "Circumstantial Evidence: An Interview with David and Albert Maysles." *Sight and Sound* 40 (autumn 1971): 183–86.

Kroll, Jack. "The World on Film." *Newsweek* (13 October 1975): 103–4.

Laporté, Dominique G. *Christo*. New York: Pantheon, 1986.

Leacock, Richard. "For an Uncontrolled Cinema." *Film Culture* 22/23 (summer 1961): 23–25.

———. "Richard Leacock Remembers the Origins of 'Direct Cinema.'" Macdonald and Cousins 251–54.

Le Grice, Malcolm. *Abstract Film and Beyond*. Cambridge: MIT Press, 1977.

Lewis, Anne S. "Stories That Tell Themselves." www.austinchronicle.com. 11 February 2000.

Loewinger, Lawrence. "Digital Recording in the Field." *American Cinematographer* June 1986): 95–103.

Macdonald, Kevin, and Mark Cousins. *Imagining Reality: The Faber Book of Documentary*. London: Faber and Faber, 1996.

MacFadden, Patrick. "*Gimme Shelter*." *Film Society Review* 6 (November 1970): 39–42.

Mamber, Stephen. "Cinéma Vérité and Social Concerns." *Film Comment* 11 (November/December 1973): 8–15.

———. *Cinéma Vérité in America: Studies in Uncontrolled Documentary*. Cambridge: MIT Press, 1974.

Mancini, J. M. "'One Term Is as Fatuous as Another': Responses to the Armory Show Reconsidered." *American Quarterly* 51 (December 1999): 833–70.

Marcorelles, Louis. "Leacock at M.I.T." *Sight and Sound* 43 (spring 1974): 104–7.

———. "Nothing but the Truth." *Sight and Sound* 32 (spring 1963): 114–17.

Marcorelles, Louis, and Andre S. Labarthe. "An Interview with Robert Drew and Richard Leacock." *Cahiers du Cinema* 24 (February 1963): 18–27.

Marshall, P. David. *Celebrity and Power: Fame in Contemporary Culture*. Minneapolis: University of Minnesota Press, 1997.

Martine, James J., ed. *Critical Essays on Arthur Miller*. Boston: G. K. Hall, 1979.

Marwick, Arthur. *The Sixties: Cultural Revolution in Britain, France, Italy, and the United States, c.1958–c.1974*. Oxford, England: Oxford University Press, 1998.

Maslin, Janet. "'Running Fence' Films Story of an Art Event." *New York Times* (11 April 1978): 44.

Mast, Gerald, and Marshall Cohen, eds. *Film Theory and Criticism*. New York: Oxford University Press, 1974.

Mattson, Kevin. *Intellectuals in Action: The Origins of the New Left and Radical Liberalism, 1945–1970*. University Park: Pennsylvania State University Press, 2002.

Matusow, Allen J. *The Unraveling of America: A History of Liberalism in the 1960s*. New York: Harper and Row, 1984.

Maysles, Albert. "Letter to the Editor." *Film Comment* 2 (spring 1964): 64.

———. Interview by the author. New York, New York, 12 November 1994.

———. Interview by the author. New York, New York, 7 February 2000.

———. "Persistence of Vision." *American Cinematographer* 73 (September 1992): 22, 24.

———. "Persistence of Vision." *American Cinematographer* 74 (January 1993): 22, 24.

"Maysles Brothers." *Film Culture* 42 (1966): 114.

Maysles, David, and Albert Maysles. "Direct Cinema." *Public Relations Journal* 38 (September 1982): 31–33.

———. "*Gimme Shelter*: Production Notes." *Filmmakers Newsletter* 5 (December 1971): 28–31.

———. "The Maysles Defend Their Film." *New York Times* (25 April 1976): sec. 2, p. 15.

McClure, William J. "Finding the 6 Families." *Film Library Quarterly* 11 (spring 1978): 16.

McGregor, Craig. "Rock's 'We Are One' Myth." *New York Times* (9 May 1971): sec. 2, pp. 15, 25.

Mekas, Jonas. "Movie Journal." *Village Voice* (3 March 1966): 21.

———. "Not Everything That Is Fun Is Cinema." *Village Voice* (10 September 1964): 21.

Michener, Charles. Review of *Grey Gardens*. *Film Comment* 11 (September/October 1975): 38.

Michener, Charles, and Katrine Ames. "The Eavesdroppers." *Newsweek* (8 March 1976): 86–87.

Miller, Arthur. *Death of a Salesman*. New York: Penguin Plays, 1987. Originally published 1949.

———. *Timebends: A Life*. New York: Grove Press, 1987.

Miller, James. *"Democracy Is in the Streets": From Port Huron to the Siege of Chicago*. New York: Simon and Schuster, 1987.

Minh-ha, Trinh T. "The Totalizing Quest of Meaning." Renov 92–107.

Monaco, Paul. *The Sixties*. Berkeley: University of California Press, 2001.

Moore, Truman E. *The Traveling Man: The Story of the American Traveling Salesman*. New York: Doubleday, 1972.

Morgenstern, Joseph. "God and Country." *Newsweek* (21 April 1969): 116, 120.

Morimoto, Stephanie. "Filmmaker Albert Maysles Address Salomon Crowd." *Brown Daily Herald* (10 October 1995): 1–2.

Morse, Steve. "Documentarian Rolls More Stones Film." *Boston Globe* (27 October 1994): 12.

Naficy, Hamid. "Richard Leacock: A Personal Perspective." *Literature/Film Quarterly* 10 (fall 1982): 234–53.

———. "'Truthful Witness': An Interview with Albert Maysles." *Quarterly Review of Film Studies* 6 (spring 1981): 155–79.

Nichols, Bill. "Getting to Know You . . . : Knowledge, Power, and the Body." Renov 174–92.

———, ed. *Movies and Methods.* Vol. 2. Berkeley: University of California Press, 1985.

———. "The Voice of Documentary." Rosenthal, *New Challenges* 48–63.

O'Connell, P. J. *Robert Drew and the Development of Cinéma Vérité in America.* Carbondale: Southern Illinois University Press, 1992.

O'Grady, Gerald. "Just Two Guys." *Fourth Annual Boston Film/Video Foundation Vision Award Ceremony Honoring Albert Maysles* 2–12.

Perez, Gilberto. *The Material Ghost: Films and Their Medium.* Baltimore: Johns Hopkins University Press, 1998.

Pezzulli, Fred A. "Saluting the Salesman." *New York Times* (12 April 1987): sec. 2, pp. 13.

Phipps, Keith. "Altamont Revisited." www.theavclub.com/avclub3637. January 2001.

Pincus, Ed. "New Possibilities in Film and the University." *Quarterly Review of Film Studies* 2 (May 1977): 169–71.

Pinkney, Tony. Introduction. Raymond Williams. 1–29.

Pirie, David. "*Gimme Shelter.*" *Sight and Sound* 40 (August 1971): 226–27.

Plantinga, Carl. *Rhetoric and Representation in Nonfiction Film.* London: Cambridge University Press, 1997.

Porton, Richard. "*Gimme Shelter*: Dionysus at Altamont." *Persistence of Vision* 6 (summer 1988), 83–90.

Primary. Dir. Robert Drew. 1960. Docurama, 2003. DVD.

Pryluck, Calvin. "Seeking To Take the Longest Journey: A Conversation with Albert Maysles." *Journal of the University Film Association* 28 (spring 1976): 9–16.

———. "Ultimately We Are All Outsiders: The Ethics of Documentary Filming." Rosenthal, *New Challenges* 255–68.

Renov, Michael, ed. *Theorizing Documentary.* New York: Routledge, 1993.

Reynolds, Charles. "Focus on Al Maysles." Jacobs 400–5.

Riesman, David. "The Uncommitted Generation." *Encounter* (November 1960): 5.

"Robe." Review of *Running Fence. Variety* (25 January 1978): 24.

Robson, Kenneth J. "Grey Gardens." *Cinema Journal* 22 (winter 1983): 42–53.

Rosaldo, Renato. *Culture and Truth: The Remaking of Social Analysis.* Boston: Beacon Press, 1989.

Rosen, Marjorie. "*Grey Gardens*: A Documentary about Dependency." *Ms* 9 (January 1976): 28–30.

Rosenthal, Alan. *The Documentary Conscience: A Casebook in Film Making.* Berkeley: University of California Press, 1980.

———. "Ellen Hovde: An Interview." *Film Quarterly* 32 (winter 1978/79): 8–17.

———, ed. *New Challenges for Documentary.* Berkeley: University of California Press, 1988.

———. *The New Documentary in Action.* Berkeley: University of California Press, 1971.

Rossinow, Doug. *The Politics of Authenticity: Liberalism, Christianity, and the New Left in America.* New York: Columbia University Press, 1998.

Rothman, William. *Documentary Film Classics.* Cambridge: Cambridge University Press, 1997.

Roudané, Matthew C. "*Death of a Salesman* and the Poetics of Arthur Miller." In *The Cambridge Companion to Arthur Miller,* edited by Christopher Bigsby. Cambridge: Cambridge University Press, 1997.

Rowan, Patricia. "Granada Meets the Maysles." *Sunday Times* (London), 16 February 1964, Arts section.

Ruby, Jay. "The Ethics of Imagemaking." Rosenthal, *New Challenges* 308–18.

———. "The Image Mirrored: Reflexivity and the Documentary Film." Rosenthal, *New Challenges* 64–77.

Ruoff, Jeffrey K. "'A Bastard Union of Several Forms': Style and Narrative in *An American Family.*" Grant and Sloniowski 286–301.

Sadkin, David. "*Gimme Shelter*: A Corkscrew or a Cathedral?" *Filmmakers Newsletter* 5 (December 1971): 20–27.

Salesman: A Film by the Maysles Brothers and Charlotte Zwerin. New York: Signet, 1969.

Salesman. Dir. Maysles Brothers and Charlotte Zwerin. 1968. Criterion Collection, 2001. DVD.

"*Salesman.*" *FilmFacts* 12 (May 1969): 178–82.

Sargent, David. "When Does Invasion of Privacy Become Art?" *Village Voice* (13 October 1975): 134.

Sarris, Andrew, "David Maysles (1932–1987)." *Village Voice* (3 February 1987): 56.

Schjeldahl, Peter, and Albert Goldman. "Delicately Handled Dynamite or a Whitewash of Jagger?" *New York Times* (3 January 1971): sec. 2, p. 9.

Schreiber, Norman. "Desire and Discovery: A Film-maker's Journey." *Amtrak Express* (August/September 1987): 30–34.

Schulman, Bruce J. *The Seventies: The Great Shift in American Society, Culture and Politics.* New York: Free Press, 2001.

———. "Taping History." *Journal of American History* 85 (September 1998): 571–78.

Scott, Nancy. "The Christo Films: *Christo's Valley Curtain* and *Running Fence.*" *Quarterly Review of Film Studies* 7 (winter 1983): 61–67.

Sekula, Allan. "Dismantling Modernism, Reinventing Documentary." *Massachusetts Review* 19 (1978): 859–83.

Shivas, Mark, and Ian Cameron. "Cinéma Vérité." *Movie* 8 (1963): 12–26.

Siegel, Joel. Review of *Grey Gardens. Film Heritage* 11 (fall 1976): 34–35.

Simon, John. "A Variety of Hells." Jacobs 466–68.

Singal, Daniel Joseph, ed. *Modernist Culture in America*. Belmont, CA: Wadsworth Publishing Company, 1991.

———. "Towards a Definition of American Modernism." Singal 1–27.

Sitton, Bob. "An Interview with Albert and David Maysles." *Film Library Quarterly* 2 (autumn 1969): 13–18.

Sklar, Robert. *Film: An International History of the Medium*. New York: Harry N. Abrams, 1995.

Sobchack, Vivian C. "*No Lies*: Direct Cinema as Rape." Rosenthal, *New Challenges* 332–41.

Spears, Timothy B. *One Hundred Years on the Road: The Traveling Salesman in American Culture*. New Haven: Yale University Press, 1995.

Sragow, Michael. "Critics." *Film Society Review* 6 (November 1970): 18.

Steele, Robert. "Meet Marlon Brando." *Film Heritage* 2 (fall 1966): 2–5.

Stein, Ellin. "It's a Wrap!" *American Film* 9 (July/August 1984): 10.

Stott, William. *Documentary Expression and Thirties America*. Chicago: University of Chicago Press, 1986.

Tammer, Peter. "A Kind of Truth." www.documenter.com. 4 March 2001.

"Third Independent Film Award." *Film Culture* 22/23 (summer 1961): 10–11.

Thompson, Howard. "Film Festival: Something for Youths." *New York Times* (18 September 1966): 78.

Tolkin, Michael. "What Makes the Maysles Run?" *Village Voice* (12 April 1976): 140–41; 144.

Tomkins, Calvin. "Chronicle." *Christo: Running Fence*. New York: Harry N. Abrams, 1978.

———. "Onward and Upward with the Arts: The Gates to the City." *New Yorker* (29 March 2004): 74–85.

———. "Onward and Upward with the Arts: Running Fence." *New Yorker* (28 March 1977): 43–82.

Tomlinson, Doug. "Gimme Shelter." In *The International Dictionary of Films and Filmmakers*, edited by Christopher Lyon. New York: Perigee Books, 1985.

Trojan, Judith. "Who's Who in Filmmaking: Albert Maysles." *Sightlines* 11 (spring 1978): 26–30.

Twelve Photographers of the American Social Landscape. Introduction by Thomas H. Garver. Waltham, MA: Brandeis University Press, 1967.

Vaizey, Marina. *Christo*. New York: Rizzoli, 1991.

Van Gelder, Lawrence. "Maysles: Filming the Impossible." *New York Times* (18 October 1987): sec. 2, p. 19.

Van Wert, William F. "The 'Hamlet Complex' or, Performance in the Personality-Profile Documentary." *Journal of Popular Film* 3 (1974): 257–63.

"Verr." Review of *Grey Gardens*. *Variety* (1 October 1975): 26.

Wakefield, Dan. "American Close-Ups." *Atlantic* 233 (May 1969): 107–8.

Ward, Ed, Geoffrey Stokes, and Ken Tucker, *Rock of Ages: The Rolling Stone History of Rock and Roll*. New York: Rolling Stone Press, 1986.

Warren, Charles, ed. *Beyond Document: Essays on Nonfiction Film*. Hanover, NH: University Press of New England, 1996.

Wiggin, Maurice. "Yeah, Yeah, Well, Maybe." *Sunday Times* (London) 16 February 1964, Arts section.

Williams, Linda. "Mirrors Without Memories: Truth, History and the New Documentary." *Film Quarterly* 46 (fall 1993): 9–21.

Williams, Raymond. *The Politics of Modernism: Against the New Conformists*. London: Verso Books, 1989.

Winster, Archer. "Rages and Outrages." *New York Post* (4 January 1971): 47.

Winston, Brian. *Claiming the Real: The Documentary Film Revisited*. London: British Film Institute, 1995.

———. "Direct Cinema: The Third Decade." Rosenthal, *New Challenges* 517–29.

———. "The Documentary Film as Scientific Inscription." Renov 37–57.

———. "Documentary: I Think We Are in Trouble." Rosenthal, *New Challenges* 21–33.

———. *Lies, Damn Lies and Documentaries*. London: BFI Publishing, 2000.

———. "The Tradition of the Victim in Griersonian Documentary." Rosenthal, *New Challenges* 269–87.

Young, Colin. "Cinema of Common Sense." *Film Quarterly* 17 (summer 1964): 26–29, 40.

Zheutlin, Barbara. "The Politics of Documentary: A Symposium." Rosenthal, *New Challenges* 227–42.

Zimmerman, Paul D. "Shooting It like It Is." *Newsweek* (17 March 1969): 134–35.

Zizek, Slavoj. *Looking Awry: An Introduction to Jacques Lacan Through Popular Culture*. Cambridge: MIT Press, 1993.

Index

Meet Marlon Brando, 16, 19, 20, 35–39, 40, 45, 155, 156, 162
Mekas, Jonas, 11, 158
Meyer, Muffie, 18, 125, 126, 127, 131, 138, 154
Milhouse, 144
Miller, Arthur, 50, 69
modernism: and American film, 10–11; definition of, 9–10. *See also* Maysles brothers, and modernism; *Grey Gardens,* modernist elements of
Monterey Pop, 17, 88, 142
Moore, Michael, 59, 171
Morituri. See Code Name: Morituri
Morris, Errol, 171
Muhammad and Larry, 18, 161–62
music, use of, 8. *See also* Christo films, use of music in

New Left, 4, 90, 154
Nichols, Bill, 147–48
No Lies, 144–45
Novak, Kim, 28–29, 30

Onassis, Jacqueline Kennedy. *See* Kennedy, Jacqueline Bouvier
O'Neill, Eugene, 8, 47
Ozawa, 18, 162–64
Ozawa, Seiji, 18, 162–64

Pennebaker, D.A., 17, 87, 140, 142, 155
Perez, Gilberto, 77, 128
Pincus, Ed, 144, 150
Point of Order!, 144
Port Huron Statement, 4
Portrait of Jason, 142
pragmatic modernism, 11–12, 19, 77, 95, 102. *See also* modernism
Primary, 3, 5, 21, 155, 156
Pryluck, Calvin, 145–46
Public Broadcasting Service (PBS), 39, 160, 170, 196n17

Quarterly Review of Film Studies, 143–44

Radziwill, Lee, 18, 124
Richards, Keith, 81, 94
Rolling Stones, 7, 17, 74–99, 161
Rothman, William, 150–51, 155–56
Rouch, Jean, 3, 147
Ruby, Jay, 147, 150, 151
Running Fence, 7, 18, 99, 111–23, 160, 164, 165, 167
Rush to Judgement, 144

Salesman, xii, 7, 11, 15, 17, 19, 21, 74, 104, 106, 119, 125, 135, 139, 152, 169, 170; background to making of, 47–49, 51; comparison to *Gimme Shelter,* 76, 98; the corruption of language within, 48, 54–68, 134; critical response to, 68–73, 145; limited release of, 68, 158–59
Sheeler, Charles, 10, 179n36
Showman, 6, 16, 19, 20, 21, 23, 24–30, 35, 36, 40, 100, 108; critical response to, 29–30
Simon, John, 69, 70, 73, 96, 146
Sleep, 11
Slick, Grace, 89–91
sound recording, 1, 8, 107
Starr, Ringo, 31–33
Swanson, Janet, 162

Tomkins, Calvin, 111, 116, 117
traveling salesman, history of, 50–51
Truth or Dare, 171, 182n33
Two Women, 23, 26, 28, 30

Umbrellas, 169
Unzipped, 171

Van Dyke, Willard, 142
Vanishing Salesman, The, 50
Visit with Truman Capote, A. See With Love from Truman: A Visit with Truman Capote
Vladimir Horowitz: The Last Romantic, 19, 162–64

Jonathan B. Vogels is the principal of the Upper School at Colorado Academy in Denver, Colorado. He has taught English, film studies, and history at the secondary and university levels and is a produced playwright. In 2000, he earned his Ph.D. in American studies from Boston University. From 2001 to 2003, Vogels organized Boston University's Nonfiction Film Festival, which featured the work of the Maysles brothers, Alan Berliner, and Lucia Small, among others.